The
Tightwad
Gazette

The Tightwad Gazette

Promoting Thrift as a Viable Alternative Lifestyle

Written and Illustrated by Amy Dacyczyn
a.k.a. The Frugal Zealot

Villard Books • New York

ISBN 0-679-74388-X

Manufactured in the United States of
America

Preface

I never wanted to write a book. Every book I have ever read on the subject of thrift or money management was as dry as . . . well . . . vacuum cleaner bag dust. As each author wrote about his or her areas of expertise, large areas were left unaddressed. And because learning is an ongoing process, any book would have to be too final and incomplete.

Within the format of a newsletter I have found that I could make my subject matter interesting and fun by balancing types of information and diversifying the manner by which I demonstrated ideas. I solicit reader participation, which provides an enormous pool of expertise to draw upon. So even if my knowledge isn't well rounded, the newsletter can be, and because I constantly learn from my readers the newsletter is a growth process for me as well.

Before accepting this offer from Villard I turned down publishers for more than a year. My primary reason for beginning a newsletter was my belief that a home business would give me more time with my children. My husband and I have six, nine years old and

under. I simply did not have the time or ambition to generate new material for a book. Doing so would shortchange my family and undermine my newsletter. However, what I had written to that point was very incomplete.

A *Tightwad Gazette* book became a possibility when Villard proposed that a compilation of articles could work. This book is a collection of the majority of the material covered in the first two years of my newsletter.

Organizing it presented problems. From the onset we saw that no one method would encompass all the material. Articles did not fit into neat obvious chapters. Some articles could fit into several categories, while others fit into none. Lumping similar material together would make the entire book dry as . . . well . . . you know. On the other hand, I knew that people who had bought all the back issues of the newsletter often read through the entire stack in a single sitting.

With this understanding we decided to assemble the book with the loosest possible structure. Because *The Tightwad Gazette* is written month to month, we organized material based on times of the year, even though only about 40% of the material is seasonal. You can therefore assume that 60% of the material included under each season may be relevant to any time of year.

This *Tightwad Gazette* compilation is not, and was never intended to be, a complete handbook on thrift. After two years of writing the newsletter I have barely scratched the surface, and I have more ideas for things to write about today than when I began. As it is only a beginning for me, likewise it is a beginning for you to rethink your lifestyle.

I have written from the viewpoint of "Give a man a fish and he'll eat for a day. Teach him to fish and he'll eat for life." This book does not contain all the answers. Hopefully, it does contain the necessary tools for you to discover answers for yourself.

Contents

A Word of Caution

A natural aspect of tightwaddery is the practice of unconventional methods to save money. We push the normal limits to make things last longer. We reuse things in unusual ways. We experiment constantly to find new, cheaper ways to do almost everything. Because this book draws upon the experiences of people throughout the country, there is a chance we will inadvertently publish information that is technically illegal or not safe. On the other hand, all of the information in this book was previously published in a newsletter that was read by thousands, maybe tens of thousands of people. Whenever any reader pointed out a concern, I thoroughly researched the question, and then made a judgment as to the validity of the concern.

Based on this, to the best of my knowledge, all of the ideas in this book are legal. Likewise I believe all the ideas meet a reasonable level of safety. I pointed out any significant hazard I was aware of, but I did not point out safety concerns if the hazard was extremely remote. For example, when I suggested turning out the lights to save electricity, I did not warn you about the hazard of stumbling over your toddler's pull toy in the darkness.

You must exercise your personal judgment when using ideas in this book and take reasonable precautions.

The Tightwad Gazette

THEY CALL ME "THE FRUGAL ZEALOT"

I am a compulsive tightwad. People who know me believe that I worry too much about money, that I don't spend enough on myself, and that I don't know how to have any fun. Even depression-era relatives think that I am too thrifty. One Christmas an aunt gave me two boxes of aluminum foil after learning that I recycled the stuff. (I made it last for years.) And when I was first labeled "The Frugal Zealot" even *I* had to smile.

It was not always this way. Before the fever gripped me I had a very normal and healthy love for spending.

The change occurred when I got married and began to pursue my dream. I had always wanted a large family and a rural pre-1900 New England farmhouse (with attached barn). I had a crazy notion that I could have both without the two-income/daycare frenzy that has become the norm for the modern American family.

Our first child was born nine months (and 15 minutes) after the ceremony. I set aside my career in graphic design to be a mom. It was during this time that I discovered daytime talk shows and first heard the commonly held myths expounded by intelligent audience members.

"Nowadays, a family has to have two incomes to make ends meet."

"Nowadays, it is impossible for a young couple to get into the housing market."

"Nowadays, families cannot afford to raise more than two children."

As if the message could magically be shot back through the television tube, I raised my fist and shouted, "It is not true, it can be done." And so began my quest . . . to prove that it could be done . . . that it was still possible to raise a large family and buy a house without two full-time incomes.

Saving money, rather than earning money, became the means to my goal. I became a recycler first of aluminum foil, then of Ziploc bags, and now, I publicly confess, I have become a recycler of vacuum cleaner bags. (No Christmas presents please.)

My challenge in life became how low could I get our food budget and still have a varied, healthful diet, or how wonderful I could make a child's birthday with a $25 budget, or how many years I could go without buying wrapping paper.

I made it my personal mission to create ways to recycle plastic milk jugs, bread tabs, brown paper bags, egg cartons, and those frozen juice lid things.

To fine-tune our spending I became a student of thrift. I routinely calculated such things as the cost of drying a load of laundry, or the cost savings in cloth diapers, or the cost difference of making food from scratch versus buying convenience foods.

When Oprah had a show featuring cheapskates I didn't laugh. I took notes.

Although I was the chief architect of our family economic plan, my husband became a willing convert. In addition he taught me the ways of scrounging and organized packratting. (A level beyond cheap is to get it for free.)

It worked.

In 1989 we realized our dream. Our family (then it was four children; now, with the advent of twins two years later, it's six) moved into our rural pre-1900 New England farmhouse (with attached barn).

Were we too thrifty?

When we got married, our joint financial assets barely paid for the budget wedding. We owned almost nothing. In other words we started from *zero*.

Over the years our average income has been less than $30,000 (including my husband's Navy salary and all allowances, plus my spotty free-lance income). In less than seven years we saved $49,000, made significant purchases (vehicles, appliances, furniture) of $38,000, and were completely debt-free! That is an annual savings/investment rate of over $12,500 per year, or 43% of our gross income.

It is difficult to compare finances of different families except in the military, where all things are roughly equal. Of the scores of families we have known, most lived paycheck to paycheck, moonlighted, or relied on a second income. I know of only one other family that were accomplished savers. Their annual savings/investment rate was about half of ours.

Without a down payment we would have been able to buy only a small starter home. Instead we purchased a wonderful house that exceeded our expectations, a house vastly superior to the 176 other houses we saw during a 15-month period. If we had saved a few thousand less we would not own it today.

No, we weren't too thrifty.

Certainly the recycling of aluminum foil did not greatly contribute to our dream. Rather it was the attention to all the thousands of ways we spent our money that made a tremendous difference.

Our success was very much a gradual learning process. We made many big mistakes. Had we known in the beginning what we know now I am sure we could have saved several thousand more.

Thus having proven that it could be done—that financial goals could be achieved through saving more rather than earning more—I have become a crusader for the causes of thrift and frugality. I have been guilty of preaching its virtues beyond the point when eyes glazed over. My ideas seemed to fall on the deaf ears of the financially strapped.

For years now my husband and I have felt we were loners . . . mavericks in the realm of personal economics.

But then one day it hit me. Maybe we *aren't* alone. Maybe there are others—penny-pinchers horrified at the holes in the pockets of those they know and love.

Maybe they feel alone, too. We need a forum for mutual support and the exchange of frugal ideas. Tightwads need to join forces!

So with my background in graphics, a joy of writing, and a conviction that the world can be saved through thrift I have decided to go where no tightwad has gone before—I have decided to write a book.

Hence, the birth of *The Tightwad Gazette*.

Amy Dacyczyn
a.k.a. The Frugal Zealot

MRS. DA...DA...?

Dear Amy,
How do you pronounce your name?

Name withheld by request
Salina, Utah

It's pronounced "decision," as in, "I made a decision to marry a guy of Ukrainian ancestry."

The week before I got married I called utility companies to notify them of my upcoming name change. The woman from the electric company asked, "What's your last name now?" I said, "Davis." She then asked, "What will your name change to?" I replied, "Dacyczyn... D-A-C-Y-C-Z-Y-N." After a lengthy pause the electric company lady asked, "Don't you want to think about this a little longer?"

Tightwaddery is not for everyone. I am keenly aware that most people really don't care a hoot about any of this stuff. Some are doing just fine, thank you. They have enough money to do everything they want. A larger segment does need to manage their finances better but are unwilling to make the needed changes. Past experience taught me quickly that I couldn't win them over. No amount of information will cause them to rethink their lifestyle.

This information is geared for the rest of the people who do not find thrift a radical concept.

Tightwads are a small elite group. But while few in number they come in endless varieties. There are borderline tightwads and spartan tightwads and all shades in between.

There are budding tightwads who feel overwhelmed and think "How does she expect me to bake bread, make wrapping paper, braid rugs and shop at fourteen different grocery stores?" Relax. It took me years to reach my level of skill and I am still learning. Choose one new idea a week. One new skill per month. When you have mastered it you'll be ready to take on a new challenge.

There are old-hand tightwads who may learn only one or two new ideas per chapter. Their primary reason for reading this will be to have *The Tightwad Gazette* to wave in the faces of spendthrift family and friends and say, "See! Look here! I'm not crazy. Someone else thinks the same way I do."

Not every tightwad is saving for a pre-1900 New England farmhouse (with attached barn).

Some live in a shack so they can afford a fleet of snowmobiles and all-terrain vehicles. As long as they are financially responsible— their kids have enough to eat, the bills are paid, and they have adequate insurance and savings for emergencies—that is absolutely acceptable.

There are working moms who want to find a way to be home with their children and there are stay-at-home moms who want to get out of the house . . . return to college or start a business. Thrift can address both these goals.

The Tightwad Gazette is for both men and women. Especially if there is a lack of spouse cooperation, tightwads need to cross over into "other-sex-dominated territories." Men can learn to bake bread, do the grocery shopping, and scrounge yard sales. Women can learn to swing a hammer and do a tune-up. Don't point a finger. Instead, do whatever it takes to reach your goal.

The size of the dream, the size of the income, and the length of time allowed to meet the goal determine the degree of thrift tightwads will resort to.

I do not expect that every reader will recycle aluminum foil, Ziploc bags, and yes, vacuum cleaner bags. *The Tightwad Gazette* will present a cornucopia of ideas, approaches, and knowledge that has worked for us, as well as for the readership. Each tightwad must weigh and decide what is compatible to his or her lifestyle.

Yeah, I've been called The Frugal Zealot, and we have had above average success with an average income. But I do not claim expert status. I still have a lot to learn but am excited about a book that serves as a clearinghouse of ideas . . . that draws upon the collective wisdom of the finest frugal minds in the country.

GOALS OF THE TIGHTWAD GAZETTE

- To give tightwaddery a good name
- To provide the widest possible sharing of the tightwad philosophy
- To be a clearinghouse of frugal ideas through active participation of tightwads everywhere
- To explode all myths wrongly associated with tightwads
- To promote tightwaddery as a viable alternative lifestyle
- To provide support to tightwads who feel they're all alone out there
- To gain recognition for tightwads as a minority
- To provide an income for the author, who doesn't want to go out and get a real job
- To demonstrate, in all sincerity, that thrift can help families of all economic levels achieve their financial goals and to have greater economic freedom

REASONS WHY PEOPLE CAN'T SAVE MONEY

I'M JUST NO GOOD AT COOKING.

MY WIFE SPENDS EVERYTHING I SAVE.

I'M JUST NOT CREATIVE LIKE YOU.

TEENAGERS ARE SO EXPENSIVE.

IT'S HARD TO MAKE ENDS MEET NOWADAYS.

I'M TOO BUSY TO CHASE AFTER SALES.

I CAN NEVER FIND WHAT I WANT AT THRIFT SHOPS.

I DON'T HAVE TIME TO...

MY FAMILY WON'T EAT CASSEROLES

WE WILL DEAL WITH THESE REASONS IN THE PAGES AHEAD.

WHAT CAN YOU DO TO GET STARTED?

The most elementary exercise for any aspiring tightwad is to record spending habits for a period of three months. Write down *everything* from the mortgage payment to the candy bar at the checkout counter.

All your expenses will be one of two types. Essential and optional. Essential expenses are things that you absolutely cannot cut. Optional expenses are nonessential. For example, your phone bill has a minimum service charge that you must pay to have telephone service and a breakdown for long-distance calls. The $10 call to your mother was optional. Your food bill contains items necessary for basic nutrition and nonnutritious items like coffee, candy, and soda, which are optional.

No one but you can say exactly where the line between essential and optional expenses falls. That depends on *your* value system. The point is to understand how much you *really* have left over to play with.

If you take home $20,000 and of that $15,000 is already allocated for essential expenses, the $5,000 remaining is what you have left for optional expenses. In that light, making a small adjustment to save $1,000 a year makes more sense. As you further fine-tune your spending, you may realize that only $12,000 of your take home is actually essential and you have even more room for savings.

By tracking your spending in this way, for the first time, you will have a truly clear picture of where your money is going and where your best options for cutbacks are. It also will give you a valuable gauge for comparison as you gain success at managing your money.

EYE OPENER

Dear Amy,

Thank you for sending the premiere issue of your *Tightwad Gazette*. As you suggested I did the necessary vs. optional lists. Wow! Just going over my checkbook, as of 1/14/91 we spent over $300 on optional items (to 3/19/91). That's not including items purchased with cash!

**Pearl Nagoshi
Budd Lake, New Jersey**

WE REGRETFULLY INFORM YOU . . .

. . . that in an effort to bring you real usable information on a limited number of pages we will *not* be able to feature the following types of articles:

Beauty makeovers
Hollywood gossip
Romance novels
$40,000 only-dreamin' kitchens
Fashions as dictated by designers that do not reside on planet Earth
Nouvelle cuisine recipes
Royal family updates

10 PAINLESS WAYS TO SAVE $100 THIS YEAR

1 Purchase 10 articles of clothing at thrift shops and yard sales this year instead of paying department store prices.

2 Hang four loads of laundry per week instead of using your dryer.

3 Once a month make a pizza from scratch instead of having one delivered.

4 Write a good letter instead of making a monthly long-distance phone call.

5 Reduce your soda consumption by four cans per week.

6 Bake one batch of bread (two loaves) per week.

7 Save $50 each on two children's birthday parties by making homemade decorations, cake, wrapping paper, and one present.

8 Reduce your smoking by three cigarettes per day (or give up smoking altogether and save even more).

9 Reduce your whole milk consumption by two gallons per week, substituting dry milk in cooking, homemade cocoa mix, and in half-and-half for drinking.

10 Pack four inexpensive school lunches per week.

Fall

EVERYTHING YOU ALREADY KNOW

Telling you how to save money is like telling you how to lose weight. Everybody knows how to lose weight. You need to eat fewer calories than your body uses. To save money you need to spend fewer dollars than you earn. In both cases you need to adjust your rate of consumption to your rate of work.

The "Don't save more, earn more" philosophy is a very one-sided approach. And it has one big flaw. Nearly everyone that earns more automatically spends more. For this reason, regardless of their incomes, many families seem to have exactly enough to get by.

Telling you to earn more instead of saving more is like saying "Don't eat less, exercise more."

When I learned that walking a mile burned up the same amount of calories as in an apple I wondered how many miles I would have to run to burn the calories in a candy bar. It made more sense to give up the candy bar.

Most Americans are running to burn up candy bars. They are running out of the house, running to the daycare center, running on the job . . . so they can *afford* candy bars and Nintendo games, meals at McDonald's, and designer sneakers.

There is no doubt that the minimum wage earner does need to earn more to afford apples—the basics of life.

But for most of us whether we choose to earn more or to save more depends on how easy, accessible, and enjoyable *more* work is.

For me, working more, especially when I had to leave home, creates a high level of stress. Juggling business and babies is a job in itself. The client's needs must come first if I am to maintain a professional image.

Likewise few dedicated fathers like to moonlight for minimum wage. In some cases more work is not available.

Earning more in the same eight-hour day often requires capital and years to make the transition to start a new business or to obtain additional education.

In the meantime, earning more boils down to working more and being away from home more hours. It means less time to call your own.

There is a point at which the quality of life and the standard of living depart . . . where earning more results in a personal cost and erodes the quality of life.

The solution is to find the right balance of earning more and sav-

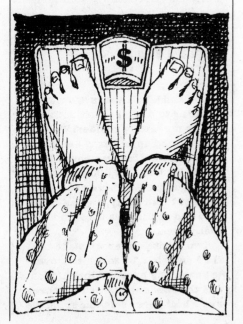

ing more. You need to couple your earning effort and your saving effort to achieve the highest quality of life.

When you do earn more, resist the temptation to spend more. Discipline yourself to saving whatever possible of what you do earn and reinvest in ways to either earn more or save more.

Sometimes I feel like I am telling you everything you already know. It is much like when I joined Weight Watchers years ago. At the time I joined I already knew how to lose weight, yet I continued to attend long after I had reached my goal. Weight Watchers' success is in their structure as a support network.

The purpose of *The Tightwad Gazette* is much the same. You will learn some new nitty-gritty strategies and it will bring into focus what you already know. But I hope you will also come to regard it as a national tightwad network, providing support as you work toward reaching your goal.

A SPENDTHRIFT HORROR STORY

Dear Amy,

One and a half years ago we felt a calling to move to Austin, Texas, where my family resides. We had no job lined up in Texas and did not know how long we would be there. We had a $9,000 check coming to us. When we received it we spent like crazy, buying furniture and appliances we didn't really need.

Two months later we made the final decision, by force, to move to Texas. My husband lost his job and the condo we rented for three and a half years sold under us. We

proceeded to put all our "new stuff" in storage in New Jersey. We have not seen these things in the last year and a half, and we continue not only to pay storage, but also to kick ourselves for spending the $9,000 on it. It would have come in handy in Texas.

Save your money. You never know what could happen in two months. Arg!

**Isabel Renbjor
Austin, Texas**

LUNCH BOX BASICS

I'm not naive. I know that while my kids might be happy now to take box lunches to school, someday the honeymoon will be over. I envision one day Alec will get off the school bus, march into the house with a mission, plunk his red plastic lunch box on the counter, and announce he wants school lunches like the rest of the kids. After six months of intensive negotiations I will lose... maybe.

In our community a grammar school lunch costs 90¢. I can prepare a box lunch for 45¢. This means that every year a child takes a box lunch I can save $81. If all six kids take box lunches through grammar school I can save $2,916.

WHAT TO PUT IT IN

If you haven't purchased a new $5 lunch box for your grade schooler you might check out your thrift shop. I frequently see several at a time.

You can refurbish a lunch box by replacing the old peeling side panel art commonly found on plastic lunch boxes. I have done this either by having a child create his own artwork or by using a large interesting photograph such as might be found on an old calendar. On one occasion a free photography magazine arrived in the mail that had a large cover photo of a dinosaur mural. This refurbished Alec's lunch box, making it the envy of his friends.

I was able to accomplish this with minimal expense since I have the proper tools and materials on hand. If you need to buy materials, realize that tools and leftover materials can be used in future projects, and so the real expense is smaller than the initial investment.

You need clear contact paper and one-coat rubber cement. One-coat dries so that it is tacky and stickerlike.

Trim out your new art to the exact size of the old art, rounding the corners. If you can remove the old art in one piece use it for a pattern.

Coat the back of the art with the rubber cement and let it completely dry. Adhere the front of the art to a larger piece of clear contact paper. Trim the contact paper ⅛ to ¼ inch larger than the art. Carefully adhere the art to the lunch box. Rub down well, paying special attention to the edges of the contact paper. Washed carefully, this waterproof sticker will last a year.

WHAT TO PUT IN IT

All of the following items are presumed to have been purchased as cheaply as possible or made from scratch.

Sandwiches like bologna, turkey, tuna, egg salad, and peanut butter and jelly cost between 10¢ to 20¢.

A cup of soup in a thermos costs between 5¢ and 10¢.

Rewarmed casserole or chili costs as little as 15¢.

Balance the "main course" with one or two of the following items, which can be put into a reused baggie or butter tub. All of these cost between 1¢ and 10¢.

Vegetable sticks
A muffin or biscuit with jam
Popcorn
Homemade cookies
Canned fruit or applesauce
Trail mix made with raisins,
    seeds, nuts, coconut, choco-
    late chips, cold cereal,
    Chinese noodles, etc.
Homemade yogurt, pudding, or
    Jell-O
Crackers
Bread sticks
Fresh fruit

A cup of juice or half-and-half milk (that is, half whole, half powdered) costs about 12¢. To ensure that it stays cold try this method:

Thoroughly wash the thermos. Pour one inch of beverage in it.

Place the cup loosely over the top (to keep out freezer odors) and put the thermos in the freezer overnight. In the morning, when you pack lunches, fill the remainder of the thermos with the same beverage. By lunch the ice should be completely melted and the beverage should still be cold. Ask your children about the lunch-time results and adjust the amount of frozen beverage if needed.

Under no circumstances use prepackaged individual-sized snack foods and juice packs. I would suggest that you fork out the money for school lunches first. Below is an example of an expensive box lunch.

GREAT QUOTES

"I would rather have my people laugh at my economies than weep for my extravagance."
—King Oscar of Sweden (1829–1907)

"To secure the greatest amount of pleasure with the least possible outlay should be the aim of all economic effort."
—Francois Quesnay (1694–1774), French economist

"The world has enough for everyone's need, but not enough for everyone's greed."
—Attributed to Mahatma Gandhi (1869–1948)

THE EXPENSIVE BOX LUNCH
(Do not try this in your own home.)

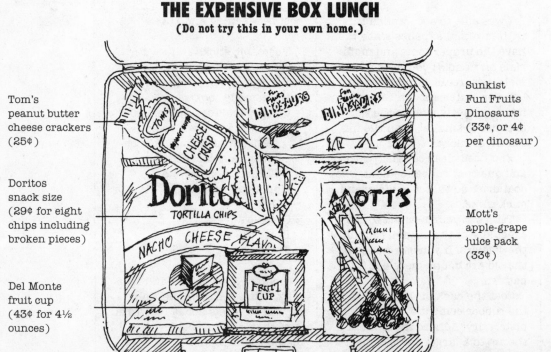

Tom's peanut butter cheese crackers (25¢)

Doritos snack size (29¢ for eight chips including broken pieces)

Del Monte fruit cup (43¢ for 4½ ounces)

Sunkist Fun Fruits Dinosaurs (33¢, or 4¢ per dinosaur)

Mott's apple-grape juice pack (33¢)

TOTAL: $1.63

"The safest way to double your money is to fold it over once and put it in your pocket."

—Frank McKinney Hubbard
(1868–1930)

"Wealth consists not in having great possessions but in having few wants."

—Epicurus (341–270 B.C.)

Here's one for the Dacyczyns:
"It is not economical to go to bed early to save candles if the results are twins."

—Chinese proverb

YOU AND THE FINANCIAL EDGE

You know someone who arrives 20 minutes late for everything. It could be late to work, to church, or for a date. He is always late because the 20 minutes falls within his margin of acceptability.

When they turn the clocks back from daylight savings to standard time, you'd figure he would now be 40 minutes early. However, he makes the mental adjustment and arrives the same 20 minutes late.

You also know people who arrive exactly on time, and people characterized by chronic earliness. Likewise these people set their mental clocks so that they arrive within a time frame that is acceptable to them. In the case of the extenuating circumstance the early bird may arrive on time, the on-time person may be 20 minutes late, and the straggler will arrive 40 minutes late.

Your personal inner clock functions in the same manner as your sense of where you are in relation to "the financial edge." You have an inner sense of how close you can come to meeting your financial obligations and still feel comfortable.

During my single working years I maintained a checking account balance of $1,000 to $1,500. When my balance exceeded $1,500 I would spend. When the balance dropped below $1,000 I would cease extravagant activity. I could have saved more, but I felt comfortable with the $1,000 to $1,500 range from the edge.

Those who feel comfortable closer to the edge frequently find themselves saying, "I have only $10 to get me to the next paycheck."

What of the individual who lives beyond his means? He builds a mental gangplank out beyond the edge where he teeters precariously.

The "$10-to-paycheck-guy" and the "gangplank-guy" will point to the extenuating circumstances

that lead to his position near or beyond the edge. When an unexpected expense comes along propelling them to financial depths, they do not accept responsibility. However, the person who maintains a cushion, given the same circumstance, will occasionally approach the edge but quickly work his way back to his comfort zone.

I have been a closet amateur budget analyst for many years. People have told me about the shortage of income that leads them to their troubles. Because my opinion was not asked for I didn't point out the Froot Loops in the cupboards, the Pampers in the bathroom, and the cable TV.

Even more responsible families on modest incomes nearly always have areas in which they could economize. They could give up red meat in favor of dried beans or whole milk in favor of mixed.

My standing as a "professional budget analyst" enjoys a briefer history. Recently I have talked or corresponded with people in the most desperate circumstances— those who have declared bankruptcy, received public assistance, or lived on the smallest of incomes. Without exception I was able to identify areas where they could save. The savings might not be enough to cure the financial shortfall, but rarely do they do everything possible.

Those who were honest admitted that I was right. If it were a matter of life and death they could resort to "desperate measures" such as eating oatmeal or changing a cloth diaper. But in truth they felt comfortable living on the financial edge.

I have not scrutinized every budget on the planet Earth, and I know rare individuals exist who live on the edge while making every frugal choice possible. However, I have not seen it.

The majority of the desperate hesitate to make the choices that our family has done routinely for years.

In the same way that the late guy still arrives late with the gift hour due to the return to standard time, many of those living on the edge or out on the gangplank fail to benefit by increased income. They might have more stuff or more fun, but they instinctively maintain the same distance to the edge regardless.

If they cannot pay a bill because "the transmission gave out," truthfully the problem is not mechanical at all. Rather the fault can be found with all the extras that they were not willing to give up in order to have the needed cushion.

For most of us our relationship to the financial edge comes down to a matter of choice. The choice may be the decisions we make today, or we may be living with choices we have made in the past. While the past choices cannot be changed, remarkably the ones we make today become tomorrow's past choices.

We can make choices that allow us to take a giant step back from the financial edge and set up a cushion. A sustained effort to scale back will result in savings for more than just a cushion. We can save for long-term goals and increased financial independence.

BUILDING MATERIALS

Dear Amy,
I am sick to death of our unfinished basement. Can you give us some suggestions as to where I can get super cheap drywall, lumber, etc.?
Lee Ann Welka
Brooklyn Park, Minnesota

Dear Lee Ann,
Jim and I usually find that shopping around for the best price is the only way we can consistently get building materials cheaply . . . if new materials are ever cheap. On occasion we scrounge small quantities of lumber, which will do for small projects and minor repairs, but for the major projects we cannot find enough.

The solution is to divert funds from other areas of finances. We routinely pinch on food, clothing, and entertainment, so that we always have money to buy the things that are hard to economize on.

I have seen advertisements for people willing to tear down buildings in exchange for lumber.

Along with that idea another reader recently wrote the following about her luck (and talent) for scrounging building materials:

Dear Amy,
Both my husband and I watch for places that are being remodeled or torn down for whatever reason, and those people generally want new stuff as replacement . . . well, there is a lot to salvage at times. Sometimes my husband is even able to help someone tear down, and he looks for useful items to salvage. We even found insulation without the backing from a fire sale that was quite useful. Also we have found windows better than ours. Most of these items were better than we had and even though secondhand we put them to good use. We even built a deck behind our house.

Time and effort have to be spent looking. With more people in the remodeling mode because of the economy you might be surprised at what you find, even in yard sales.
Ann Gardner
Conway, New Hampshire

DRYER SHEETS

Dear Amy,
Dryer sheets do not require a full sheet to reduce static. I've found I can tear one sheet into four strips and use one strip per load, thus making one box last four times as long.
Deb Knight
Westbrook, Maine

Dear Amy,
Make dryer sheets by using a big bottle of Downy and old face cloths. Pour 1 to 2 tablespoons on the face cloths and use the same as you would use a dryer sheet. You don't have to rewash the face cloths often.
Polly Dzurak
Quincy, Massachusetts

Dear Amy,
I don't buy dryer sheets anymore. I live in an apartment building. I just reuse the dryer sheets other tenants have discarded. They work great.
Kathy Ranta
Coon Rapids, Minnesota

(I asked Jim, "How come we don't use dryer sheets?" Jim replied, "We don't use our dryer!" Air-dried clothing is so stiff it couldn't possibly cling. FZ)

THE SCHOOL RECYCLER

Charlotte Johns of Bison, Oklahoma, sent in an idea for making a "new" carrier for "old" school supplies. I thought it could be used for other applications as well; a kit of small tools, a manicure set, crochet needles, etc.

Use heavyweight fabrics. Examples include denim (from last year's cutoffs) or quilted fabric. Charlotte has used seed sacks.

Fabric should be double layered. Sew two layers, right side together. Leave one end open and reverse. Press into a workable square or rectangle.

To finish, fold up bottom flap and stitch. Make spaces for pencils, pens, crayons, a paint box, scissors, etc.

Stitch on the pocket for the eraser and sharpener. The opening will be on the inside at the top when it folds down.

Finally, sew on a tie made of the same material, or a ribbon.

A possible modification to this design might be an additional flap sewn from the top to prevent any supplies from falling out once the recycler is tied.

stitch on pocket

sew tie on here

fold up and sew

rolled up and tied

pencils   small ruler

eraser   sharpener   ?

pocket flips up

water colors

scissors

crayons

"HOW CAN I SAVE ON BABY FORMULA?"

Many readers have requested a homemade baby formula recipe. These queries coincided with the following baby formula recipe sent in:

2 12-oz cans of evaporated milk
32 oz water
2 Tbsp Karo syrup
3 ml Poly Vi Sol vitamins

Commercial formula costs roughly three times as much as this recipe, or between $816 and $967 per year.

In the interest of passing along good information, I began a phone call trek to verify the appropriateness of this recipe, or to find an approved recipe.

I called the American Academy of Pediatrics and spoke with two of their advisers. They gave me the name of a lab that develops baby formula. I also spoke with three other nutritionists, including one from Women and Infant Children.

None of the professionals I spoke with felt that homemade formulas were a very good option. Prepared correctly, they rank a distant third behind breast-feeding and commercial formula. They are probably adequate but not optimum.

However, under certain circumstances homemade formulas may be fine to use. Before considering its use you need to know more about infant nutrition, and formula in general.

A generation ago most of us were fed formula made with evaporated milk. It was the best formula available at the time.

Parents in many other countries still make their own today. However, the new commercial formulas more closely resemble breast milk and are more complete.

Homemade formulas use evaporated milk because it has been sufficiently heated to denature or break down the protein of cow's milk, in the same way that commercial formulas are manufactured. No newborn should be fed regular cow's milk, which is too hard for the child to digest. Ten to 20% of the infants will suffer from minor stomach bleeding, which would be undetectable and could lead to an iron deficiency.

Evaporated milk is on the low end of the range for essential fatty acids. Concern was expressed over prolonged use of evaporated milk for that reason. A generation ago this issue was not as great because children started solid foods as early as four months. Essential fatty acids are found in a variety of foods. However, it is now believed that the introduction of solid foods too early can cause lifelong allergies. Today many doctors advise waiting until at least six months before introducing solid foods.

Essential fatty acids are important to brain development.

Homemade formula contains Karo syrup. There has been some concern raised over the possibility of infant botulism, such as is the case with honey. The AAP was not aware of any documented cases, and therefore did not feel that there was any need for concern. The lack of documented cases may be a result of the fact that very few babies are fed Karo syrup today. The WIC nutritionist thought that granulated sugar might be a better addition.

The formula lab felt that infant formula would need a vitamin supplement that contains vitamin C, iron, and folic acid. Poly Vi Sol vitamins have vitamin C and iron, but no folic acid. (Folic acid aids in the absorption of iron.) The vitamins should be given to an infant separately if the formula is heated up beyond room temperature, since heat destroys many vitamins.

The professionals I spoke with felt concern over the preparation of the homemade formulas. If a parent were highly conscientious this need not be a factor, but incorrect mixing could be a problem, especially if the milk were not sufficiently diluted. The same argument could be made about mixing powdered commercial formulas.

When asked about the cost difference, and whether the savings could justify use of homemade formulas, the reaction was mixed. They truthfully pointed out that most household budgets include many nonessentials. A potential annual savings in the hundreds of dollars could be important to "the working poor," but most

families should look to other cuts first.

What of the argument "We were all raised on it and we turned out fine"? One expert described that as the Dr. Welby approach to medicine. The theory is cozy and warm but not very scientific. The same applies to the argument "My children look healthy, so I must be doing it right." The best information currently available points to specific nutritional guidelines. While experts frequently disagree, and new evidence always comes along, we should not discount the opinions of those who have studied the question for years.

Where does this leave us? Breast-feeding is still the best option for feeding infants, from a nutritional and economic standpoint. A breast-feeding mother needs an additional two cups of milk per day, which costs about a quarter. If you are having difficulty, call your local chapter of the La Leche League for help. Statistically only about 10% of mothers are physically unable to breast-feed infants. The remainder of mothers who use formula do so by choice or because of problems with work schedules.

Some of the nutritionists feel that babies who eat a well-balanced diet of solid food twice a day can be switched to a homemade formula, and some pediatricians may approve whole milk around eight months.

The interest in reviving the old recipes stems from a real concern over the dramatic rise in the cost of commercial formulas. The Federal Trade Commission is currently investigating three major formula manufacturers for price fixing. However, this does not invalidate the product.

If a mother cannot breast-feed, commercial formula remains a strong second. Before using any homemade formula recipe, consult your pediatrician.

BABY FORMULA UPDATE

Dear Amy,

I am writing concerning the article "How Can I Save on Baby Formula?" As you pointed out, only 5% to 10% of women are physically unable to breast-feed, meaning that the majority of women who do choose to bottle-feed do so for personal reasons. I would like it noted for your cost-conscious readers that the expense of feeding breast-milk substitute to a baby must also include added medical expenses. A recent study in *The American Physician* found that artificially fed infants are treated by their doctor three times as often as breast-fed infants. In their first year, only 25% of breast-fed infants were brought to their doctor for illness, while 97% of artificially fed infants needed medical treatment. With the cost of doctor visits ranging from $30 to $50 per visit, breast-feeding could save a family a lot of money and a baby from a lot of unnecessary pain.

> Beverly Wilder
> Lawrenceville, Georgia

(Without having read it, I don't know the criteria for this study. It occurs to me that formula-fed babies are more likely to be in daycare, and thus more likely to be exposed to germs. This may account for some of the higher incidence of illness of the formula-fed babies. FZ)

TACKY & CHEAP

Dear Amy,

Use duct tape, or masking tape, for taping jobs where the tape does not need to be clear. Duct tape is also excellent for package sealing. The P.O. frowns on it, for unknown reasons, but many people are using it. Masking tape does not have the strength needed for most packages.

> John Etter
> Hood River, Oregon

(OK, this tightwad sends me in this idea, and in the interest of passing along good information, I, the greatest mathematical midget of all time, have to work out how to compare:

Duct 2 in × 60 yds. for $6
Masking 1 in. × 60 yds. for $1
Clear ½ in. × 12.5 yds. for 69¢

I finally figured based on ½ in. × 1 yd. After at least 30 minutes of intense calculations I have determined that a hunk of duct tape would cost 2½¢ (2.5¢), masking tape would cost under a penny (.83¢), and clear tape would cost over 5¢ (5.7¢). Phew! FZ)

HOW BIG IS A CORD OF WOOD?

I have a friend, and subscriber, who sells wood part time. He tells me that from time to time he finds that people do not get their money's worth when they purchase firewood.

The problem arises over confusion between a "full cord" and a "face cord" of wood.

A full cord of firewood is a stack of wood that equals 128 cu. ft. Although usually defined as 4′ × 4′ × 8′, obviously it can be an equal dimension, such as 2′ × 4′ × 16′.

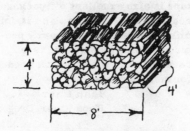

A face cord is a stack of firewood where the "face" is the traditional 4′ × 8′, but the depth is not the 4′ measurement. This can occur when the wood has been cut in an odd length so that it stacks up to an odd depth. Such as two rows deep of 18″ wood adds up to 3′ deep. If you have purchased a face cord, which equals 3′ × 4′ × 8′, you've only bought 75% of a full cord.

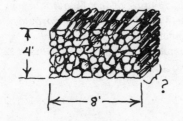

PRESCRIPTIONS

Dear Amy,

I am sensitive to certain medicines and sometimes get side effects. Many times after purchasing a full bottle of prescription pills that is outrageously expensive, after taking one or two, my doctor would switch me to another brand. I'd be stuck with the bottle of pills.

When I complained to my pharmacist, I learned I could buy as few or as many pills as I want at a time. Since then, I have purchased as few as three at a time. This has saved me lots of money, plus I can stick to my budget and buy pills by the day or the week.

Doreen Gully
Silver Spring, Maryland

PILL POINTER

Dear Amy,

A reader wrote in about buying prescriptions in small amounts. That is fine for people who are worried about allergic reactions, etc. However, you do end up paying more per pill that way. The pharmacy not only charges for the pills but also a dispensing fee (of about $3) each time they fill a prescription. If you have insurance you pay the copayment each time you get it filled. I know this because I used to work in a pharmacy.

Chris Bean
Sevartz Creek, Michigan

CALCULATING THE NET VALUE OF THE SECOND INCOME

Some time ago I met a woman at a party who told me she worked because she *had* to. I should have let this comment slide by, but I didn't. Instead I interrogated her mercilessly until I was able to get her to admit she worked because she *wanted* to. She did not appreciate my attempt to enlighten, and I did regret doing it.

If you have concluded that I think mothers who work outside the home are subhuman, you are wrong. I just get a little off kilter when middle-income families do not assume responsibility for their choices.

This woman, it turned out, was a teacher, and she was genuinely enriched by her job. She just had unresolved feelings about her role as a parent.

Families choose a two-income lifestyle for very good reasons. In the lowest-income groups it is usually an economic necessity. I know of many cases when the wife works because her husband's job lacks security or sufficient benefits. Usually the purpose of the second income is to elevate the standard of living.

All these reasons can be valid. It would be clearly stupid of me to nitpick the choices of working moms when I am indebted to many. Some wonderful school-teachers and delivery room nurses come to mind.

This lengthy prelude is, admittedly, literary clutter because this article is not about values. My biggest concern about the traditional two-income structure is that it can be extremely inefficient.

To illustrate this I am using a scenario of a family of four with two incomes of $25,000 and $15,000. Neither spouse is self-employed (thereby paying less social security), and both have equal benefits.

The most complicated factor to figure is the bigger tax bite. I am presuming my couple does not

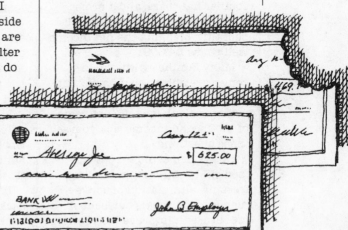

itemize. A $15,000 income loses about 12% to federal and state income tax, and social security. A $25,000 income has about 18% withheld. But as these two incomes combine, our couple moves into a higher tax bracket. A $40,000 income has about 22% withheld. In reality what this means is that the $15,000 loses 27% to the tax bite. To determine this I figured the couple's taxes with a $40,000 income and a $25,000 income. The difference is then subtracted from the $15,000 income.

$40,000 income pays $8,638
$25,000 income pays $4,516
additional taxes = $4,122

When the difference is subtracted from $15,000, the net is $10,878.

My couple has two children in daycare at a cost of $120 per week. (Daycare costs exceed $100 per child weekly in urban areas. Infants cost even more.) After factoring in the child care tax deduction, the income drops to $5,838 annually. Transportation, costlier hair care, and a professional wardrobe can further impact this, bringing the net income well below $4,000.

Many families with two incomes are able to economize, but the reality is that most do not. If you are calculating the net value of the second income, ask yourself these questions:

How much could we cut our food bill by gardening, canning, freezing, elimination of convenience foods, meals out, school lunches, and improved shopping skills?

How much could we save by spending more time shopping for better prices on the purchase of household goods?

Could we eliminate services we currently buy because of a lack of time, such as home maintenance and renovation, tax preparation, house cleaning, tutoring, etc.?

How much could be saved on birthdays and holidays by making gifts?

How much could be saved by writing letters instead of making long-distance phone calls?

How much could we save on clothing by yard saling, watching sales, sewing, and repairing clothing?

How much could we save by using cloth diapers and hanging laundry?

If wood heat is a factor, how much could we save by 100% wood use and providing some labor?

In addition to the endless ways to save money with more free time, families with lower incomes qualify for special benefits. In Maine families earning $30,000 or less qualify for subsidized loans if they are a first-time home buyer. (Our income was low enough, but we were disqualified because we had saved too much money!) As children reach college age they can obtain more loans and scholarships.

When you calculate the net value of your second income, work out your taxes both ways. State taxes and individual deductions will vary.

If you decide you want to scale back to one income, you must be sure you are willing to actually economize in the ways you factored in.

If you are single or newly married and wish to achieve a single income lifestyle, be aware that it requires aggressive planning. It is not a matter of luck. Many double-income families who believe they work because they have to are in reality paying for past choices.

If you both love your jobs . . . great. But if you would like to work less or leave your job altogether, an evening with a calculator may turn up a pleasant surprise.

TWO INCOMES

Dear Amy,
It seems that you have started your gazette at just the right time. People are beginning to

wake up and realize that they are not saving a lot by working two jobs. I know I wished I had stayed home with our son. We could have saved so much. Since I gave up a full-time job in favor of a part-time weekend job, my husband has admitted that the quality of our lives has improved and that we are doing better now.

Matilda Carreras
Malden Massachusetts

(She also included an article that appeared in the August 1990 issue of Parents *magazine called "Can You Afford to Quit?" It came to an identical conclusion as my article "Calculating the Net Value of the Second Income." Check your library for back issues of* Parents *magazine. FZ)*

PIGGYBACK POSTAGE

Dear Amy,

To save on postage, form a neighborhood group to use a common envelope and stamp to mail bills. In our neighborhood all the telephone bills are due on the 4th, water bills on the 10th, etc. When three neighbors combine their bills with a fourth neighbor, 87¢ is saved. This is not a big savings, especially when divided by several families, but can foster a spirit of "community tightwaddery."

Connie Tefteller
La Vernia,
Texas

HOMEMADE GRANOLA

The homemade granola contributions from several readers and the gift of a few pounds of Georgia pecans inspired me to dig out my granola recipe. Presuming that you buy the ingredients cheaply enough and you avoid the option of nuts, this recipe will make a 2-oz. serving for about 10¢ to 12¢, or half the price of name-brand cereals and less than a third of many commercial granolas.

¾ cup brown sugar
⅓ cup vegetable oil
⅓ cup honey
5 cups oatmeal
½ cup raisins*
½ cup dry milk
¾ teaspoon cinnamon
pinch of salt

Mix brown sugar, oil, and honey in a saucepan. Heat until the sugar is dissolved. Combine dry ingredients in a large cake pan. Pour sugar mixture over dry mixture and mix well. Bake at 375° for 10 minutes. Let cool in pan. Store in an airtight container.
Optional: add nuts, wheat germ, coconut, dates, etc.
* add raisins after cooking

TOILET PAPER STRATEGY

Dear Amy,

This is what I discovered when my umpteen grandchildren came to visit: The bathroom was in constant use and I had to run to the store to renew my supply of toilet paper. That roll of paper was letting them grab miles of it at a time, and so before I replaced a roll, I stood on it with one foot. It was no longer round like a circle but was creased instead. When the roll was put back it would

turn around three times and tear off easy. It saves money, trees, and a stuffed-up sewer line.
Mrs. Mary Fedorka
Jamestown, New York

(Not to mention that this could potentially dampen the thrill that a toddler receives from gleefully unwinding a whole roll, stuffing it in the toilet, flushing half a dozen times, flooding the upstairs bathroom to the extent that all the kitchen ceiling lights fill with water before spilling into the kitchen during the major monthly mailing. FZ)

THE SCROUNGED HALLOWEEN COSTUME

Chances are that you will not be creating a Halloween costume for a six-year-old boy who wants to be a robot. In fact, it is possible to live one's entire life without being pressed into any costume designing.

This article is really about creating something from nothing. The process is the same as putting together a gourmet meal from leftovers or building a wheelbarrow from salvaged materials.

If it happens that there is a six-year-old in your house that does want to be a robot, do not read this as a "paint by numbers" how-to article.

The creative tightwad method requires that you draw from your own resources—your talents and materials you can obtain cheaply or are in surplus. You do not have the same materials on hand that I did. You may not have the same skills or husband waiting in the wings willing to lend technical support.

Before asking your child what he wants to be this year, access your resources. One year the only material I had to make costumes was from a pile of old black Navy uniforms. I told the children they could be anything they wanted to be as long as it was something black. When you are stuck for an idea, let your available materials be your springboard.

The following year Alec told me he wanted to be a transformer. I accessed my resources and decided even I wasn't that creative. We compromised with a robot design. The springboard was a milk jug mask design I had developed a few years before. Having just moved we had a surplus of cardboard boxes and a discarded dryer duct. I had a can of silver spray paint and I gambled that Jim would have some electronic or mechanical stuff kicking around.

The result was a successful collaboration of Jim's and my skills. We made our community debut at the church Halloween party. Alec won the "Most Creative Costume" award, but the real prize was seeing him surrounded by a crowd of older boys checking out the front door panel. One voice

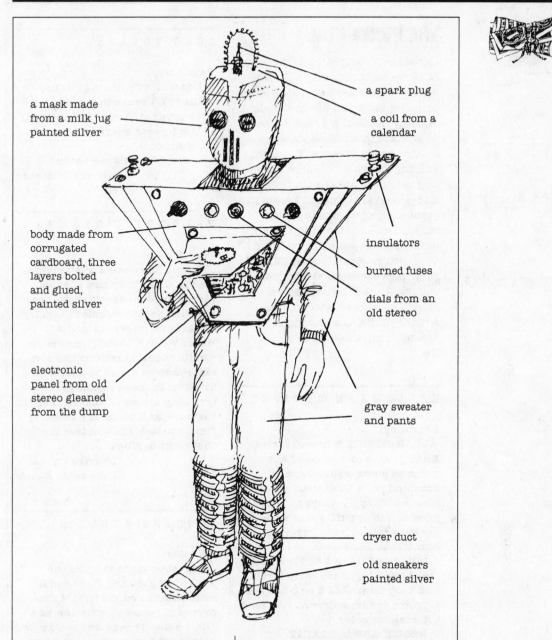

a mask made from a milk jug painted silver

a spark plug

a coil from a calendar

body made from corrugated cardboard, three layers bolted and glued, painted silver

insulators

burned fuses

dials from an old stereo

electronic panel from old stereo gleaned from the dump

gray sweater and pants

dryer duct

old sneakers painted silver

announced, "This is the best costume any kid could ever have!"

My children are not always clad with award-winning efforts. The two-year-old was shortchanged with a fire hat and red raincoat.

This kind of quality-time project has value beyond the production of a good costume. The dime store ones are cheap enough. But by observing you, children learn how to create and they learn craft. These powerful memories imprint a more important message. They come to understand the superiority of the creative tightwad method.

THE PUREE PLAN

Carve your pumpkin on October 30. Save all the cuttings. On November 1 salvage the jack-o'-lantern. Cut it up and discard peels and any blackened areas. Prepare as you would winter squash by cutting in small cubes. Fill a pot and add 2 inches of water. Cover and boil until soft. Drain water and process in blender. Freeze in (reused) Ziploc bags in 2-cup quantities. Save for Thanksgiving pumpkin pie, pumpkin pudding (pie with no crust), or muffins. After puree is thawed it is often watery, unlike the canned version. Use excess water to mix with dry milk to make mock cream or milk needed in your recipe.

HALLOWEEN RECIPES

Dear Amy,

SCAR TISSUE. Mix unflavored Knox gelatin and drops of hot water to make a paste. Apply drooping open flesh with a spatula. Gently apply a layer of baby powder with a puff. Paint with acrylic craft paint to resemble scar tissue and blood.

WHITE GREASE PAINT. Mix 2 tsp shortening, 5 tsp cornstarch and 1 tsp flour. Add 2 or 3 drops of glycerin for smoothness. Add food coloring for color.

BROWN GREASE PAINT. Mix 1 tsp shortening and 2½ tsp cocoa. Add 2 or 3 drops of glycerin.

Both grease paints wash off with baby oil, cold cream, or Crisco.

Merrie Hallman
Liv Manor, New York

COLD ROLLER

Dear Amy,

I do a lot of painting (walls, ceilings). I reuse the same roller with cover still on it by putting it in the freezer overnight. Just thaw to reuse.

Elaine Levine
Scarborough, Maine

HALF-PRICE STAMPS

Dear Amy,

People buy sheets of all stamps issued. Then they tire of them, die, or need money. The stamps are then sold to a dealer (usually as part of a larger collection). Usually older, the stamps are in smaller denominations and considered to be a pain to deal with. The dealer doesn't want them unless they are rare, and will sell them for half price. It's worth it for me to lick a few extras for that basic savings.

Charles Tanner
Falmouth, Maine

SUCCESS STORY

Dear Amy,

I must write to tell you the kind of impact *The Tightwad Gazette* has had on my life. My father sent me a subscription as a gift. I actually received two issues. In the past several weeks I have read each at least six times and highlighted the main points.

Last Monday I went shopping, keeping in mind your suggestions for savings. My normal bill for 10 days' worth of food for 3 was about $110. This past Monday I purchased the same amount of food, just different types. To my total glee the bill was $60.94! Almost half. And, yes, I did buy the dry milk and so far my family has not noticed the switch.

Morgan M. Franks
Hackettstown, New Jersey

(Learning how to feed a family for as little as we do can take a year or more to learn, especially if gardening is to be a part of the plan. Morgan's ability to nearly cut her food bill in half in a matter of weeks is terrific. FZ)

AIR FRESHENER

Dear Amy,
   We find that instead of using the highly perfumed and expensive room refreshers, such as Airwick and Glade, we can easily get rid of unpleasant odors by simply lighting a match. We have not yet tried it as an underarm deodorant!

Jim Spaulding
Northfield, Massachusetts

STAIN REMEDY

Dear Amy,
   My father-in-law had made me savvy to the dishwasher detergent/all-fabric bleach combo* years ago. But for even tougher stains, a paste of Barkeeper's Friend cleanser on the stain for about five minutes has had remarkable results for me.

Anne Fairfield
Wiscasset, Maine

(This reader refers to my stain recipe on page 272. FZ)*

GETTING A BARGAIN EVERY TIME

We had a burst of company the first summer after we bought the house . . . relatives coming to see our new home for the first time. Part way through the umpteenth house tour I realized that every other sentence coming out of my mouth started to the effect of: "We bought this at a yard sale" or "Jim scrounged this. . . ." After taking a quick inventory of our household stuff, it became obvious of the high percentage of goods we have obtained as the result of expert bargain hunting. I could more easily single out the items purchased in department-store desperation.

Our style of acquisition is strikingly different from most families I know. Typically people tend to notice today that they will need a new something tomorrow, run to Kmart, and put it on a charge card. They purchase, paying full price with interest. If they change their mind about their rushed purchase, they yard sale it for a 90% loss of their investment. (And someone like me buys it.)

If you are an impulse buyer, the first strategy you need to employ is *foresight.* You need to anticipate needs as far in advance as possible. Time is the key to finding bargains. It is not unreasonable to spend years shopping for a house, a year shopping for a car, or six months shopping for a tool.

During this period you should do extensive research. You need to determine your exact needs. Decide if you can get by with the inexpensive simpler model or if you really need the more expensive one with all the features. Will a used item serve your needs as well? If so spend time in thrift shops, flea markets, and at yard sales, etc. to determine the "going price." Also look into your local swap magazine.

Only after you have done extensive research will you be certain you have found a genuine bargain.

It goes without saying that during this time you should plan your finances so that you have the available cash at the time you need it. If you know you will purchase a house in three years, do the homework to determine the down payment you'll need. Sometimes people miss smaller bargains for lack of funds. As a woman once told me, "Yes, I saw that sale on chicken, but I didn't have $10 to spare at the time."

Patience is the second element. It takes time to find your bargain. You need to stretch out your "looking-around time" as much as possible. Do not even consider paying full price for anything, and persist with your hunt.

Third, *improvise*. Often you will not find your bargain before the need comes due—the camping trip is next weekend and you are short two sleeping bags. Can you temporarily borrow the item you need? Can you rent the tool for one or two occasions? Can you make a widget that will do for a short time? In other words, bedrolls work almost as well as sleeping bags.

It does happen that some items never go on sale or turn up at a yard sale. When you get to this point you will be confident that you have done your best in finding a bargain. Pay full price only when you are certain that you have exhausted all possibilities.

How long is too long to wait? A good rule of thumb is to buy when it costs you money *not* to own it. Examples include a car, a washer, or a new business suit.

Otherwise, be stubborn and persistant.

I ruined our $14 teakettle by allowing the water to boil out. (Murphy's Law dictates that you will destroy new expensive purchases first.) We improvised by using a coffee perker (minus the guts) until I ruined that one two weeks later. In the following months we limped along boiling water in a pot, waiting for a bargain.

Then Jim found another perker (minus the guts) for $1 in a thrift shop. Since the destruction of two hot water vessels (and a couple of pots over the years) constitutes a habit, we are employing foresight. We are continuing our search for other cheap teakettles.

THE PRICE BOOK

I was four years into my thrift quest before I realized I needed to develop some sort of book to keep track of prices. I often wonder if all the various sizes and brands is part of a huge conspiracy to confuse consumers. With this possibility in mind, I set out to beat them at their own game.

Although prices on many items can vary widely from store to store, they probably average out overall. But what if I could buy only the cheapest products at each store?

We shop at a supermarket, a natural foods store, a day-old-bread store, a warehouse store, a smaller overpriced store with terrific sales, and we buy a few items from local farmers. (We don't shop at the Navy commissary because it is located an hour away from us and the savings are marginal.)

My price book is a small loose-leaf binder. Each page contains prices for one item, and the pages are in alphabetical order for quick reference. I include my code for the store name, the brand, the size of the item, the price, and the unit price.

I began by writing down prices on sale flyers and from my grocery slips. I made a few trips to compare prices of specific items.

It quickly became evident that not every sale was really a sale. But when I did find

a good buy, and I could verify it with months of records . . . what power! I could stock up with confidence.

At first you may think this is too much work and the idea of shopping at so many stores will be inconceivable. It will pay off. A good strategy is to shop at different stores each week of the month so that within a 30-day cycle you can hit them all. We have our shopping system down to once a month with only a few short trips to hit unbeatable sales.

The keeping of a price book revolutionized our shopping strategy more than anything else we did. For the first time we had a feeling of control over our food budget.

PEANUT BUTTER

SNS GENERIC 18oz./99¢   .88¢/lb.

CM GENERIC 4lb./3.38   .85¢/lb.

CW PETER PAN 2lb 8oz/3.67   1.44¢/lb.

16A STORE BRAND 18oz/99¢   88¢/lb

MS ALL NATURAL 1lb./1.79   1.79 lb.

AN URBAN EXCURSION

Twice a month I venture into the "city" to pick up or drop off printing. Each 50-mile round trip saves money on the cost of printing my newsletter. To make this effort more profitable I hit thrift shops, day-old bread stores, yard sales, discount stores, etc. On page 33 is a table that depicts the results of a real outing. The entire trip, with all the stops, took three hours. We estimated our savings based on typical supermarket or department store prices.

If you travel to an area other than where you regularly shop, I recommend that you make a  point of investigating any stores that might offer a discount, and record items into your price book. In the future when you make a trip, make it a point to pick up items with worthwhile prices. Always compare prices with your price book (see below) and never assume any discount store offers best prices on every item.

Not including the savings on printing and factoring in gas, this trip earned (saved) us a tax-free $32 per hour.

GROCERY PRICES

Dear Amy,
   Thanks for the idea on pricing all area stores. I was so surprised when my impressions were completely wrong. Even the discount warehouse was higher than our local store on a few items. Also the food co-op we participate in had some great bargains and some items way overpriced!
   Joyce Bussell
   Jensen Beach, Florida

SOURCE	ITEM	COST	EST. SAV.
Wholesale Depot, a large warehouse store	2 gal. generic shampoo	$ 4.18 ea	$ 7.48
	1 gal. generic conditioner	4.18 ea	3.74
	1 ltr soda	free	1.00
	50 lbs Purina dog food	15.99	1.09
	12" x 2,000' plastic wrap	4.83	9.07
	40 lbs generic detergent	9.99	12.50
	1 gal. Murphy's Oil Soap	7.63	1.93
	1½ lbs dog chews	4.88	.49
Caswell's, a liquidation center	8 12-oz apple juice conc.	.57 ea	2.00
	24 20-oz cans of pineapple	.49 ea	6.00
Marden's, a salvage store	5 rolls of clear tape	.20 ea	2.50
	25 mailing envelopes	.11 ea	3.25
Yard sales	27 qt. canning jars	3.00	9.50
	soup thermos	.25	1.75
	snowsuit	.50	24.00
	boys' denim jacket	1.00	14.00
	Total	$76.12	$100.30

HOW TO BUY FOOD IN BULK

The typical American shops once a week. Each trip includes a walk down every aisle as he puts enough in his cart to last seven days. This shopping style is time consuming and expensive.

We have fallen into this pattern perhaps because we tend to be paid weekly, or because a small percentage of groceries (milk, produce) has a shelf life of about a week. Sales also run weekly.

Even if the shopper were to stop in weekly for produce, milk, and the unbeatable sale, touring each aisle need not be necessary.

Bulk buying, or stocking up, saves money, and although you may shop at more than one store it need not require more time, and will probably *save* time.

The first rule of bulk buying is to know your prices. Never assume that one source of food has the lowest price on every item, regardless of the type of store. To effectively determine the lowest price you must establish some method of tracking prices and frequency of sales. We use a price book system, as discussed in the preceding article. This information tells you which store to buy each item from and how much to buy. A few hours spent doing this research can save you hundreds of dollars over the year. Do not forgo this step, thinking it is too much work. I have had many readers write saying they tried the price book and "It works!"

Secondly you must investigate all sources of food in your area. Aside from grocery stores, check out warehouse stores, salvage stores, food co-ops, and even local farmers. As a general rule the loss leader sale items, which appear on the cover and back of sale flyers, will beat the prices of any wholesale source of food. The grocer takes a loss on these items figuring you will buy other products at the regular price. However, many staples never go on sale, so you will look for other sources for these items.

Bulk buying isn't just for big families. Simply put, buy enough to get you to the next sale or enough until it's convenient for you to stop there again. For example, we go past a bakery thrift shop twice a month. Each time I buy two weeks' worth of bread. We never make a special trip. Obviously a large family buys more than a single person. Each buys in bulk according to his need.

Note the date of any rare, unbeatable sales. In some cases you might detect a pattern of frequency. If you determine that peanut butter goes on sale once every three months, you should buy a three-month supply.

Many bulk foods are packaged in large quantities. The 50-pound sack of oatmeal will not be practical for the small family. Co-ops came into existence to address this need. Generally in the form of a buying club, groups of families band together to buy large quantities and split them up into smaller ones. As formal organizations, members are usually asked to donate a few hours of labor per month.

Food co-ops vary greatly in character. Some deal only with organic foods while others carry a line of frozen and prepackaged foods. Finding one that suits your needs may prove difficult.

An alternative is the informal co-op. A small group of friends, who buy similar foods, agrees to split up large quantities or pick up large quantities of sale items for others in the group. This saves time, gasoline, and money. These options address the needs of the smaller family units and those people with storage and time limitations.

To find additional room for bulk foods, rethink the spaces in your home. If you were offered $50 per month to rent out the space under your bed would you do it? People tend to think that all food must be stored in kitchen cabinets. However, a closet can be converted to a pantry and unused spaces, such as under your bed, can store a case of bargain canned pineapple. Buying in bulk can save the average family at least $50 per month.

To buy in bulk most effectively you should have a freezer. Used for garden surplus as well, the savings far outweigh the cost of electricity. The largest Sears freezer costs under $6 per month to operate. If you do not have a garden, you should select a smaller model. While some families and singles genuinely may not have room for a freezer, I have known renters who worked out arrangements to leave their freezer in the apartment basement. Freezers come with a lock.

Many people do not buy in bulk because they live paycheck to paycheck. Available dollars must be used to buy food for this week, not next month. The inability to bulk buy is one of the many ways that being "poor" makes your lifestyle more expensive. Make a small beginning. Eat more meatless meals or eliminate some nonessential grocery items. Use the surplus to begin buying in bulk. The savings will provide more spare cash to reinvest. Within a few months you should not have to think twice about affording to buy in bulk.

To make the most of buying in bulk you will probably have to let go of budgetary guidelines (allowing yourself only a very strict amount to be spent per week). You should not miss a great sale because you've already spent your quota. Instead work toward an average. As you begin to buy in bulk your food bill will be high the first month, but eventually the average will drop to a new low as you gradually eat a larger percentage of foods purchased at the lowest possible price.

After three years of living in this area we still find new sources of inexpensive foods. Even within the past few weeks we have found less expensive sources of cheese, chicken, and powdered milk. Two of these sources were through word of mouth. Ask around, especially of those people you know to be shrewd shoppers. Try to find wholesale distributors in your Yellow Pages. One in our area primarily sells to bakeries, and is listed under "Bakery Supplies." A wholesale distributor may or may not sell to individuals. Or they may have minimum order requirements. However, they can give you the names of a storefront co-op or buying club that they sell to.

If you are unable to locate sources of bulk foods send an SASE to:

Co-op Directory Services
919 21st Ave. South
Minneapolis, MN 55404

This service will provide you with the name of a regional wholesaler who can give you the names of local co-ops, buying clubs, or storefronts.

Learning to bulk buy, like the acquisition of any new skill, requires an initial investment of time. The long-range dividends are unquestionable.

RIBBON TRICK

Dear Amy,

One tightwad tip that you might not have heard of is to spray faded (but not torn) typewriter ribbons with WD-40, which renews some oil used in typewriter ribbon inks.

Joseph Hagedorn
Cincinnati, Ohio

FREE RIDE

Dear Amy,

In 25 years of driving over 30,000 miles a year, I haven't spent a cent to own the cars.

When I first started in business, I called the local commercial credit office to inquire about repossessed cars. They had dozens, and I bought two for a total of $500 . . . sold one for $600, and that began my odyssey of not spending money for cars.

When I tired of that car (remember I got that car and $100 to start) I ran an ad to sell my "Classic 1959 Plymouth" and sold it for $400. I used that $400 to buy a 1962 Volvo, drove it two years, ran another "classic" ad and sold it for $600. I bought another Volvo for $500 . . . and I've repeated the process about 15 times.

Part of the formula involves negotiating. I might look at 10 cars (all private sales, no dealers) before I find one I like that can be bought right. I pull out my money in $100 bills, explain that I'm on my way to look at another car, but if I could buy theirs for X (usually half of what they are asking) I can give them cash now.

Sometimes I have to drive away and look at more cars, but 15 times they accepted my offer.

I prefer Volvos, as they last, hold value, and give great service. I do my own maintenance, using a Chilton's guide or the manual for that model car. I change the oil every 3,000 miles, keep them clean, had several Maaco $100 paint jobs, and always have whitewall tires.

Bill Niland
Topsfield, Massachusetts

GOOD DEAL

Dear Amy,

I recently discovered "price adjustment policies." I first learned of them from a discount department store. If I make a purchase and that item goes on sale, within 30 days, I can take my receipt to Customer Service for a cash refund of the difference. I have already received $5 back on school supplies.

I called other larger department stores and specialty shops in my area and learned they also had the same unwritten policy. One store even has a policy that if I make a purchase of an item that I know had been on sale within the past 30 days, they will give me the former sale price. All the stores I researched also gave a price adjustment for items that are on layaway that go on sale.

Some stores make the offer for seven days after the purchase only. Only one store wanted to see a dated sales receipt and the merchandise. Some stores have exclusions, such as for clearance of special-event sales. One store would make a price adjustment if a competitor had the same item on sale.

D. T. Mercer
Loma, Colorado

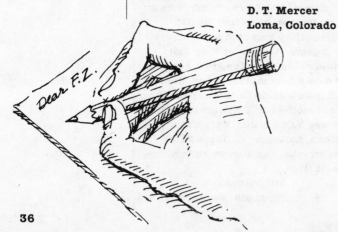

PAPER SAVER

Dear Amy,

I work in a busy office that utilizes personal computers and printers that use up a lot of paper. There is an extraordinary amount of paper wasted after printing. I save any blank or unused sheets. By the end of the day I might have 5 to 10 sheets. I use these to make envelopes.

Make a template from a piece of cardboard the same size as a business- or letter-size envelope. Then cut the paper 10″ × 10″ for legal size, or 7½″ × 7½″ for a letter-size envelope. Place the tem-

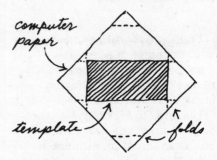

plate in the middle of the paper on an angle. Using the template as a guide, first fold the sides, next the bottom, and finally the top. Use glue or glue stick to secure.

Margaret Williams
DeLand, Florida

A READER QUESTION

Dear Amy,
I am interested in finding out how your husband purchased a new car and saved so much money. I am desperate for some ammo when dealing with car dealers. It's a jungle out there!

Judith Perry
Lee, Massachusetts

Dear Judith,

Purchasing a new car can only be considered economical if you plan to own it for more than 10 years, you maintain it meticulously, and you buy it with cash. The exception would be if your cash is invested in a safe plan that has a higher interest rate than the interest rate you could get for a car loan. At least try to pay off the loan quickly.

Figuring that you expect to own this vehicle for 10 or more years, plan ahead. Don't buy a compact car if you are planning a family. Carefully consider the options you want. When purchasing our Horizon we decided to save $250 and not get the rear window wiper and defogger. However, there were many frigid mornings of

frost scraping that we wished we had gotten it.

The ammo to which you refer can be found at bookstores . . . a new car buyer's guide. Find one that pertains to the type of vehicle you want, tells you the suggested list price and dealer's cost. The dealer's cost is broken down by models and options.

After you decide on the model you want, visit a dealer to learn the codes for options and which options go together.

Make up a list of options with the codes, dealer's cost, and the suggested list price. Total up the prices. From this determine what you feel is an allowable profit, bearing in mind that the dealer will get further discounts below the dealer cost. A $200 to $500 profit will be adequate.

Start making the rounds of dealers and tell them what you would be willing to pay. If they do not want to meet your price, go elsewhere. To speed up the process you can mail copies of your specifications and price you are willing to pay to other area dealers.

Also check on buying clubs or organizations that can get you a group discount.

In general, remember that sometimes at the end of the month dealers become desperate to make a sales quota. Don't let dealers talk you into buying something other than what you have decided you want.

Avoid trading in. You'll get a better price for your old car through a private sale.

Ignore sales and rebates. These are designed to confuse you.

If you buy "off-the-lot" you will likely pay for options you didn't really

want, and not get ones you really wanted. The dealer has money tied up in a lot car and won't give you as good a deal.

In general, dealerships will not sell any car at a loss. They don't operate like grocery stores, which sell one item at a loss to get you to buy several more. You will buy only one car from them. However, they will cut their profits to the bone.

Your only consideration should be the bottom line. How much you "save" is not as important as how much you spend.

Using this method Jim has gotten roughly 20% off the sticker price of two vehicles.

MYSTERIES OF THE MODERN WORLD

Why is it that if I had placed my six children in daycare at a cost of about $250 per week, and I worked a job grossing $100 per week, our family would have qualified for a larger mortgage loan?

Why do people moonlight for a few more dollars to make ends meet and then buy convenience foods because of a lack of time?

Why is it that people won't donate to charities, but will buy overpriced merchandise they do not need because it's for a good cause?

THE SPIDER WEB GAME

The standard games for Halloween are always great ... they're traditional. Here's one you might never have heard of. This is called the Spider Web Game.

You are having a small party with about 10 people. You need a few balls of white string and 10 prizes. You tie an end of string around a prize and hide it. Then you unroll the ball of string and wind it around the room, wrapping it taut around chair legs, door knobs, window hardware, etc. Make a complex design. The string should not be loose on the floor. Tie the other end around a stick or small piece of cardboard. Repeat until you have made 10 string trails that crisscross and tangle up together. Design your game so that all the trails begin near the door. When your guests arrive they get their own stick to wind their string on as they follow their own trail.

This game is appropriate for guests of all ages (as long as they are limber enough to crawl under and over the string maze). You can make shorter trails for younger kids and longer, more difficult ones for older kids and adults. You can also choose specific prizes for age and sex. Just

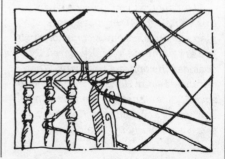

label the stick or cardboard with a name as you finish each trail.

I used this idea for a birthday party game one time. By the time I finished setting up the game I figure I burned up a few thousand calories. I finished at the front door. Then I realized I had forgotten something in one of the bedrooms . . . on the other side of the string web. It took a full 10 minutes to get across the room and back.

(Naturally, when you finish the Spider Web Game you must save the string.)

NEW/OLD QUILTS

Dear Amy,

Everyone loves handmade quilts; however, with the rising cost of material and batting, they become very expensive to make, and with the rising cost of heating they become very necessary to have.

To save money and recycle you can take an old quilt (factory made or handmade) that is stained or getting frayed and re-cover it. Yard sales often have stained quilts for very low prices.

You can use sheets for backing purchased at white sales and factory outlets. Use scraps of material collected over time (shirts ready for the rag bag usually have a nice square or two, as well as material left over when you cut off jeans).

After winter you can use this to display in your frugal country home.

**Betty Candage
Auburn, Maine**

CORN CASSEROLE

Dear Amy,

I had three ears of leftover corn, and ½ onion in the fridge. I cut the corn off the cob, chopped the onion, and threw them into a bowl together with a big handful of stale crackers, an egg, dry milk, a tablespoon of sugar, a little water, and blended it. Cooked it about ¾ hour in a 350° oven. My crew loved it!

**Attalie Boynton
Readfield, Maine**

SPENDTHRIFT HORROR STORY

Leeds, Maine, is a very rural farm community. Most of the families have practiced thrift for generations as a matter of survival. In this tightwad environment I am finding my fervor slipping and feel a need to go to a mall just to get my batteries recharged. Therefore I appreciate spendthrift horror stories like the following submission.

Dear Amy,

A friend and I were talking about sorting through fall and winter clothing for our sons. She thought she had done well in only paying $700 for school clothes and an additional $150 at department stores for her three-year-old. She also threw out all her son's size 5 clothes. My son has just outgrown his size 4 clothes. I would have happily traded my 4's for her 5 and 6 clothes. We would have both benefited. Of course she put her new purchases on credit cards. Ouch!

**Matilda Carreras
Billerica, Massachusetts**

THREE WAYS TO SAVE

There are three basic methods to save money.

1. Buy it cheaper
2. Make it last longer
3. Use it less

Using all three strategies may not work or be desirable in all situations. For instance, you shouldn't brush your teeth less. Or maybe you prefer the taste of the more expensive brands. But if you can combine strategies the results are dramatic.

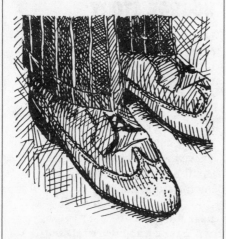

EXAMPLE:

You currently wear out one $75 pair of business shoes every six months, for an annual shoe cost of $150.

STRATEGY OPTIONS:

1. Before your shoes wear out you find a sale of your favorite brand for $60. You buy two pairs.

2. You double the life of the shoes by getting them reheeled for $10.

3. You double the life of your shoes by wearing last year's old shoes for street use.

RESULTING ANNUAL COST:

Strategy 1: $120
Strategy 2: $85
Strategy 3: $75

Strategies 1 and 2: $70
Strategies 1 and 3: $60
Strategies 2 and 3: $42.50

Strategies 1, 2, and 3: $35

EXAMPLE:

You are buying one can of coffee per month at $5.12 per can.

STRATEGY OPTIONS:

1. You switch brands and purchase coffee with a coupon.

2. You make your coffee go farther by reusing your grounds with half as much fresh grounds added to the old ones.

3. You decide to drink half as much coffee.

RESULTING MONTHLY COST:

Strategy 1: $1.18
Strategy 2: $3.84
Strategy 3: $2.56

Strategies 1 and 2: $.88
Strategies 1 and 3: $.59
Strategies 2 and 3: $1.92

Strategies 1, 2, and 3: $.44

EXAMPLE:

You currently spend $75 per month for gasoline.

STRATEGY OPTIONS:

1. You switch to pumping your own gas, and you learn where the cheapest stations are and fill up when in the area for a 10% cost savings.

2. You get a tune-up, change your oil, and make sure your tires are pumped to the right pressure. Even when the cost of the service is factored in, your improved mileage saves you 15% on gas for the year.

3. You reduce your transportation cost a third by car pooling, combining more errands, and walking more.

RESULTING MONTHLY COST:

Strategy 1: $67.50
Strategy 2: $63.75
Strategy 3: $50.00

Strategies 1 and 2: $57.37
Strategies 1 and 3: $45.00
Strategies 2 and 3: $42.33

Strategies 1, 2, and 3: $38.25

EXAMPLE:

You get your hair cut every six weeks for $25, including tip, for an annual cost of $216.67.

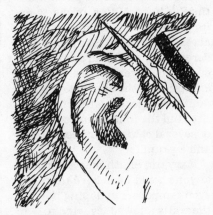

STRATEGY OPTIONS:

1. You shop around and find a less prestigious salon that does as good a job for $12.50.

2. No savings here. I haven't figured out how to make hair grow slower yet.

3. You trim your hair around the ears yourself so that you need to get a professional cut once every eight weeks.

RESULTING ANNUAL COST:

Strategy 1: $108.34
Strategy 3: $162.50

Strategies 1 and 3: $81.25

LIFESTYLES OF THE FRUGAL AND OBSCURE

Dave Smith told me he would have been better off burning the place and starting from scratch. I wondered at his sincerity, as the 43-year-old electrical contractor takes obvious pride in owning a home appraised at four times his investment.

The Smiths' home is a prime example of how ingenuity and a willingness to work can yield huge savings in home remodeling.

In 1988 the Smiths purchased the Readfield, Maine, property for its picturesque six and a half acres, planning to tear down the derelict house. It had been unoccupied for several years, with the exception of the short stay of a family who lost their home in a fire, and the long-term occupancy of several cats, sundry rodents, and a skunk.

Maryann Smith marveled that anyone could have lived there, even temporarily. Gaping holes in the walls allowed icy wind to blow through, the ceiling was falling down, and the critter invasion had left it less than sanitary. Judging from the pictures in

their scrapbook, I, too, would have doubted the building's salvageability.

But something stirred Dave's Scotch instincts, and one day he lifted a crowbar. During the following three years he gutted the main house,

and dismantled and rebuilt the addition. Today the home has a new roof, a shingled gray exterior, and a wrap-around deck. The interior features arched doorways, a new kitchen, two new baths, and a cathedral ceiling in the living room.

With a passion, Dave reused old materials. He pulled out the worn floor joists, turned them over, and reinstalled them for a fresh nailing edge. Maryann spent endless hours pulling nails out of old boards. Dave used scraps of old lumber to make new trim for windows and doors. He used wood in rougher condition for the internal structure of cabinets and other places where it would not be seen.

To purchase new materials cheaply, Dave learned which lumber yards would negotiate on materials they had been unable to sell. He bought five interior doors for the price of three because the packaging had been damaged. He bought odd lots of ceramic floor tile reduced in price because of barely visible color differences. The home has marble details purchased from an out-of-state factory outlet. Typically, a one-foot square that might cost $9 locally, cost 50¢.

Dave's job provides ample opportunity to scavenge discarded materials. The cellar lighting came from stores that were replacing and disposing of their old fixtures.

He constructed a water tank from a section of 18-inch-diameter stainless-steel pipe with a plate welded on the top and bottom. Most of the fittings were also scavenged. A new-looking sink for the laundry room came from another job site.

The house's unique feature, a two-floor spiral staircase, is a feat of engineering and welding. Dave scrounged scrap electrical conduit for years before he had enough to complete the framework.

Dave also keeps a lookout on trips to the dump. An old set of drawers provided porcelain knobs for the laundry room cabinet.

He scavenged some 15,000 old bricks from a burned mill and other sources to build walkways, steps, and garden walls.

Dave saves all leftover materials. He built an attractive kitchen countertop from scraps of hardwood flooring laid on a 45-degree angle. He used leftover ceramic floor tile from the kitchen for the countertop in the laundry room and leftover ceiling lumber for flooring in a bathroom. The lack of huge piles of surplus materials bears witness to his persistence in finding ways to use them.

Dave took advantage of inexpensive alternatives. He used dowels, which are low cost and versatile, to make spindles for his staircase and uprights for bookcases. By ripping them in half, Dave made counter trim for a fifth of the price of ready-made trim. Stucco, made from cement and sand, made a smooth covering on the interior of the cement-block foundation downstairs.

The Smiths' resourcefulness extends to some of the things within their home. Dave made a coat rack by soldering together leftover copper pipe. They were given a 28-year-old washer (fixed with $6 worth of parts) and a dryer (fixed with a few minutes of soldering). They bought televi-

sions for $10 and $45 from a local handyman. The workshop has a large rubber mat—formerly a conveyor belt—on the floor.

In the warmer months Maryann's green thumb provides the flowering plants for the deck while Dave provides the audio treat. He makes wind chimes from copper and aluminum pipe, and experiments with different designs for optimum resonance.

During my December house tour I couldn't help notice the lush 9-foot Christmas tree, and silently wagered it cost a bit more than the Charlie Brown special our family hauled from the woods. In Maine such a tree might go for $50, but few people have a ceiling high enough for one as big. I learned Dave waits until just before Christmas and dickers for a tree that didn't sell. This one cost $9.

The Smiths' home needs one more purchase to make it complete . . . they have not installed carpeting yet. When I asked when they would, Dave stroked his full auburn mustache and answered, "When we find a good deal."

EASY ZIPPER REPAIR

One of the best thrift shop/yard sale bargains can be an article of clothing with a broken zipper. They are frequently marked down because most people shy away from "the monumental task" of replacing a broken zipper. However zipper repair can involve only a few minutes to an hour of time.

I will purchase an item with a broken zipper if it's practically free (maybe 25¢) and it's a hard-to-come-by commodity, such as a child's jacket, a snowsuit, or a backpack. If I point out the damage to the yard sale or thrift shop proprietor I might get the garment free.

There are several cases in which zipper replacement isn't feasible. I wouldn't replace a zipper on an article of clothing that could be easily found again, such as pants. Some zippers were sewn into the garment from the inside before it was finished, such as zippers on pockets. In this case, a zipper replacement might be extremely complex and time consuming. Some coats have zippers in combination with large snaps. Zipper replacement may be impossible if the snaps would get in the way of machine sewing. I wouldn't bother replacing a zipper on a garment that has other undesirable qualities such as stains, excessive wear, or a dated look.

I also look closely to make sure the zipper really needs replacing. A close-ended (or dress) zipper with a break near the bottom may be repaired without replacement. My daughter broke the zipper on her backpack an inch from the

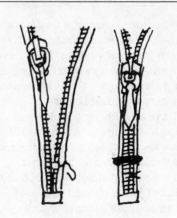

bottom (or beginning). By snipping off the damaged and stretched plastic zipper teeth I was able to restart the zipper. Then I hand sewed the zipper securely just above the break to prevent it from coming apart again.

A separating zipper, such as on a jacket, with a break at the top that allows the zipper pull to come off track, can also be repaired with thread. Simply make a new "zipper stopper" by sewing several layers of thread below the break.

If the zipper pull is missing you can replace it with a small metal ring, a tiny metal ring with some type of charm, or even with a paperclip.

Before replacing an unfixable zipper, consider other possible alternatives. My daughter's jacket had a broken zipper covered by a large flap with Velcro fasteners. If the coat had a zipper in combination with snaps I could have simply removed the zipper. I also considered adding buttons to the jacket by making buttonholes on the flap. Ultimately I decided that replacing the zipper would be best.

If you determine that a zipper must be replaced completely, carefully look at the construction of the garment. Usually the broken zipper can be replaced by ripping out only two or three seams. If the procedure looks more complex, make notes as to the sequence that you follow to rip out the seams. You will want to put in the new zipper by reversing the sequence.

A new zipper, especially a heavy one for a jacket, can cost as much as $4. You can save money by scavenging a zipper from another garment. In the case of Jamie's jacket, I scavenged a zipper from a worn windbreaker, which I purchased at a $1-per-bag sale at a thrift shop. Because I purchased several other items, the zipper was essentially free. (You can save money on buttons this way as well.)

Used zippers offer two basic advantages. They are preshrunk, and because they've held up for a period of time already, they probably will continue to hold up. I would try to get a metal zipper over a plastic one, because of the durability factor.

When scavenging a zipper it might not be necessary to get a precise color match, especially if the zipper is hidden by a flap. In the case of Jamie's jacket, the black scavenged zipper looked fine with a multicolored design. The old zipper in her

jacket extended to the tips of the collar. I stopped the new zipper at the throat, and stitched the collar closed.

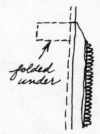

folded under

In addition, the zipper doesn't have to be the same length—it can be longer. You can use a longer zipper by cutting it at the precise length needed and sewing "zipper stoppers" or you can cut the zipper ⅜ inch longer than needed and fold the surplus under at a 45-degree angle. When you sew the zipper in place you will secure the end in the seam.

The trick to replacing a zipper is good preparation. First pin the zipper into position and then baste. (Basting is hand sewing with a large running stitch.) Remove the pins before machine stitching, and the basting afterwards. If the zipper lies flat, lines up well, and works well in the basting stage, you ensure the best result when you machine stitch. Basting is especially important if the garment has an inner and outer piece of fabric to line up when stitching the zipper in place.

Always machine stitch from the visible side. It can be hard to make both the inside and outside perfect, so remember that you want the outside to look best. Be sure to keep the material a uniform distance away from the zipper so it can't get caught when zipping.

A sewing machine is an important tool to save money in clothing repair. First attempts to learn new skills can be frustrating, but they're an important time investment that can lead to future savings.

BAGGIE BASICS

Letters from readers lead me to believe that there is some mystery about the proper method to wash out plastic bags. Here are a few pointers to illuminate this basic tightwad task:

I only wash out sturdy Ziploc (or other brand equivalent) bags. The flimsy sandwich bags do not seem to dry as well.

I never save any bag that was used to store meats. Greasy bags are hard to wash as well. I store meats in other bags or plastic wrap. Most important, I never, ever reuse any bag that stored raw poultry.

Due to these precautions, I can personally report that in nearly 10 years of Baggie washing I have yet to lose a family member to food poisoning.

Wash bags in the same dishwater in which you wash dishes (so that the cost of water does not become a factor). Wash bags while the water is still fairly clean.

To wash a bag that held something goopy, such as pumpkin puree, turn it inside out over your hand and wash with a dishrag. Ones that contained something relatively dry and solid, like carrot sticks, require only minimal swishing.

Entrepreneurs have devised several kinds of plastic-bag drying racks that you can buy. The problem is I don't want such an odd contraption taking up space in my kitchen.

I drape washed bags over kitchen utensils already drying in the dish rack. If I run out of utensils to hang them on, I whip out a skewer or chopstick and prop it in the drainer.

Most of my Baggies are used for school lunches. With two kids in school I wash as many as six per day. When I have six kids in school my dish drainer is an unsightly tower of as many as 18 Baggies, assorted utensils, skewers, and chopsticks.

(As I was writing this article an idea came across my desk. Janet Groleau of Menominee, Michigan, wrote that you can make a noodle dryer out of

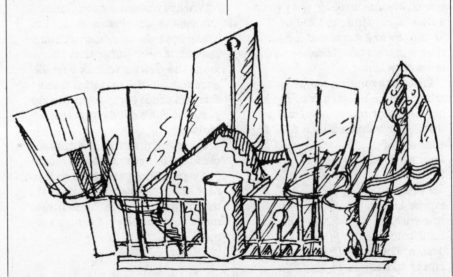

Tinkertoys. A vision of a Tinkertoy bag dryer came to me. OK. Far-fetched, but funny.)

Dry bags inside out. That way, even if the bags don't completely dry, any remaining droplets will be on the outside.

There are several ways to squeeze more life from bags. During a radio interview, a caller told me that when the seams on the "zipper" start to split on the edges, he fuses them with the tip of an iron.

If the zipper begins to separate completely from the bag, cut it off altogether and use a bread tab to close it.

If a bag has a small hole, don't throw it away yet—use it for foods that don't need to be air-tight, like popcorn.

Here's my answer to the most critical Baggie-washing question: When do you throw it away? When washing the bag, fill it with water and hold it up. If the bag resembles a sprinkler you may throw it away. I've never tracked an average Baggie life span, but I have used them until the white block (where you write the bag's contents) has worn off.

One could argue that we should use plastic freezer containers and plastic food containers for lunch boxes. The argument has some merit, but I couldn't fit three plastic containers and a thermos in one lunch box.

Except for the Ziploc bags we buy for freezing garden produce and recycle for household use, we never buy any plastic bags. Think about the plastic bags you throw away daily. Panty hose comes in a bag with a sheet of cardboard. I reuse the bags that brown sugar comes in. One of my staff takes lightweight produce bags back to the grocery store and refills them (even though they're free . . . this is an environmental tip, not an economic one).

Any bag with paint, such as a bread bag, should not be used inside out.

For all of you longtime tight-wads, who can't believe I have devoted space to such basic information . . . be patient with me. I'm educating novices as well. (You should read my mail.) For you folks, I'm including some information you probably don't know—how much money washing plastic bags saves.

One reader enlarged upon my Time and Money Chart on page 102, where I show that to determine the hourly worth of any money-saving activity, you calculate how many times you could do the task in an hour and multiply that figure by the savings per task.

In her study, which she did for a class she is taking, she calculated the savings from washing out plastic bags:

"I can wash out a plastic Baggie used to store broccoli in the freezer in 11 seconds, saving .05¢ per bag . . . or I can throw the bag away and reach under the counter to get a new Baggie in 5 seconds."

Figuring that she spends 6 seconds to save .05¢, she calculated the savings rate of washing Baggies is $30 per hour.

So if you get nothing else from this article, you can at least stop feeling crazy for washing plastic bags.

EPITAPHS

Dear Amy,

For me to consider becoming a tightwad is almost revolutionary. My husband used to say that he'd put two phrases on my tombstone: (1) Nothing feels like real gold. (2) My wife wasn't happy unless she paid full price.

Janet Stanhope
Auburn, Maine

AMAZING REFUND

Dear Amy,

My best bargains are usually at the reduced rack at the grocery store. I went in one day and they had 12 boxes of Tide (39 oz). They had been damaged by a blade used to open the cartons. The reduced price was $1. I had coupons for $1, so all I paid was 5¢ tax. My mother cut the net weight from the boxes and sent them in for a $2 refund each.

Patricia Williams
Rockland, Maine

HOMEMADE WEIGHTS

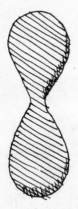

Dear Amy,

To make dumbbells of different weights take long, strong, plastic bags and fill with sand to the required weight. Put into cloth bag (you may have to sew these), or leg sections from pants, sleeves, long socks, or stockings. Distribute sand equally at each end leaving a narrow section in the center for a hand or foot.

Arnie Anfinson
Seattle, Washington

NOT JUST LENTILS AND OATMEAL

People frequently express astonishment at our family's food budget and have requested a menu. (We feed Jim, myself and our six children, ages 9 to 1-year-old twins, on $180 per month.)

You asked for it, you got it. I recorded the meals we ate during a 14-day period in March. Because I wanted to depict the way we really eat, I purposely did not plan special meals for the benefit of publication.

While the menu shown opposite is typical, it doesn't reflect our entire repertoire. We tend to eat according to what foods happen to be on sale. For example, during previous weeks we ate less cheese and more turkey.

The lunch menu shows what I put into school lunches. All sandwiches were made with whole-wheat bread. I didn't record the weekend's every-man-for-himself lunch menu.

I put an asterisk on foods that were homegrown.

Our diet does have its share of humble meals and repetition, due in part to a lack of time. We still manage to avoid all convenience foods, and counter with meals that require very little preparation time.

While our diet may not be glamorous, it's nourishing and offers a reasonable amount of variety. Jim and I also have excellent blood pressure and cholesterol numbers.

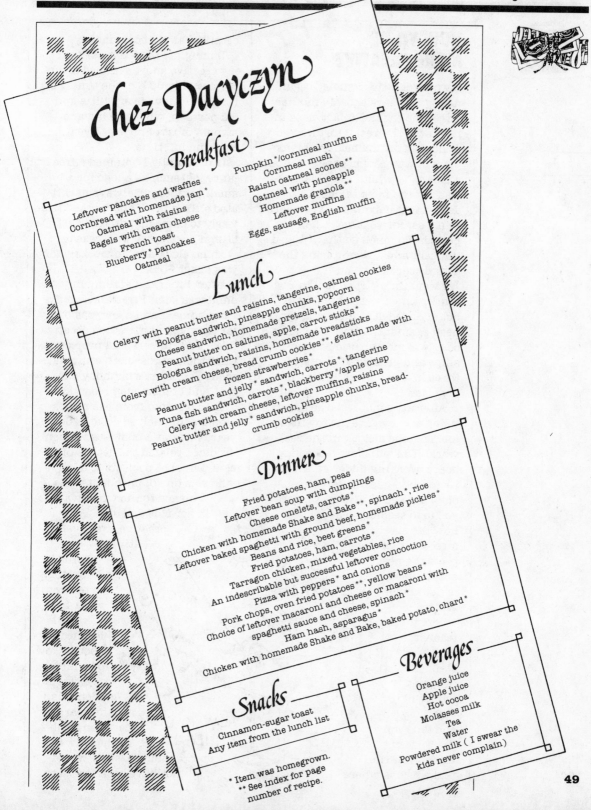

Chez Dacyczyn

Breakfast

Leftover pancakes and waffles
Cornbread with homemade jam*
Oatmeal with raisins
Bagels with cream cheese
French toast
Blueberry* pancakes
Oatmeal
Pumpkin*/cornmeal muffins
Cornmeal mush
Raisin oatmeal scones**
Oatmeal with pineapple
Homemade granola**
Leftover muffins
Eggs, sausage, English muffin

Lunch

Celery with peanut butter and raisins, tangerine, oatmeal cookies
Bologna sandwich, pineapple chunks, popcorn
Cheese sandwich, homemade pretzels, tangerine
Peanut butter on saltines, apple, carrot sticks*
Bologna sandwich, raisins, homemade breadsticks
Celery with cream cheese, bread crumb cookies**, gelatin made with
frozen strawberries*
Peanut butter and jelly* sandwich, carrots*, tangerine
Tuna fish sandwich, carrots*, blackberry*/apple crisp
Celery with cream cheese, leftover muffins, raisins
Peanut butter and jelly* sandwich, pineapple chunks, bread-
crumb cookies

Dinner

Fried potatoes, ham, peas
Leftover bean soup with dumplings
Cheese omelets, carrots*
Chicken with homemade Shake and Bake**, spinach*, rice
Leftover baked spaghetti with ground beef, homemade pickles*
Beans and rice, beet greens*
Fried potatoes, ham, carrots*
Tarragon chicken, mixed vegetables, rice
An indescribable but successful leftover concoction
Pizza with peppers* and onions
Pork chops, oven fried potatoes**, yellow beans*
Choice of leftover macaroni and cheese or macaroni with
spaghetti sauce and cheese, spinach*
Ham hash, asparagus*
Chicken with homemade Shake and Bake, baked potato, chard*

Snacks

Cinnamon-sugar toast
Any item from the lunch list

Beverages

Orange juice
Apple juice
Hot cocoa
Molasses milk
Tea
Water
Powdered milk (I swear the
kids never complain)

* Item was homegrown.
** See index for page
number of recipe.

49

HOW TO BE MORE CREATIVE

My own creative journey began nearly 20 years ago. My mother forced me to take an art class in high school. I recall tortured occasions of sitting before a blank piece of watercolor paper without a clue as to what I should paint. I was not the most talented student, and receiving the art award in my senior year was unexpected. (So much so that I was delinquent and absent during the awards ceremony.)

I went on to art school in Boston. At times ideas came easily but often it felt like beating my head against the wall. I did snag a couple of merit-based scholarships and graduated as one of three in a dead heat at the top of my class.

After art school a large advertising agency gave me my first job. There is a clock in the real world. You sit before a drawing board, working under an art director who has a different sense of what is good. The task before you is to second guess how the art director interprets the needs of the client. It is not kindergarten, where the teacher understands the fragile nature of creativity and tells you every idea is wonderful. The real world is where

creative failure costs money.

During my professional peak my creative effort satisfied art directors only 50% of the time. As a result I designed very little and did pasteup, typespecking and layouts most of my eight years working full time.

Occasionally I obtained a freelance job, such as a logo for a small company. I always negotiated a fixed price and worked tirelessly to come up with the best design possible. My success rate with no clock and no art director was about 95%.

After I married and my first child was born I freelanced only from home. I had a few jobs but for the most part put my creative energies into personal projects. Christmas cards, birth announcements, children's birthday parties, and homemade presents.

This freedom from the professional grind helped greatly. Some years later, at a business women's dinner, I related the details of recent personal projects to a lady who was one of my clients. She turned to the woman at her side and said "Amy is creative, creative, creative."

This is a long story to tell you what I have learned about "How to be more creative." My credentials are the years of success and failure. If it had always come easily I would not have been forced to

START HERE

FINAL OBJECTIVE

TA DAH!

HOW TO GET AN IDEA

analyze. But through my roller coaster ride I have come to understand something of the nuts and bolts process of creativity.

People tend to believe that creativity is a mystical gift reserved for a few. They think this mistaking creativity for "craft." Creativity is the process. Craft is the product. When there is a lack of a recognized outlet, such as writing, art, or music, creativity goes unnoticed.

Creativity is nothing more and nothing less than solving a problem in an original way. As humans we all have this spark. We string together words to express our thoughts. We do not memorize and repeat the sentences that we speak. We put together new word combinations continually.

Creativity occurs in subtle ways. While preparing a familiar recipe and you realize that you lack an ingredient and make a substitution. Or while folding laundry the way your mother taught you 20 years ago, you discover that by rearranging piles in a different order you can save time. Or you have a problem with a co-worker and attempt a new strategy to make the relationship work better. Or you figure how to build a lathe out of salvaged materials and a washing machine motor. These are all forms of creativity.

TEN STEPS TO A MORE CREATIVE YOU

Step 1. Realize that you *are* creative. Look for it in your daily life and nurture that part of yourself.

Step 2. Give yourself mental space, a clear field. We tend to fill up our days with the TV, car radio, reading the paper, chats with friends on the phone. Instead do that "mindless task" in quiet. This type of activity dominates my life . . . housework, mowing lawn, scraping paint. Boredom never strikes, as the mental gears whirl continually. I write only after mentally rehearsing paragraphs a dozen times.

When someone says, "I'm just not creative like you," I reply "No, I just thought about it longer."

Step 3. Never *ever* compare yourself to others, but rather enjoy your own innovations. I stumbled over this block working in the shadow of many award-winning designers. No matter how good I could become there would still be someone better. Later I realized that no matter how bad I was there was always someone worse. Compare yourself only to yourself. "This is how good I am today. I am better than I was yesterday and I will be better tomorrow."

Step 4. I use a strategy I call "putting the problem into the mental computer." Your brain functions continually, even as you sleep. Study the parameters of your problem and then let it rest for a few days. Very often your mental computer will spit out the solution unexpectedly as you shower or drive to work. This works much better than trying to perform as the clock ticks away. If you are trying to come up with a great party idea, give yourself a couple months of mental back-burner time.

Step 5. Brainstorm. Toss the idea around with another person. Be flexible and say or write down every "stupid" thought that comes. Very often another person can take your idea and add a twist that makes it great. Jim is my brainstorming partner. He is very good at telling me when my idea is good and I should run with it. Sometimes something isn't working just right and he can look at it and come up with a better sentence or illustration idea.

Step 6. Find a springboard, a starting place. For the tightwad this usually means determining which resources are cheap or in surplus. Build from that point.

Step 7. Do not share your creative ideas with anyone who continually tells you they are dumb. This is often a spouse or a parent. Professionally I should have switched jobs until I found an art director who shared a similar creative style. The art directors that didn't like my ideas were not more creative than me. Often they were *less* creative. Mostly it was a matter of seeing things differently. But, the constant message that I was doing it wrong took its toll. A mouse does not go down the same hole over and over if he fails to find cheese.

After I stopped working under art directors and created for myself, or for my clients in my own way, I began to realize that I was creative after all.

Step 8. Practice. As with any skill, accessing your creative ability improves the more you do it. You will develop your own methods and strategies to fall back on when tackling new problems.

Step 9. Avoid negative stress. This also tends to block creativity, as your mind focuses on that problem instead. Try to limit contact with individuals who bring on these problems. If it is some-

one within your household, try to limit your reaction to their actions.

Step 10. Start small. When you bite off more than you can chew you set yourself up for failure. Instead set small easily attainable goals to build a sense of success. In subsequent projects stretch yourself to slightly more ambitious undertakings.

Sometime as you were reading the beginning of this piece you thought, "What the heck does creativity have to do with thrift?"

Tightwaddery without creativity is deprivation. When there is a lack of resourcefulness, inventiveness, and innovation, thrift means doing without.

When creativity combines with thrift you may be doing it without money, but you are not doing without.

HEADBAND HOW-TO

My daughter Jamie, at the age of six, had a field day with a pair of shears and cut off a lock of her (already thin) hair at the earlobe. Rather then resorting to a drastic short haircut I thought I'd have her wear headbands until it grew out.

Remember those cloth headbands we wore in the 60s and 70s? You can't buy them anymore. The sweat bands now on the market work, but are limited. The plastic ones don't stay on well, and a younger sibling snaps them in half within a week.

As I pondered this dilemma I saw a classmate of my daughter's wearing a pretty cloth headband.

I asked, and her mother admitted that she made it.

She made a tube of fabric from a 2½" × 32" strip, sewing the right side together, about a half inch from the edge. She turned the tube inside out and inserted a 19" × ¾" piece of elastic. Then she machine sewed the elastic ends together, and then hand sewed the cloth tube ends together, neatly tucking under the cut edge.

The resulting headband has a ruffled or gathered look. Her headband was of a calico material. I have some pink satin I'd like to try first. The length of elastic and strip of cloth are based on a six-year-old head size.

REAL MAIL

When the price of the first-class stamp soared to 29¢, Ralph Nader complained on television talk shows, and perhaps a few subscribers wondered if *The Tightwad Gazette* would cost more. (It didn't.)

Despite concern over postal rates, the first-class letter remains one of our best bargains. By comparison the instant the telephone receiver clicks back into position a long-distance phone call becomes an expensive intangible memory.

For this reason nearly all my long-distance communication takes the form of *real mail*.

I regard the letters I receive to be a gift from the sender, and from the best writers, a treasure to be savored.

I spend more time writing letters than most people I know, and I am told (seldom by return mail) that they are wonderful. Friends have been known to read choice excerpts to their mothers, who have never met me, during long-distance phone conversations. (Yes, I have befriended a spendthrift or two.)

A business envelope with about five sheets of paper can be mailed with a first-class stamp. Using 15-pitch type, small margins, single spacing, and two sides of the paper your entire autobiography can be mailed first class as far as such remote areas as Alaska, Guam, or Leeds, Maine.

My mother saves my letters and returns them by the stack, which double as a journal for me. When rereading a letter written only a few years ago I am amazed at how many events I had forgotten.

Writing letters helps to develop writing skills. For any beginning writer the best material comes from personal experience, making letters a perfect training ground. And any acquired skill is a potential money maker.

Any researcher of genealogy knows how important letters are in providing insight to an ancestor who might otherwise be known only through birth and death records. In terms of more recent family members, it is a real trip to read the "gee whiz" literary style of your then 20-year-old father.

If you are blank-page-phobic, a few suggestions to get you going are shown below:

WOOD AND OIL

We have an efficient wood/oil furnace and an ample supply of wood purchased at $60 per cord (go-get-it-yourself), but we need some oil for when we are not home.

It seems like a sure bet that wood burning will be cheaper

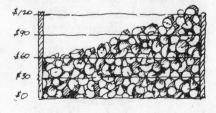

1 For a day or so before you plan to write, keep a pencil and paper handy to jot down ideas of items to include in your letter.

2 If you think there is little newsworthy in your life, remember that those who love you are interested in the "dull" goings on, too.

3 Try to include humorous stories. While I often have soapbox topics on my mind, I try to remember that grandmas are more interested in childhood comic action.

4 My mother and I write what we call "familygrams." These are a sort of general letter that go out to about 25 people. They can be photocopied or reproduced on a memory typewriter or computer. This enables us to communicate more in depth with a larger group of people. Though it sounds impersonal, considering the rarity of real mail, it is easy to see how people enjoy them.

5 Write as if you were speaking to the reader using common everyday language. Think of how your letter will sound to the recipient. Use descriptive and colorful images.

6 Former generations considered a typed letter inappropriate. Now home computers are commonplace. Use whatever technology you have available to make letter writing easier. Typing gives them a more polished look and improves readability. You will have a greater sense of accomplishment than if you pen several pages of chicken scratchings.

7 Include other items like a joke you heard recently, a new recipe, clippings, a child's drawing, and photographs.

8 When you reread your completed letter and think it too lackluster, mail it anyway. Any letter is better than no letter.

than oil. If you are thinking you might buy wood this fall and fire up the wood stove to avoid the rising oil prices you will also pay high prices for wood.

The question becomes, When is wood cheaper than oil?

Depending on the variety of hardwood, a cord of wood equals 130 to 200 gallons of oil.

Fall prices for dry wood are about $120 per cord, or even higher. Let's say that you buy wood of average quality and it produces the same heat as 165 gallons of oil.

To figure the break point you need to calculate when 165 gallons of oil equals $120 or . . .

$120 divided by 165 equals 75¢

. . . so when oil costs 75¢ per gallon and wood is $120 per cord they cost the same. As oil and wood prices stand, even a late purchase of wood will be cheaper than a late purchase of oil.

THE SCOOP ON COUPONS

It feels like tightwad sacrilege to suggest that there might be anything wrong with coupon use. But consider that manufacturers provide coupons to entice consumers to buy their products. Multiple coupons for a single product, which have decreasing values, such as 75¢ off, 50¢ off, and 25¢ off, are a dead giveaway that they hope to hook you by creating a habit.

There's a right way and a wrong way to use coupons. All coupon users believe they are using coupons the right way. "I never use a coupon to buy something I wouldn't buy anyway." However, if a majority of users did it the right way, manufacturers would be losing money and would stop offering coupons. So, consider the following questions:

HOW MUCH DO COUPONS REALLY SAVE?

Readers frequently send me sales slips to demonstrate how much they save using coupons. With bold sweeps of colored markers they circle the figure that shows how much the coupons used added up to. They're circling the wrong figure. The most important figure on your sales slip is how much you spend on groceries . . . not how much you save using coupons.

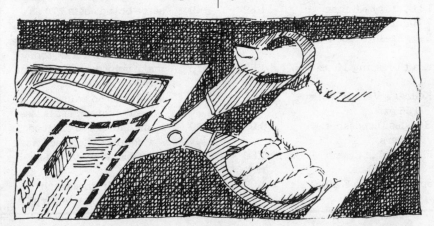

Sometimes, even with doubling your coupons you might be spending more money on items than if you had resorted to a different strategy. Always compare the price after coupons with alternative products, making the same item from scratch, or not buying the product at all (as in the case of things like soda, candy, etc.). Below is a table that demonstrates this. ("A.D.C." stands for the price "after double coupons.")

Even if the price after coupon is less than an alternative coupon, users frequently fail to calculate the true savings. Let's say you get $1.00 off brand A spaghetti sauce, which costs $1.89. Brand B, a sauce of equal quality, costs $1.29. Obviously you buy brand A, but your savings is not $1.00—it's really 40¢. This may seem like I'm quibbling. But it's important to understand your genuine savings because coupon use takes time. You need to know how much extra time you're spending compared to how much money you're saving. You also need to factor in the cost of obtaining the coupon, if there is any, such as the purchase of magazines and newspapers.

HOW MUCH TIME DO COUPONS REQUIRE?

Reports from readers vary. Some claim they only spend a few minutes extra per week. These individuals are moderate coupon users who tend to be very organized. An excellent way to do this is to keep your coupons in a small file box and organize them by type. On about the 20th of each month you should go through

PRODUCT	PRICE	A.D.C.	ALTERNATIVE STRATEGY
Lite & Lively Yogurt 6-pk.	$1.67	$1.16	store brand costs 80¢, homemade costs less
Aunt Jemima Syrup 24 oz.	3.19	2.44	store brand costs $1.99, homemade costs 66¢
Betty Crocker Scalloped Potatoes	1.09	.59	prepared from scratch costs less
Dixie 5 oz. Kitchen Cups 100 ct.	1.69	.69	use plastic, permanent cups instead
12 Country Kitchen Hamburger Rolls	1.39	.99	same brand costs 77¢ at bakery thrift store
Baby Fresh Wipes 84 ct.	2.99	2.39	make your own version . . . a washcloth works, too
Kraft Dressing 16 oz.	1.55	1.15	make your own version for 30% the cost
Kellogg's Variety Pack 9.58 oz.	3.19	2.19	at 22¢ per box almost any scratch breakfast is less
Huggies Disposable Diapers	9.99	8.99	home-laundered cloth costs a couple dollars per week
Philadelphia Cream Cheese 12 oz.	1.89	1.59	store brand costs $1.29
Special K Eggo Waffles 8 ct.	1.29	.69	prepared from scratch costs less, freeze surplus

your coupons looking for ones that might expire. Always take your file box with you when you shop. You might run across an unexpected sale or a good deal in the damages bin.

On the other end of the spectrum, very serious coupon users, those who also spend time refunding, can spend as much as 10 to 15 hours per week clipping coupons, studying sale flyers, soaking off and filing labels, and saving packaging and receipts. Serious refunders also subscribe to refund newsletters. Through these they swap "complete deals" or the refund with the required proof of purchase and receipt to get the refund. The most diligent can reap more than $100 per month in refunds and rebates. They also may get enough free gifts to make a significant dent in their Christmas budget. Sometimes refunders boost their coupon and refund results because family and friends save their proofs of purchase and coupons for them. In this case the coupon user/refunder benefits because an original purchaser paid an inflated price.

Another time element often not considered is how much additional time is spent in the supermarket. It takes more time making individual price comparisons and purchases. In contrast, other strategies, such as bulk buying of sale items, reduce shopping time.

WHAT DO PEOPLE BUY WITH COUPONS?

Our family generally uses coupons to buy nonfood items, and food items that cannot be pre-

pared from scratch. But most food coupons are for convenience foods. Often the foods are more processed. Even when these items can be purchased cheaply, it should be considered that your family is acquiring a taste for these more expensive and less healthful items. This could potentially create bigger grocery bills in the future. Many of the products have more packaging as well. So even when Jell-O Pudding Snack Paks are near free, I seriously question these purchases because of the environmental issue of the excess trash created.

WHAT ABOUT THE "COUPON QUEENS" FEATURED BY THE MEDIA?

Most of us have seen newspaper articles or television shows featuring coupon experts who demonstrate their skills by taking reporters shopping and buying $134.86 of groceries, but after all the coupons are subtracted pay only $54.73. This type of shopping trip requires months of planning, and is not typical of these shoppers' usual trips to the store. On the average these shoppers claim their real savings is closer to 25 to 40%. Again, it's important to remember that these are savings on the prices of products that may be inflated in price.

Consider the real figures sent in by Mary Kenyan of Independence, Iowa. She saves 10% to 30% on a grocery bill of $385 per month. She feeds a family of six, with four children ages 2 to 11. Her grocery bill does not include her husband's work lunches, but they never eat out.

Figuring that she saves an average of 20% on her grocery bill using coupons, she actually spends about $308 per month. She receives $110 per month (after postage) from refunds. Of that figure roughly 65% comes from refunds from items she purchased at the grocery store, or $71.50. She has offsetting expenses of about $12.54 for additional postage and magazine and newspaper subscriptions. She gets her refund newsletters free in exchange for credits for submissions. This works out to a bottom line grocery bill of $249.04 per month. In addition she receives roughly 10 free gifts per month of varying values through refunding.

The average family of six spends $500 per month on groceries. In comparison, Mary's grocery budget compares well. However, with very little coupon use many families of equal size spend under $200 per month on groceries. A mixed approach, which includes some coupon use, will produce the lowest possible grocery bill. Readers have written that when they began to incorporate other strategies, they used fewer coupons and their grocery bills dropped.

If you genuinely dislike couponing and refunding, use other strategies (like gardening, bulk buying, and baking from scratch) that will save you as much if not more money on your grocery bill.

If, however, you find that refunding and couponing is an enjoyable hobby, and you genuinely are saving money, this is a valid way to spend your time. To read more about the coupon/refund strategy look for *Cashing In at the Cash Register* by Susan Samtur, commonly available at the library.

Refund newsletters include:

Money Talk
P.O. Box 1677
Kingston, PA 18704

Refunding Makes Cents
Box R
Farmington, UT 84025

Roadrunner Refunder
6535 West Ellis
Laveen, AZ 85339

WHAT TO DO WITH . . .

Pickle Juice.
A. Use in marinade or create your own salad dressings.

B. Sweet Pickled Chops. Arrange four chops in a shallow pan and sprinkle with salt. Place a slice of onion and a tablespoon of catsup on the top of each. Pour ½ cup of sweet pickle juice around chops. Cover and bake for 1 hour at 350°.

Bread Bags. Use as
freezer bags for short-term storage, especially when re-packaging family packs of sale meats. Knot excess to close, and cut open when ready for use. Never reuse any plastic bag that has stored meats. Don't store food in inside-out bags.

Toilet Paper Tubes. Use to
gather up unsightly loose excess electrical cord on kitchen appliances, lamps, entertainment center, etc.

A Half-Eaten Apple. Cut off remaining good parts and save to make an individual apple crisp. To make crumb mixture combine 1 tsp each of brown sugar, flour, oatmeal, and margarine. Add a dash of cinnamon. Top apples and microwave.

Milk Jug Rings. Use to keep socks together when laundering. Store in drawer with rings. When taking socks out, keep ring on bureau. Replace ring around soiled socks before tossing in hamper.

Dried-out Bread. Save slices in a freezer container or bread bag until you need to make bread crumbs. Grind up in your blender or food processor. When using as a topping toss in melted margarine, and season.

Dryer Lint. My neighbor and organic gardening expert was out for her evening stroll when I bounded down to the road with a breathless query, "Can you compost dryer lint?" Her official answer is yes, if the lint is from cotton material. Synthetic lint can be composted for flower garden use.

Yellow-flowered Broccoli.

A. Tell your family it is a rare gourmet variety.

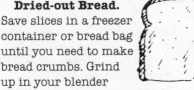

B. If they're not quite that gullible use in quiche. The yellow egg and cheese mixture combine to create an effective camouflage.

Crayon Bits. Place a variety of colors in a muffin tin and melt in the oven. Cool. This makes a scribble cookie. Each one has its own unique color and pattern. Use for an inexpensive stocking stuffer.

Carrot Peels, Onion Skins, and Celery Leaves. Jeff Smith, the frugal gourmet, (no relation) uses these when cooking up turkey and chicken bones for soup stock.

Worn Towels and Washcloths. A worn towel can be cut lengthwise into strips to make a back washer. (Contributed by Alma Trider, Leeds, ME.) Washcloths can be cut in quarters to make reusable "handiwipes" or "baby wipes." Store damp in a plastic bag when traveling.

An Old Yellow Pages. Use for a gluing surface. Once the top page is used tear off for a fresh surface. The yellow color makes it easy to spot tiny pieces of white paper that would otherwise become lost on white pages or newspaper.

Mesh Onion Bags. Cut off metal clip and knot. Use to store soap bits. The mesh and soap combine to form an effective cleaning agent when washing hands. (Contributed by Polly Davis, Shirley, MA.)

A Tuna Fish Can. Use to make cookie cutters. Cut off bottom of can and shape with two pliers, preferably needle nose. When making a symmetrical design begin working at opposite points of the can.

Leftover Rice. Make a rice crust for a quiche by combining 1½ cups of cooked rice, 1 ounce of shredded cheese, and an egg. Pat out in a pie plate. For a larger quiche dish increase rice and cheese portions slightly. Do not Pam or grease the dish. Bake at 425° for 20 minutes.

Old Cloth Diapers. Obviously these make excellent cleaning rags; however, I have found their best use is for washing windows. Because they are highly absorbent they beat paper towels and newspaper for a streak-free final wipe.

A Coat Hanger. Make a Baggie dryer by bending as shown. This idea is for the man in my church who said to me, "Have you any idea what you've started? Now when I wash dishes

my wife has me hanging Baggies on a clothesline in the pantry!"

A STOLEN THANKSGIVING SOAP BOX SPEECH

Most of this article is a direct steal from a lay sermon preached by my neighbor.

Charlie Woodward works for the Rural Community Action Ministry, which provides a variety of services for low-income families. He serves as the chairman for the Maine Coalition for the Homeless, frequently meets with state officials, and is considered to be an expert on rural poverty.

I had heard bits and pieces of this sermon before. I have picked his brain on a number of occasions to understand why poor people are poor. Invariably the conversations have concluded as Charlie patiently reminded me that we have not all been born with the same gifts.

A gift is anything that we have that we did not work for. People born to wealth have more advantages than those born in poverty. People with a high intelligence will probably fare better than those born with low intelligence. It is known that people who are blond, tall, and good-looking will be more likely to succeed than those who are not.

Most of us feel that being born in the United States is a gift. While not all of us are rich, we are likely to have greater opportunities for education, health care, and employment than those living in Third World countries.

Health is a gift, at least the health with which we were born. Most of us are botching it to some degree or another. But our genetic package plays a large role in why some can abuse their health and never get sick while others work at being healthy and still get sick.

Those of us who were raised in good families have a gift. Not everyone was raised with love, security, positive feedback, and values. Charlie believes that the "work ethic" is also a gift. Some parents taught it to their kids and some parents did not.

Many examples come to mind of individuals who have overcome a lack of gifts. These people always have a variety of other gifts.

The bottom line is to understand that what we have and who we are has a lot to do with factors we received in a package deal when we came into the world. If that realization doesn't make you thankful, nothing will.

I believe we need to use all our gifts as well as we can to provide security and quality of life for our families. Most of us do this well enough to have a surplus of either time or money.

Clearly some people are short on gifts and some have gifts and do not use them well. For both groups their security and quality of life runs a deficit. All the grumbling about those who receive public assistance is really about deciding into which

group people fall. The questions I have asked have only yielded the knowledge that experts do not agree and there are many murky gray areas.

But what of the rest of us whose gifts (and usually some effort) have yielded a surplus? It is easy to find people who have surpluses . . . most of us do. And most of us squander huge amounts of surplus money or time on personal gratification and give very little or nothing in return.

The attitude of "I worked hard and I deserve . . ." does not consider the very large degree that our gifts contributed to what we have.

The frugal lifestyle allows us to engineer the maximum surplus of time, energy, and/or money while using a minimum of resources. Since we are gifted differently, our surplus will also be different. We can, and should, use our surpluses to help smooth the peaks and valleys or unequal gift distribution.

Clearly I do not advocate squandering of resources, but neither do I advocate hoarding or stinginess.

By donating some of our surplus time, energy, and money we express thankfulness for the abundance of gifts with which we were born. (See, Charlie, I *was* paying attention.)

A VOICE FROM THE PAST

Had I known there were so many books written on the subject of thrift I probably would not have begun *The Tightwad Gazette*.

In the past several months readers have suggested or mailed some of these to me. One sent by a sister, probably in fun, is a reproduction of an 1833 work.

The American Frugal Housewife, written by a Mrs. Child bears a curious subtitle. She dedicated the book "To Those Who Are Not Ashamed of Economy."

Although frugality may have enjoyed a larger general acceptance during her time, clearly she felt it was falling out of fashion. She frequently quotes Benjamin Franklin's words on thrift. After pondering that I also wondered at the 18th-century attitude of thrift, since Franklin felt compelled to write his thoughts on the subject.

Mrs. Child wrote: "Economy is generally despised as low virtue, tending to make [characterize] people ungenerous and selfish. This is true of avarice; but not so of economy. The man who is economical, is laying up for himself the permanent power of being useful and generous."

Mrs. Child's observation of the negative attitude toward thrift might also be seen from earlier times. Since the development of the English language, we have no positive nouns for a frugal person. Instead we have "cheapskate," "skinflint," "penny-pincher," "miser," and "tightwad." Even the positive adjectives that the English language gives us, like "frugal" or "thrifty," have come to have a dull or boring connotation. We associate these words with Depression-era fuddy-duddy thinking.

(My choice of the word "tightwad" reflects my belief that thrift is not dull, but actually fun, and defies the attitude of our culture. If I had called my publication "The Frugal Person's Newsletter" the media wouldn't have paid attention.)

The American Frugal Housewife is not to be considered required reading. Much of it reads like a 19th-century Heloise, offering tips that have little relevance for our time. The essays sound like something one might have heard from an elderly schoolteacher. And as the title suggests, the book is by no means gender neutral.

However, I was also struck by the similar overall strategies and philosophies that still apply (and parallel ideas that I have written).

"It is wise to keep an exact account of all you expend . . .

Buy a barrel of really strong vinegar . . .

it makes you more careful in spending money, and it enables your husband to judge precisely whether his family live within his income." (Record spending.)

"If you have two dollars a day, let nothing but sickness induce you to spend more than nine shillings; if you have half a dollar a day, be satisfied to spend forty cents." (Regardless of your income level do not spend everything you earn.)

"Let [women] prove, by exertion of ingenuity and economy, that neatness, good taste, and gentility, are attainable without great expense." (Use creativity and thrift to improve the quality of life, rather than spending more money.)

"Make your own bread and cake. Some people think it is just as cheap to buy of the baker and confectioner; but it is not half as cheap." (Avoid convenience foods and instead prepare food from scratch.)

"It is poor economy to buy vinegar by the gallon. Buy a barrel, or half a barrel, of really strong vinegar when you begin housekeeping." (Buy in bulk.)

"It is a great deal better for boys and girls on a farm to be picking blackberries at six cents a quart, than to be wearing out clothes in useless play. They enjoy themselves just as well." (All family members should develop hobbies that save money rather than ones that are nonproductive . . . or ones that cost money.)

"Patchwork is good economy. It is indeed a foolish waste of time to tear cloth into bits for the sake of rearranging it anew in fantastic figures; but a family may be kept out of idleness, and a few shillings saved, by thus using scraps of gowns, curtains, etc." (Whenever possible reuse materials you already have rather than buying new materials at craft shops.)

"To associate with influential and genteel people with an appearance of equality unquestionably has its advantages, but like all other external advantages, these have their proper price, and may be bought too dearly. Self-denial, in proportion to the narrowness of your income, will eventually be the happiest and

FZ's World

DARN, A HOLE RIGHT IN THE FRONT OF A PERFECTLY GOOD JERSEY!

HMM... WHAT COULD I MAKE WITH ALL THAT JERSEY MATERIAL?

JAZZY UNDERWEAR?

OF COURSE I WOULD NEED ABOUT 50¢ WORTH OF ELASTIC . . . AND IT WOULD TAKE A COUPLE OF HOURS TO SEW . . .

AND YOU CAN BUY A PAIR OF NEW UNDERWEAR FOR $1.

SOMETIMES I THINK I'M TREADING DANGEROUSLY CLOSE TO THE EDGE OF THE GREAT ABYSS OF SKINFLINTIAN COMPULSION.

I'LL MAKE JAZZY RAGS INSTEAD!

AmyD

TAKE THE TIGHTWAD TEST

Are you a tightwad or a spendthrift? Read the questions and circle the most appropriate answer. After you have completed the test, compare your answers to those below.

1. A movie that you would *love* to see is playing. You . . .
A. Drop off the kids at the sitter, pay top dollar for tickets, and buy overpriced theater popcorn and soda.
B. Wait for the movie to come to cable TV or on video to rent.
C. Wait 10 years for the movie to come to primetime TV.

2. Your children are thirsty. You say . . .
A. "Help yourself. There's plenty of soda in the fridge."
B. "Help yourself. There are plenty of juice packs in the fridge."
C. "Help yourself. There's plenty of water."

3. Your family is midway through a four-hour car trip. You pull into McDonald's and . . .
A. Order a round of Happy Meals.
B. Order a round of burgers and shakes.
C. Use the restrooms only. Later you break out the peanut butter and jelly sandwiches in the car.

4. Your spouse says your family needs to increase its food budget. You say . . .
A. "No problem."
B. "What food budget?"
C. "Wouldn't this be a great time to start that diet, dear?"

5. You think the most perfect toy for your four-year-old is . . .
A. A battery-powered riding toy.
B. Nintendo games.
C. A cardboard box.

6. A thrilling family outing for you typically would be . . .
A. A day at the amusement park.
B. A day on the ski slopes.
C. A trip to the double-coupon store to combine coupons, sales, damaged goods, and store brands for the maximum possible volume of groceries.

7. Your teenager says he will die if he can't have a $75 pair of designer sneakers. You say . . .
A. "Anything for you, kid."
B. "If we have any money left over at the end of the month."
C. Nothing, being unable to speak through the peals of laughter.

8. If you and your spouse receive a gift coupon for a rare romantic dinner at a restaurant, your conversation would include . . .
A. Recollections of your courtship.
B. Compliments on your spouse's stunning appearance.
C. Calculations of how cheaply this meal could be prepared at home.

ANSWERS: If you had to turn this page upside down to learn the right answers *you failed the test.*

most respectable course for you and yours." (Don't try to keep up with the Joneses. Instead live within your means.)

CREDIT UNIONS VS. BANKS

A reader suggested that I write an article comparing credit unions to banks. I thought, "Great idea! This will give me another of those heavyweight financial-type articles."

In theory, no one should ever use a bank. Credit unions are nonprofit organizations, and they return surplus funds to their customers in the form of less expensive services.

I actually discovered that the rates between the two types of institutions often overlap to a large degree. Some credit unions are too small to offer better rates than banks, but if you have access to a large credit union the advantages are unquestionable.

The chart on page 66 indicates 1991 rates and fees based on three large credit unions and four major banks in our area. I have indicated the ranges where they existed.

Although interest rates on mortgages, checking, and savings accounts are similar, there is a significant difference in car loans and interest on credit cards. These credit unions offer free checking and a lesser annual fee (or none at all) for credit cards.

While most banks resell mortgage loans to loan institutions often credit unions do not. This can work to your advantage since loans that are resold must meet tighter requirements. We were able to get a mortgage based against 34% of our income rather than the standard 28%.

Loans through a credit union frequently are repaid with an allotment system. This can work to your disadvantage since a bank may not recognize the loan as part of your credit history. Because you didn't write a check each month, in theory, you have not demonstrated personal responsibility. As a result you might have trouble getting a loan through a bank in the future.

Credit unions often do not have automatic teller machines. Banks that have a national network offer the advantage of ready cash anywhere, at anytime. Credit unions have fewer branch offices, making them less convenient.

Comparing banks to credit unions is much like comparing supermarkets to warehouse stores. Generally one is better

than the other, but not always. In the same way that supermarkets run sales, banks can offer great deals to entice customers. At one time we had our sizable nest egg in a bank savings account with an interest rate of 8½%.

It is a fairly simple matter to join a credit union. One needs only to open a savings account with a minimum of $25 (or less in some cases). Therefore you can have a checking account in a bank and a credit union if both offer options that you need.

SERVICES COMPARED	BANKS	CREDIT UNIONS
30-year fixed mortgage	9.125% to 10%	9.5% to 9.9%
used car loan interest rate	12.75% to 16.75%	10.9% to 12.5%
new car loan interest rate	12.75% to 13.25%	10.9% to 11.5%
checking account fee	$6 per month under minimum balance	free
checking account interest rate	4.75% to 5.25%	5% to 6%
savings account interest rate	5.25%	5% to 6%
annual fee for credit cards	$12	$0 to $8
credit card interest rate	18% to 19.8%	12% to 14%

YOUR POULTRY PURCHASE

1. Buy your turkey several months in advance, when the price bottoms out at 39¢ lb.

2. If you didn't do that you will likely pay between 69¢ and 79¢ per pound. If you purchase a larger turkey (over 18 to 20 lbs) the price usually drops as much as 20¢ per pound. Many smaller households are reluctant to purchase the larger turkeys. But often a larger turkey will be cheaper than a smaller turkey.

Buy the larger one and freeze the leftovers in meal-size portions to eat during the next few months.

3. Beware of "the deal." A few years ago one store advertised a "free turkey" with the purchase of brand A ham. We discovered that brand B ham was far cheaper than brand A. After about 10 minutes of intense calculation we found that the cost difference was such that we could purchase brand B ham and a separate turkey (which was on sale at 29¢ per pound) and save money.

SQUEAKY WHEEL GREASED

Dear Amy,
Several times I have taken it upon myself to critique a product and send in my opinion to the address on the box. I usually tell them what I feel could be improved on or the benefits of using their products. I have always received something free back, whether it be more of the same product or coupons for free products, and all it cost me was a stamp.

**Name withheld by request
Lincoln, Nebraska**

DRYER POINTERS

Our family washes about 50 loads of laundry per month—100% dryer use would add at least $20 to our electric bill. Our attic clothesline allows us to air dry laundry year-round.

The only clothing still dried the conventional way (in the dryer) is the cloth diapers. Air-dried diapers resemble shingles, both in appearance and texture. I regard happy babies to be a bargain.

I heard, secondhand, from an energy expert, that smaller dryer

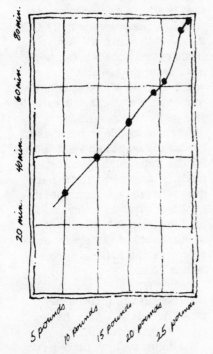

loads are more efficient. This was contrary to what I thought, so I devised an experiment to test this theory. Cloth diapers made an excellent control load, providing uniform consistency. Since they are also small items, I was able to precision-weigh loads in five-pound increments on my doctor's

scale. I checked the drying loads frequently and removed the diapers at the brink of dryness. The chart above shows my results.

According to my findings 20 pounds of laundry appears to be the most energy-efficient load, with only a slight upturn (loss of efficiency) beyond that point. The important thing to note is that under 20 pounds the loads *are* inefficient. You can see that 10 pounds required 40 minutes of dryer time and 20 pounds required 60 minutes of dryer time. One large load versus two small saves 20 minutes of dryer time; 25 pounds of diapers equals a very full laundry basket and is all my 18-gallon washer will handle. It is also all the diapers, except two, that we own. (Actually I had to toss in a dampened washcloth to weigh in at exactly 25 pounds.) I did not test beyond that point, and perhaps a more dramatic loss of efficiency would be evident.

Your electric dryer costs about 44¢ per hour to operate based on 9¢ per KWH. Your iron, in comparison, costs about 9¢. Aren't we all guilty of using our dryer for an iron?

Air-dried clothing does come out wrinkled. I have found that about half a day of wear removes most wrinkles. If this method undermines your public image, try drying the clothing in the dryer for a few minutes before hanging. You'll find this works very well.

When I have to iron I save it for when I want to watch something really stupid on TV. This provides me justification for the mental mush.

Finally, these parting words of wisdom. *Clean your lint trap!*

THE EGG-CARTON PRINCESS CROWN

When my daughter, then going through her fairytale stage, asked me to make her a "princess crown," I went to my craft material bin (some folks call it a trash can) in search of some sort of discarded carton that would be suitable. An egg carton was on the top and the idea came to me.

I cut the egg carton through the cups lengthwise. I also cut the two rows of cups apart. This gave me four strips. By bending the strips in half circles, two could be stapled together to form a circle or crown. (Use insides with insides and outsides with outsides so the two sections will be the same.) I cut away a little on the end of each strip so they would overlap to make a better joint. The crown is exactly the right size for the head of a small child.

We spray painted ours silver with a can of paint that I found beside the road while collecting cans. We also used glitter left over from a Christmas project.

I have found that some egg cartons lack enough flexibility to bend properly. You'll have to experiment. Some carton designs have dips in the lid. These cut in the same way make a different sort of crown.

Decorate your crown with materials you have on hand—bits of colored paper, buttons, ribbon, stickers, etc. Be creative!

A REALLY DULL ARTICLE ABOUT HEALTH INSURANCE

> WARNING: The following article contains important but boring information. Reading it may be hazardous to your alertness. Reader discretion is advised.

Health insurance rates continue to climb dramatically, in part because the costs of the uninsured are passed on to those who have insurance. Like a ship that is sinking, the more water that fills the ship, the more likely it is that the ship will sink. As health insurance increases in cost, fewer people and businesses will be able to afford it, and the more those who carry insurance will pay.

As inaccessible as purchasing health insurance appears to be for the individual, if you're healthy it may be within your grasp. In fact, a catastrophic health insurance policy could be paid for from the amount of money that's routinely wasted on groceries and expensive consumer items.

People fear high-deductible policies because they think they won't be able to afford the deductible if they become ill.

To illustrate how high-deductible policies work I obtained rates for a woman my age in my part of the country. I compared rates of policies with a $500 deductible, a $1,000 deductible, and a $2,500 deductible. After the deductible is met the policy holder must pay 20% of the bills up to $5,000. This 20% is called the copayment.

DEDUCT-IBLE	MONTHLY RATE	ANNUAL RATE	WORST SCE-NARIO
$ 500	$158	$1,896	$3,396
$1000	$137	$1,644	$3,644
$2500	$105	$1,260	$4,760

The above table shows what it would cost with the three plans.

The annual rate is the "best scenario"—you have no medical bills and pay only the insurance premium.

I calculated the "worst scenarios" by using this equation:

The annual rate + the deductible + 20% of $5000 = your total cost

For example, to figure the worst scenario for the $500 deductible.

$1,896 + $500 + $1,000 = $3,396

If you choose the $2,500 deductible over the $500 deductible and have no medical expenses, you will save $636 over the year. If you have a medically expensive year the worst that could happen is that you would have to pay an additional $1,364. Although you have to pay the first $2,500, in reality you are not "out" the entire $2,500. In less than two healthy years your premium savings would pay for the additional $1,364.

The chart below shows that if you incur $1,500 of medical bills your annual cost will be about the same regardless of the deductible you choose.

Many people who are looking at insurance will not opt for the higher deductible because they don't have that much cash in the bank. However, most doctors and hospitals will work out a pay-

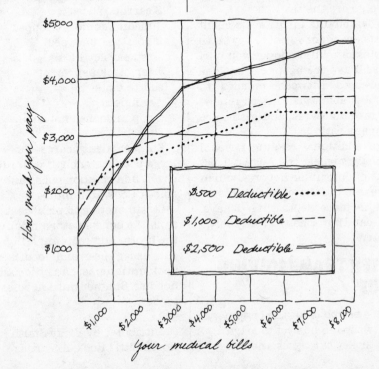

Your medical bills

ment schedule if you are caught short. So get the higher deductible and discipline yourself to save the premium difference. Do not bank on the generosity of the medical establishment, for although they might be flexible, the cost of your unpaid bills gets passed on to other consumers.

If you're purchasing insurance for a family, the deductibles get scarier and it becomes more confusing to calculate the worst scenario. Companies vary in how they handle multiple deductibles. Many offer a cap...once three family members meet the deductible, the other family members don't have to. However, you must keep these huge numbers in perspective. In healthy families it's rare for one family member to have a high medical cost, let alone for one family to have three separate major illnesses or accidents. And while the worst scenario is huge, so are the savings.

When buying insurance consult an independent agent. They have no stake in which policy you purchase. Have the agent explain the differences between policies to you. Ask about guaranteed renewals, rate increases, and insurance company ratings.

For additional reading I would strongly suggest the August 1990 issue of *Consumer Reports,* which discusses pitfalls of health insurance in more depth than I have. You can find a copy at any large library.

AFTER THANKSGIVING SOUP

This recipe is for the beginner tightwad who has yet to learn that turkey carcasses and bones from other meats should be used for soup making. Leftovers from this soup should become the first ingredient in your grand adventure of refrigerator stew cookery.

Longtime practitioners of the Zen of Advanced Tightwaddery not only do this as second nature but also regard soup recipes to be an unnatural restraint, preferring instead to fly by the seat of their pants. Here's a tip for those folks:

Add vinegar to the water when you cook bones for soup. It will draw out calcium from the bones into your soup broth. Add 1 oz of vinegar to 1 quart. of water up to 4 oz of vinegar no matter how much water you use. You won't taste the vinegar in the final soup.

1 turkey carcass
4 chicken bouillon cubes
2 ribs celery, chopped
3 carrots, sliced
1 medium onion, chopped
2 potatoes, chopped
1 tsp parsley flakes
1 tsp black pepper
salt to taste
1 can peas
1 cup uncooked noodles

Simmer turkey carcass in a large pot with enough water to cover. Add bouillon cubes and spices. Cook 45 minutes.

Strain broth and pick meat from the bones. Return meat to the broth. Add remaining ingredients except peas and noodles. Cook until tender. Add peas and noodles. Simmer until noodles are tender.

(Contributed by Vicky Smith, North Little Rock, Arkansas)

KIDS' CLOTHES

Dear Amy,

I always buy my children's clothes at the end of the season for the next year. I buy one size larger than they are now. Around Labor Day there are still some summer items not sold. Last year I bought $10 pajamas for $1 and $2. And $5 and $6 tops for 75¢ to $1. Later in the fall there are still odds and ends left and I got several shirts for 50¢. I store clothes for next year in a closet in a trash bag.

Diana Meyer
St. Louis, Missouri

PLASTIC LIDS

Dear Amy,

In summer, we made our own Popsicles in plastic cups. We inserted recycled sticks (boiled to sanitation) in the little circles we cut out of large plastic lids to hold the stick upright in cup until frozen.

At Halloween we'd use the same plastic tops, especially the white ones, and cut vampire teeth, which one could put across one's gum and lip. These were also used as party favors.

Jean Grover
Oregon City, Oregon

TRANSCENDENTAL WOOD REFINISHING

I am a novice on the subject of refinishing wood in general, but when it comes to stripping old varnish, it seems I know of a method that few others do.

I learned about it when all other attempts to remove the old darkened varnish from our 100-year-old home's woodwork failed. Like most people would, I first tried all sorts of expensive chemicals. These made the finish gummy, and it still would not come off.

It turns out, as another owner of a Victorian home told me, old varnish can be removed with a simple paint scraper. I raced home to try it, and son-of-a-gun, it worked like a charm.

I had worried that it would scratch the surface, but several refinished doors, yard upon yard of trim, and a walnut bookcase later, I got compliments ... and not a botched job yet.

If I were beginning a new project, I would first try denatured alcohol. Sometimes this will remove old varnish with no scraping. I had an antique bureau with stained, darkened varnish sitting around for a year before I tried denatured alcohol. Three hours later I had removed all the finish with ease. I just applied the denatured alcohol, let it sit for a minute, and wiped off the dissolved finish with a rag.

If the varnish proves to be more stubborn, scraping is the next option. Old varnish scrapes off in a powdery form with relative ease. I scrape very lightly.

I use a standard paint scraper with disposable blades, which I sharpen on a bench grinder (bought at a yard sale for $10). If you don't have access to a grinder, you might try a whetstone. New blades, just out of the package, are not as sharp as ones sharpened on a grinder.

I discovered that if I grind the blades so that they have a slight convex curve, they work much better on flat surfaces.

I scrape concave curves with a sharpened spoon, and grooves can be scraped with the tip of a small screwdriver.

Once I have scraped an entire surface, which takes maybe three hours for a paneled door, I wipe the scraped area with a little denatured alcohol on a rag or a piece of steel wool. This dissolves and smooths out any varnish residue. After it dries I look for shiny spots, which indicate remaining varnish, and scrape those areas again. Then I hit rescraped areas with a little more denatured alcohol.

For the final finish I favor the low-luster look of linseed oil. It wipes on easily with a rag.

I like the scraper method because it's cheap, I can work small sections at a time, and I can clean up with a little quick sweeping and damp mopping. If I get the urge, I can pick up the project by getting the scraper out of the kitchen drawer. I don't need to get out chemicals, rubber gloves,

newspapers, etc. Other methods produce more waste . . . more gunky steel wool, dirty rags, and sometimes wastewater (the toxic chemicals should not be dumped down the sink).

The denatured alcohol/scraper method does not work for all finishes, and predicting which method will work for a piece of furniture you're contemplating buying is difficult. But try the least expensive methods first.

Scraping might require a little more time, but I enjoy the peace of mindless work. After about three days of scraping I enter a (chemical-free) trancelike state. Lofty and profound thoughts flow into my consciousness. The scraper, the wood, and I become one.

THE POPCORN CHALLENGE

As the crack staff investigative reporter, I am planning a series of articles exposing the practice of the food industry to make healthful and cheap food more expensive, all in the name of—yes, you guessed it—*Convenience!*

The focus of this article is microwave popcorn.

To illustrate the factors of cost versus savings of time we devised a race—a pop-off—pitting a nationally recognized "gourmet" microwave popcorn against 15-year-old homegrown popcorn popped in a hot-air popcorn popper.

My husband, Jim, went undercover to a chain grocery store, where he would not be recognized, and made the actual purchase of the microwave popcorn.

Jim became the competitor designate of the Microwave Team, while I headed up the Homegrown Team.

He placed the microwave popcorn on a handy pantry shelf while I did a final check to be sure all was in place for traditional popping.

I wore track shoes and loosened up with stretching exercises while Jim relaxed, cocky and confident in hiking boots.

We assumed like starting positions on the sofa (couch potatoesque). Our oldest son fired the toy starting gun, and we were off.

The Microwave Team cheated shamelessly, holding, elbowing, and blocking my path. Forced to abandon my preplanned route, instead I sped down the hall, dodging four excited cheering children, and arrived in the pantry with a two-second advantage.

With fluid catlike movements I prepared my popcorn while Jim fumbled with unfamiliar packaging before getting his popcorn into the microwave.

The commotion settled into a tense stillness as we waited to the competitive hums of popper and microwave.

Being a knowledgeable tightwad, you have probably ascertained that the microwave popcorn is far more expensive. The packaging boasts 12 cups of popcorn per bag. This is a gross exaggeration. Fully popped the 75¢ bag yielded only 6 cups (12½¢ per cup). Traditional "gourmet" popcorn costs 30¢ per batch of 10 cups (3¢ per cup). Generic popcorn can be purchased for as little as 9¢ per batch of 9 cups (1¢ per cup).

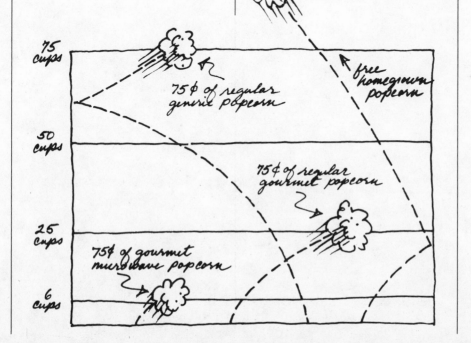

75 cups

50 cups

25 cups

6 cups

75¢ of regular generic popcorn

free homegrown popcorn

75¢ of regular gourmet popcorn

75¢ of gourmet microwave popcorn

If your family pops two batches of traditional generic popcorn per week, instead of preparing an equivalent amount of microwave popcorn, you will save nearly $100 over the course of the year.

But how much *time* does microwave popcorn save?

Meanwhile, back in the pantry, the competitive humming gave way to the explosive fury of the Homegrown challenger: 3½ minutes into the race the traditionally popped popcorn was buttered and salted while the microwave popcorn emitted its first humble bursts. Jim had to wait an additional two minutes in the pantry for his to finish popping while the Homegrown Team relaxed victoriously on the sofa (couch potatoesque) in time for the start of the next program.

Note: some people spray a paper bag with cooking spray to make "homemade microwave popcorn." This is more flammable than the store bought type, and if attempted should be watched carefully.

Winter

THE CHRISTMAS FULFILLMENT DRAMA

In December most of us who share the holidays with children will observe a drama called the "fulfillment curve," played out within the space of two or three hours.

This drama, or idea, is one of many great insights in the book called *Transforming Your Relationship with Money and Achieving Financial Independence* by Joe Dominguez.

His theory is that when we spend money on the basics of survival—food, shelter, warmth, clothing—we receive maximum fulfillment for the dollars spent. To a slightly lesser degree we are fulfilled as we begin to spend on a few comforts and luxuries. Beyond this, however, the curve peaks and begins to drop so that we receive *less* fulfillment for the dollars spent (see chart below).

THE FULFILLMENT CURVE

It is not that spending money stops being fun altogether, but that the ratio of dollars spent to fulfillment received drops off. Ideally we should recognize where the peak is and consciously taper our spending beyond that point. If we do continue to spend we trade more hours of work to earn money to buy less and less fulfillment.

His book further outlines the way this works in relation to a scenario couple over a period of years.

Simpler examples come to mind, such as the fulfillment received from the first spoonful from a half gallon of ice cream versus the last one scraped from the bottom of the carton 20 minutes later. Or the fulfillment received from the first $200 car as a teenager versus the $20,000 car bought 10 years later. The new car was nice . . . but not 100 times as nice.

When I first read this book I instantly recognized the truth of the fulfillment curve as I thought about Christmas mornings (and birthdays) I have witnessed with children. Every parent who has overshot the peak knows exactly what I'm writing about.

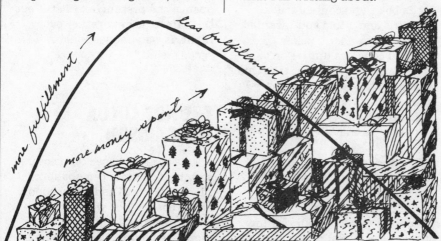

more fulfillment →
less fulfillment
more money spent →

The Christmas morning fulfillment drama opens with a scene of the Smuckster family gathered around an enormous stack of gifts. Clyde and Bunni anxiously anticipate the reaction of their son Hubert.

Act I. Hubert opens up two presents—a Sno-Boggan and the King's Mountain Fortress Lego set. He is ecstatic and wants to play with the Legos, but Clyde insists he must open all his presents first.

Act 2. Hubert continues opening presents and receives a Creepy Cruiser Car, Beetle Juice Neighborhood Nasty figures, and a Mario Brothers pinball game. His eyes are big as saucers as he exclaims, "Cool! What else is for me?"

Act 3. More tearing and flinging of paper reveals a Hasbro WWF Wrestling Ring, the Jetsons videotape and a Nasta Air Guitar. Hubert's inner monster begins to show itself as he disdainfully points and says, "I didn't want that wrestling thing."

Act 4. Hubert opens Teenage Mutant Ninja Turtle figures, a Nintendo Game Boy, and a Nikko Big Bubba radio control truck. "Not this one. I told you I wanted the Black Thunder truck."

Bunni consoles him, "Don't worry, sweetie, we'll just take this one back and get the one you want." Hubert sulks, pokes through the empty wrappings and says, "Is that all I got?"

The peak of the fulfillment curve is different for every family. The drama may play out more subtly in your family. Sometimes the only indicator is a lessening of enthusiasm. But wherever it is

for you, spending beyond the peak fails to add significantly to your holiday experience. The Smucksters' Christmas would have been perfect had it been a one-act play.

The peak seems to vary depending on the age of the child. (Your teenager may deny there is any such peak.) It is largely determined by our current culture, as any senior citizen will verify. When children have become accustomed to a large volume of material goods, more presents are required to satisfy them.

I am not suggesting that we revert to Dickensian holidays. We have found that Christmas and birthdays lack the "Wow!" when we have relied solely on scrounged and homemade presents. We seem to hit the peak when we focus on the purchase of one special new item of about $20, especially for the older children, and fill in around the edges with other things.

One Christmas our daughter, Jamie, desperately wanted P.J. Sparkles, a doll that lights up when hugged. We didn't locate the doll until her birthday in March. Jamie danced with joy when she opened the present, and I still put the pair to sleep together every night. It was unquestionably a "good spend."

THE HOT COCOA COMPARISON

This chart is based on price per serving, but that does not show the real story. Whenever we look at the cost of food we must consider how much nutrition our money is buying. The percentage

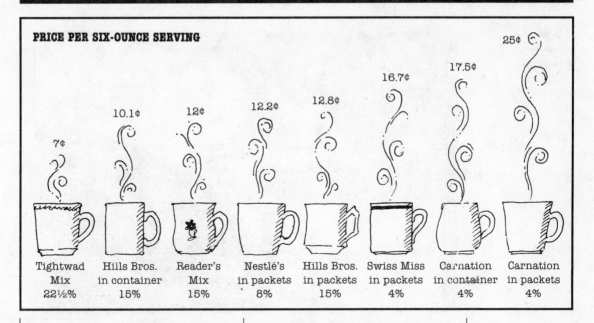

PRICE PER SIX-OUNCE SERVING

7¢	10.1¢	12¢	12.2¢	12.8¢	16.7¢	17.5¢	25¢
Tightwad Mix 22½%	Hills Bros. in container 15%	Reader's Mix 15%	Nestlé's in packets 8%	Hills Bros. in packets 15%	Swiss Miss in packets 4%	Carnation in container 4%	Carnation in packets 4%

figure under each type of cocoa indicates the percent of the USRDA (U.S. Recommended Daily Allowance) of calcium each 6-ounce serving contains. Milk products do contain other nutrients, but we primarily look to them for calcium.

According to the information on a box of dry milk, 6 ounces of milk provides about 22½% of the RDA of calcium. The packaging information of the commercial mixes lists nutrition.

A reader sent in a homemade mix recipe, but when I made it up I found that, although it tasted very good, it was about the same price per serving as some commercially prepared brands. I calculated the volume of dry milk to nonnutritious ingredients to determine the percent of USRDA of calcium.

To determine how much nutrition your money is buying, divide the cost per serving by the percent of USRDA of calcium. I found that the tightwad mix provides about 3% per penny spent while the next most nutritious mixes, Hills Bros. and the reader's mix provide 1½%. Swiss Miss and Carnation are the bad guys coming in at under ¼% per penny spent.

Tightwad Hot Cocoa Mix

I mix ⅓ cup of dry milk with 1 teaspoon of cocoa and sugar each. Add 1 cup of hot water. Or mix with cold water and prepare in the microwave.

The Reader's Hot Cocoa Mix

10⅔ cups dry milk
6 oz of nondairy coffee creamer
1 pound of Nestlé's Quik
⅓ cup confectioner's sugar

Mix the ingredients in a large bowl and store in covered container. To prepare hot cocoa, mix ½ cup of the mix with 1 cup of hot water.

THE ENVELOPE RECYCLER

Dear Amy,

Want some cheap return-address labels? Here's how to get some. Cut out all of the mailing labels from your junk mail that have your address all nicely pre-printed. Attach them to your envelopes with a glue stick, white glue, or tape.

**Pat Flewelling
Leeds, Maine**

(This is one of those things we tightwads do even though we know they don't contribute much to our financial dream. One of my other readers takes this a step further. Homemade labels can be made big enough to cover old return addresses. He reuses an envelope by patching it with one of these, and a blank label over the other address, and then adds a new stamp. The letters come with a double postmark. FZ)

CLEANING SOLUTION

Dear Amy,

This was given to me by a home economics teacher. It is just as effective as high-priced cleaning solutions.

½ cup ammonia
⅓ cup vinegar
2 Tbsp baking soda
1 gallon water

**Alice Kinsman
Auburn, Maine**

A TIGHTWAD QUERY

Dear Amy,

Still haven't figured out how to recycle toilet paper. I keep wondering about toilet paper that is advertised as recycled!

**Arnie Anfinson
Seattle, Washington**

Dear Amy,
   My husband never believed me until he tried it, but drying your razor after you rinse it clean saves tons of shaves. My blades for my legs last for months.
                    Marina Andrew
                    Forest Lake, Minnesota

D O   O N E   B E T T E R

Dear Amy,
   In reference to the "Saves on Shaves" contribution, I can do one better. After you clean and dry your razor blade, coat it with that ever-present-in-your-medicine-chest Vaseline or cold cream. This keeps the air from coming in contact with the cutting edge and causing rust. It also helps to lubricate the next shave.
                    Louis Pifer
                    Delano, California

THE INVESTMENT PURCHASE AND THE DISPOSABLE PURCHASE

During our honeymoon Jim and I went antiquing and stayed at country inns. Although we bought a few other items we primarily searched for an antique cannonball bed (a wooden bed frame with a ball on the top of the ornately turned corner posts).
   We poked through scores of shops over a period of 10 days and turned up only a dozen in various conditions, costing between $300 and $800. After criss-crossing our way through the New England states we finally located one in perfect condition only a few miles from Jim's parents' house. Because we had shopped so thoroughly we knew the $425 price tag was perhaps not a steal, but certainly fair.
   The bed, being a genuine antique, was too short and needed to have the rails lengthened by a woodworker. Then we had a custom box spring made to fit. Before we slept in it we had spent $700.
   About this same time we also became very conscious of our food bill and refused to pay 59¢ for a can of tuna fish. We knew it would go on sale for 49¢ the next week.
   Was this craziness or true tightwaddery?
   The tuna fish is a disposable purchase. The bed is an investment purchase, not only because antiques appreciate in value but also because we will own it for 50 to 60 years. This bed annually costs us about the same as a pair of movie tickets.
   Disposable purchases are those things that we buy for short-term use, such as food, clothing, and entertainment. Certainly food is an investment in nutrition, but tuna fish provides a similar food value to lobster. A business suit may be an investment but children's clothing can only be considered a disposable purchase. Entertainment is an investment in family time, but generally free entertainment can be as fulfilling.
   Some purchases fall into a gray area. Automobiles, for example,

may be either depending on your car ownership philosophy.

Early on we recognized it was poor financial management to spend most of our money on disposable things. In the same way it did not seem wise to compromise on intermediate-priced items that we didn't like. As a result the cannonball bed remains our most extravagant household purchase. Other than half a dozen items that we have paid more than $100 for, the remainder of our house is furnished in an Early Marriage (thrift shop) style, liberally accessorized with wooden crates. We have temporarily shifted some of these purchases from the investment to the disposable category.

When I was single most of my discretionary income went for disposable things. Over an eight-year period I spent about $5,000 just on movies and meals out. Today I cannot name one tenth of the movies I saw and recall very few meals out.

During the same time I spent less than $400 on three chairs, a coffee table, and a cabinet. Now, 10 years later, these items still see daily use.

Without resorting to deprivation we try to spend a minimum on disposable purchases. In 1990 we spent less than $250 to clothe six people, less than $350 on birthdays and Christmas, and I am hard pressed to think of anything spent for entertainment. I know of only one family that spends less than we do for food.

By comparison we spent about $2,000 on a used garden tractor and several tools, which will save us many times their cost.

When we do spend on an investment purchase we shop for months, or even years. We look for the best value, not necessarily the cheapest solutions. If we plan to live with an item, perhaps forever, we do not compromise on what we like.

Although my $5,000 expenditure on movies and dinners

out is shocking it also typifies the down-the-drain spending habits of many people. They merely have not added it up yet. The lack of financial progress over a period of years dramatizes the long-term result of this type of spending. When gratification depends on the purchase of disposable things, spending must continue at the same level forever. Factoring in growing families and inflation more money needs to be spent to achieve the same level of gratification.

Although I have illustrated this concept with material goods, investment purchases can include less tangible things, such as education as well as the buying of financial freedom through a variety of strategies.

Jim and I are working toward a mix of acquiring material goods and buying financial freedom. We have done this to a degree when we bought a "two-income house" on one income. As inflation shrinks the value of the mortgage and as we pay it off early a smaller percentage of our income will go for housing.

The prudent (and restrained) expenditure on lesser investment purchases works toward this same goal. The first few years we were married we spent a great deal on investment purchases. The "extravagant" investment purchases, such as our cannonball bed, will never need to be replaced. Good appliances and tools save money. Today we need to spend far less on things of permanence.

As toddlers inevitably grow to be teenagers we expect our budget for disposable purchases will in-crease. (Although, amazingly, tuna fish still goes on sale for 49¢ a can.)

Some who are not lovers of antiques will argue the merits of our expenditure for a cannonball bed, pointing out that a mattress can be supported equally well by the floor. Nevertheless our financial plan continues to include the replacement of wooden crates with real furniture.

BOOK SMARTS

Dear Amy,

My main entertainment is reading. I use the library a lot, but I also like to own certain books. One bookstore in town offers 25% off all new books in July and December. I keep a list and buy during these two months.

I also frequent used-book stores. I trade in books I no longer want for "new" ones. When I run low on books to trade in, I go to a flea market or garage sale and offer to buy all their books for 10¢ each. I can get 100 books for $10. After reading the ones I am interested in I take the rest to the used bookstore to trade in.

I generally get $100 to $200 in credit this way, and can exchange it for other books, which I read and exchange again. For $10 and 100 books I can get 150 to 175 books to read. This is a lot of entertainment for $10. (Bookstores generally don't accept the small romance books because they have hundreds of them.)

Barbara Turner
Colorado Springs, Colorado

BARGAINS IN BACK

Dear Amy,

I work in a drugstore. We are always repricing items in our store, which means, in general, *raising them.* Yesterday I repriced Solarcaine at $5.49, and in the process noticed that there was some Solarcaine on the back of the shelf still at $3.95. It had missed being marked up for some time.

So, don't buy the product right in front. Look at all the packages, especially the ones in the back. This works best in older stores that don't use a laser reader.

Tightwad Jim
Phoenix, Arizona

LIGHT TRICK

Dear Amy,

My 74-year-old father lives in an 1867 home with only a very few conveniences. The elderly have always "made do" and so "does" my father. A ceiling kitchen light pull chain was pulled off one day when the light was "on," and so he couldn't turn it off (or off and on again). Rather than call in an electrician to fix the problem, my father found a green plastic garden pot, placed a styrofoam cup inside, which he then nailed to an old broom handle. As the old fixture is up on a 10-foot or so high ceiling, my parents have no problem turning the bulb to the right or left for "on" and "off." You see, the styrofoam cup gets a good grip on the bulb.

So goes life at my parents' house. There is a special place on the wall beside the kitchen table for this conversation piece, which they have used now for years!

I think an award should be given to this senior citizen tightwad.

Suzanne Foster
Winthrop, Maine

THE GIFT WHEEL

This inspiration comes from Duane and Muriel McIntire of Rolling Hills Estates, California, They have seven children. With all the grandchildren, gift giving had become too expensive. While many families draw names, this wheel method is superior because no family member will get the same person more than one time in eight years.

The McIntires' wheel (see opposite) is divided into eight sections—one section for each of their children and one section for them. You will divide yours by the number of people in your family.

Cut a large circle (about 5") and a small circle (about 4") from a piece of cardboard. Trace the correct size jar lids if you don't have a compass. Divide each circle into the appropriate number of sections. Poke a hole in the center of each of the circles and attach them with a brass fastener. Write names of family members around the outer edge of each circle. The sequence of names should be the same on each circle.

In the outer circle write this year's date in the first section, next year's date in the second section, and so on around the circle. With a different color mark an index line on any of the section lines on the inner circle.

Each year you rotate the wheel by realigning the index line with the new date. The name on the inside wheel gives to the person on the outside wheel.

SEEKING THE MINIMUM LEVEL

People are creatures of habit. We do things because we have always done them that way, or because our parents always did them that way, or because a teacher taught us that way, or because an "expert" said to do it that way. We seldom challenge why we do things the way we do. As a result we persist in expensive behaviors, purely out of habit.

To form new, frugal habits, develop an awareness about all the small actions you do every day. Explore new ways to do things ... seek the minimum level. Scale down step by step until the

process does not work satisfactorily for your standards. Then bump it up one level.

When you wash dishes, do you always fill the sink to the top? If you're doing a small number of dishes a sink half full of water may suffice. Do you always put a two-second squirt of dishwashing liquid in the water? See if a one-second squirt will work. Or measure it in a teaspoon so that you have an accurate gauge.

When you wash laundry, do you always put the recommended amount of detergent in each load? Isn't it handy the way the manufacturers provide you with a plastic scoop in each box so you never think about using less? Think about how dirty each load is and add detergent accordingly. Often a half scoop will work as well.

Our grandmothers boiled cloth diapers. Our mothers bleached them. Experiment with your laundering procedure. Can you use less bleach? Do you need bleach? Will the ultraviolet rays from outdoor air drying be sufficient? Do you need to wash in hot water? Keep bumping down the procedure until it seems to bother your baby. Then move back up one level. It seems mean, but it may take three years before your child is potty trained, so you could save hundreds of dollars.

If your dryer doesn't have a moisture sensor, do you always set the dial at a certain point? Try setting it for less time, until you find how little time you really need to dry your clothes. Record your findings for the different lengths of time required to dry different types and amounts of laundry.

Do you use an inch of toothpaste because a brush has inch-long rows of bristles and every toothpaste advertisement you've ever seen portrays a neat, full, bristle-length swath? Experiment to see if a ½ inch of toothpaste works as well.

When you pour bath water, do you habitually fill the tub to eight inches deep when four would do the same job? When you shampoo, do you experiment to find the least amount that will work? If you pour a quarter-sized dab in your palm, try using a nickel-sized one. When you shower, do you need to wash your hair each time? Do you need a shower every day or would a sponge bath suffice on days you're not going to work?

If you blow-dry your hair, are there days when air drying would be suitable? Do you need the full makeup regimen every day? Maybe some days you could scale it down—not use eye makeup or not use any at all.

To avoid the expense of canned shaving cream, a friend of mine put a chunk of soap in the bottom of a mug and used a shaving brush to whip it to a froth and apply it. He got good results, but one day, fresh from the shower, he tried shaving his still-wet face with no cream at all. Because his beard is relatively light, it worked. Now he only uses the mug and brush on days when he doesn't shower.

CHEAP

CHEAPER

CHEAPEST

When you are baking, do you always set the timer the recommended time? Maybe your oven thermostat is high, and your oven bakes faster. Try checking for doneness a few minutes early. Do you follow recipes exactly or do you experiment? In baking you can try using less sugar, eggs, and oil. Find the point where you notice a significant taste difference, and then increase the sugar, eggs, or oil slightly.

When you eat and drink, do you always fill plates and cups full? Maybe a partial cup of coffee or a smaller portion would satisfy you as much. If you have a chocolate craving at the checkout line, do you really need the extra-large-size chocolate bar? Maybe a small Peppermint Patty would satisfy you.

Do you always buy brand-name foods because your one experiment with store brands was unsatisfactory? Keep experimenting to find lower-cost brands that work for your needs. And bear in mind, just because a brand tastes different, it doesn't mean it tastes worse.

Could your heat thermostat be set lower? Move it down and put on a sweater. How high is your water heater set? Turn it down to 125°. (Do not experiment lower—it needs to be this hot to kill bacteria.) Could any of your lights be a lower wattage, especially in hallways? If you find the dimness of the lower-wattage bulbs bothersome, put the brighter ones back in.

How many gifts do you give for birthdays? Would fewer be as satisfying? We set a $50 limit on the total cost of gifts and the party, but found we were often able to do an entire birthday for about $25. If you find your reduced spending level is not quite satisfactory, increase the budget slightly.

Most important, when you establish your budget, do you always spend the allowed amount, or do you try to spend less on the areas of your budget that are flexible?

When you seek the minimum level you may be breaking old habits. Give yourself time to get used to the new lower level. It may take a few months to adjust so that the change feels comfortable. And at that point try the experiment again.

RAISIN OATMEAL SCONES

- 1½ cups flour
- 1 cup uncooked oatmeal
- 1 tsp baking soda
- ½ tsp salt
- ¼ cup softened margarine
- ½ cup raisins
- ¾ cup sour milk (milk with 2 tsp of vinegar added)
- 1 egg, beaten

Preheat oven to 400°. Mix dry ingredients; cut in margarine and raisins. Stir in enough sour milk just to moisten. Divide the dough in half. Flour hands and pat dough into two circles on a greased cookie sheet about ½ inch thick. Cut into quarters. Bake for 10 minutes. Brush on egg and then bake until golden brown. Serve with honey, margarine, or jam.

This hindsight wisdom translates into "expensive is good" and "inexpensive is bad." If it were true there would be no bargains.

Consumers are so deeply conditioned with this notion that they are suspicious when goods and services are "too low."

Did you ever wander down a store aisle of expensively priced shampoos and think, "Who buys this stuff?" In fact buyers of "quality" products are often purchasing advertising, glitzy packaging, and high corporate overhead.

Certainly there are times that my good deals turn out to be not so good and I hear that little voice whisper the familiar hindsight wisdom: "You get what you pay for." But those times are rare and the financial risks are small compared to all the savings that have come from the bargain hunting.

Every tightwad has a list of favorite steals. Here's a few of our recent good deals.

- A year-old probably-purebred German shepherd from the animal shelter for a $20 donation.
- Bulk purchased yeast at about 7% of the price of those little packages.

- A like-new Battleship game for 39¢ at the thrift shop.
- An antique wood cookstove found buried in a garage, rusted and in pieces. This, purchased for $100, is now worth about $500 after a few hours of elbow grease.
- An unopened half gallon of carpenter's glue for $3, originally priced at $17.95.

Finding bargains requires experimentation, research, and a little patience. Basing your purchases on the "you get what you pay for" presumption is easy, effortless . . . and expensive.

BEST BARGAINS

Toothpaste. Next time you sit in the dentist's chair, think about how much toothpaste could be purchased for the cost of that filling.

The Public Library. This remarkable institution makes information, knowledge, and self-education available to everyone at no cost.

Thinness. Despite the enormous weight loss industry, thinness is in fact very cheap. It does not require expensive diet foods, clubs, or counseling. One simply eats less. In many cultures only the wealthy can achieve the desired weight.

Paper. In an interview Bette Midler spoke of the extravagant presents fans send to her daughter. Sending these to children of low-income families seemed more logical to her. She added, "Besides, I kind of think the best present for a kid is a pencil and a piece of paper."

Public Places. Within any geographic area there are a number of places of interest that are free and open to all. Among my personal favorites are Trinity Chapel in Boston and Halibut Point in Gloucester, MA.

Television. Advertisers pick up the tab for this form of free entertainment. Note: this is only a bargain if you select worthwhile programming and if you have the presence of mind to ignore the commercials.

A 29¢ Postage Stamp. Consider the volume of information that can be included under an ounce and that the U.S. Postal Service will carry it thousands of miles for the same price.

A Single Zucchini Seed. As most of us wrap up the gardening season this is self-explanatory.

TWO CHRISTMAS PROJECTS

If you're like me, by this time you are frantically looking for one more good, last-minute idea that doesn't require learning a new skill. And you are vowing to start earlier next year. Here is a project for this year, and one to begin for next year.

Bread Bears

(This recipe comes from the Rodale Press Christmas magazine.)

- 1 package dry yeast
- ¼ cup warm water
- ½ cup softened butter
- ¼ to ½ cup honey
- 3 tsp freshly grated lemon peel

- 1 tsp pure almond extract
- 3 tsp lemon juice
- ½ tsp salt
- 3 eggs
- 3 eggs, separated
- ½ cup warm milk
- 5 to 6 cups unbleached flour
- cinnamon sugar

Combine yeast with water; stir with fork until dissolved and set aside.

In a large bowl of an electric mixer, cream butter, honey, lemon peel, almond extract, lemon juice, and salt until mixture is fluffy. Beat in eggs and egg yolks one at a time. (Reserve three egg whites for glaze.)

With a spatula, blend in milk and yeast mixture.

Beat in two cups of flour to make a smooth batter. Add enough flour to make a stiff dough.

Turn dough onto a lightly floured surface. Knead it until the texture is smooth ... about 10 minutes. Place in a buttered bowl, cover lightly with a cloth, and allow it to rise in a warm place for an hour, or until doubled in bulk.

Turn the dough out onto a lightly floured surface; punch it down and let it rest for 10 minutes.

To assemble bears:

Each recipe makes two 12" bears, or four 8" bears. Or you can make a number of smaller ones. Divide your dough into circles, one for each bear. Each circle is divided according to the directions below to get the right proportions. (Or you can eyeball it.)

Divide each circle in half. One half makes up the body. Divide the second half into sections. One section becomes a head. The remaining section is used for body parts. Pull off a quarter of it to make a snout. The remainder of the dough is divided in half. The first half is divided into thirds— one for the two ears and two for two arms. The last of the dough is divided in half to make two legs.

Roll the body section into a smooth ball and place in the center of a greased cookie sheet and flatten slightly. Roll the head section smooth and attach it to the body. Roll the snout and ear sections and attach them. The arms and legs sections are rolled into cylinders and attached. Use a small amount of water to stick together bear parts.

To finish the bear, press indentations with your index finger to make eyes and belly button. Put a blanched almond in each eye socket so that it will hold its shape while baking.

Cover the bear with a clean cloth and let it rise for one hour in a draft-free space.

Preheat the oven to 375°.

Beat one egg white with 1 tsp of water. Using a pastry brush paint the entire top surface of the bear with the egg glaze. Sprinkle with cinnamon sugar. (To make cinnamon sugar mix ½ cup granulated sugar to 1 tsp cinnamon.)

Bake the bears, 30 to 45 minutes, or until golden brown. (Smaller bears take less time.) After baking remove the nuts from the eyes. Let cool for 1 hour. Place raisins or candies in the eyes.

Tie brightly colored ribbon around the bear's neck. Place a large bear on a foil-covered cardboard and cover with plastic wrap. Or give several small bears in a basket. If you feel really inspired you could make an entire bear family to correspond with the sizes of family members you are giving to —a mommy and daddy and baby bears. Use red ribbon for girls and green for boys.

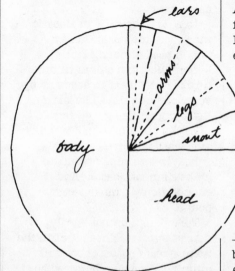

A Fruit Stone Wreath

Contributed by Nancy Wilson of Warren, Maine.

The stones or pits from peaches, prunes, and cherries have differing textures and natural colors. These can be saved to make a unique and attractive wreath.

After collecting a large number, wash the pits well. Soak briefly in bleach and rinse.

The pits are then glued to a sanded circle of ¼-inch plywood using Elmer's glue. Before beginning the gluing, plan a design using the different colors and textures of the pits.

To complete your wreath wire it over an evergreen wreath. It can be hung or laid flat as a centerpiece with a candle or made to fit around a punch bowl.

DEALING WITH DESIGNER CLOTHES

1. Give your child a clothing budget ample enough to cover his basic needs. Provide him with special jobs he can do to earn the difference between the $25 sneakers and the $75 sneakers. The pay scale should not rise above slave labor.

2. Form a parents' group specifically to strike against this unfair demand. If fewer parents caved in, fewer children would have designer clothes. Simple mathematics reveal that if fewer kids have designer clothes, more kids must wear generic clothes. Therefore, fewer designer-clad kids are around to pressure everyone else.

3. For those of you who have kids living in the real world, try this idea. Save designer labels from worn clothing and sew on to new generic clothing. If necessary get old designer clothes from yard sales and thrift shops. One of my helpers told me her mother used to save alligators when she was in high school.

INTERIOR DECORATING FOR TIGHTWADS

I have had this same experience on several occasions: I visit the home of someone on a small income, frequently a senior citizen. The home is tidy, orderly, and inviting. I like being there.

Maybe the hostess asks me to get the milk. Only then I notice that the refrigerator is of a vintage bordering on antique. The paint has worn through near the handle from decades of openings. But the refrigerator is also lacking in fingerprints and the litter of shopping lists and phone messages adhered with cute magnets and clear tape. An attractive arrangement of dried bittersweet in a stoneware jug replaces the usual crown of permanent clutter.

A further tour throughout the home would reveal a similar pattern. Furniture might be mismatched but good-looking. Woodwork might need to be repainted, but it is clean. Nothing is brand new, but somehow the entire home has an appeal.

Where we live has a marked effect on our sense of well-being. If we are happy in our home we have less need to leave it and spend money. As tightwads, how we feel about where we live is important. But we approach interior decorating in a unique manner—money *is* an object. Therefore, we must resort to the strategies that yield the most improvement for the least money.

Housecleaning. This should be your first interior design consideration. Without investing any money you can achieve the most dramatic results.

Make a concentrated effort to eliminate the permanent pile of clutter, minimize eyesores, and put things away. If things are out of place because you don't have a place for them, then designate a place.

People who live in small places should eliminate unnecessary items such as the multicolored mushroom candle that has been sitting on your counter for years, that you never liked in the first place, and serves no useful purpose. Smaller places are harder to keep clean, so the less stuff you have the better.

When you eliminate stuff, hold a yard sale, donate, or ask around to find someone who wants it.

Rearranging. Redecorate by putting old things in new places. I saw a television program about an interior designer who could makeover a home without buying anything new. She worked on the assumption that whatever her clients already owned was there by their choosing, so they probably liked it. Instead she focused on using the things the clients already owned in more pleasing arrangements.

Recently I noticed that I had been storing a nice basket in the basement. I brought it upstairs where it could be seen in the kitchen. We repotted some of our plants and one found its way to a new spot in the living room. I had a frame with artwork that I didn't like. I replaced the art with a decorative card someone had sent me. That picture filled an empty spot on the kitchen wall. In each case the small change felt satisfying.

When you clean house and rearrange you can still keep the decorative items that please you, but try to group your treasures to create a focal point. Rooms also need areas that are clutter-free and restful to the eyes. You might put your collection of baseball memorabilia on one set of shelves. Your collection of baskets can hang in a grouping on one wall. Don't scatter them evenly around the room.

Eclecticism. This bona fide style of interior design allows you to mix furniture of all types. It lends itself perfectly to the tightwad approach. We tend to collect mismatched stuff from yard sales, the curb, the secondhand shop, and Great-Aunt Ethel's attic.

Eclecticism defies the expensive approach of buying an entire room of furniture direct from the Ethan Allen showroom (and buying it on time). Some people feel compelled to buy things that match because they lack confidence in their own tastes. While being "safe," purchasing furniture in sets can result in a sterile and impersonal look. Your home should reflect you and not a designer.

Eclecticism is a great liberator. You can't make a mistake as long as you choose things that you like. It doesn't have to match or conform to someone else's standard of tastefulness. (This means if you really love it, you can keep the painting of bullfighters on black velvet.)

The Potpourri Approach. A potpourri is a grouping of items that are similar but not identical.

Rather than having one large picture, collect a variety of small frames and paint them the same color. Hang these in a grouping. You might like vintage silverware but find only a few pieces at a time. Collect a variety and set your table with a mix of pieces. If you can't afford a set of china pick up odd pieces of the same color (most likely white). Mismatched but similar dining chairs can be painted the same color.

You don't want to hide the mismatches, but rather take pleasure in the diversity.

Do-It-Yourself. When you refinish furniture, paint your own art, or grow your own houseplants from seedlings, you invest part of yourself in those items.

They feel more personal to you because you have a history with them.

You can save a lot when you learn to see the potential of something that needs work. It might be priced low because other potential buyers lack vision.

The first time we laid eyes on our house, our enthusiasm wasn't dampened by the disastrous kitchen. So we bought the house and forged ahead. We removed all the peeling wallpaper, patched the old plaster, and painted over the dingy yellow with white paint. We repaired the holes in the ceiling with a large piece of Sheetrock we found in the barn. We removed the old cracked floor tiles and sanded and finished the wood floor underneath. We found a section of counter from an old country store in the shed, painted and refinished it, and use it as a work island. The total cost of our make-do-for-now redecoration was only $200.

Flexibility. Your interior design plan should be flexible. Carefully choose things over time and as bargains come your way. As you acquire better things you will want to be able to use your earlier acquisitions in other parts of your home. Our "entertainment

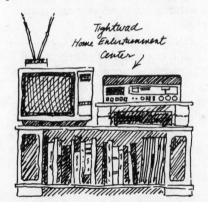

Tightwad Home Entertainment Center

center" is made of boards, cement blocks, and bricks.

When we replace it, the materials can be reused for other projects. We bought four small reproduction oriental rugs at a yard sale. (They are worn enough to look almost authentic.) We have used these in a grouping on our living-room floor. If we buy a large rug the small ones can be used in other parts of the house.

If you move frequently you'll want to acquire smaller, more versatile things. I had a friend who secretly sawed and replaced the banister of her new apartment house so she could get the couch up the stairs. More responsible friends have sold their couches at a loss. Large pictures, rugs, and furniture lack flexibility and may not work well in a new home.

Breaking with Convention. In a letter that contained pictures and descriptions, one reader shared a number of unconventional ideas that work well. She and her husband bought a surplus library card catalog, refinished it, and use it for silverware, napkins, placemats, wrapping paper, dominoes, etc. They have an interesting old street light for a lamp. An old chifforobe became a cabinet for their television and stereo.

If you accept the unconventional, the range of inexpensive alternatives increases. Some types of outdoor furniture work well indoors. A glass brick can become a vase. Discarded lockers can be painted and used for storage in a child's room. A restaurant booth can become a breakfast nook.

Stick with Classics. Interior design, like clothing, undergoes style changes. With clothing, black is the classic color. In interior design the classic color is white. The harvest golds and avocados have long since enjoyed their heyday. But the white appliances from the '50s go with the ones from the '90s.

Likewise, white painted walls are not only the cheapest solution but also highly universal and timeless. Look through magazines that feature country and contemporary homes. Roughly 75% of the featured rooms have white painted walls.

The colors in design change every few years. The bright colored countertops of the '70s look dated today. The Williamsburg blue and salmons of the '80s will give way to something new.

Clear finished wood is also classic, as are most natural colors. Accessorize with colors in ways that you can change easily if you tire of them.

Avoid trendy design motifs. A few years ago mushrooms were popular. Today's cows and cats seem to be gaining ground on the "ducky decor" of more recent years. We have a nation of folks continually replacing matching canisters, potholders, and toaster covers.

Think. (It's cheap.) I have often suspected that people haven't really identified what it is about their home that bothers them. The general sense of confusion, frustration, or dissatisfaction they feel about their homes might be resolved by a good cleaning, a move of the furniture, or a fresh coat of paint.

Dear Amy,

My aloe vera plant supplies me with better burn ointment than I've ever bought. Its juices erase the minor burns my careless fingers get while cooking, and heal cuts and scrapes, too. This plant has also been reported to absorb household air pollutants. In a north window, with no direct sun, my aloe vera energetically produces offspring, which make lovely free gifts.

Westy Melby
Boone, Colorado

BABY FOOD

Dear Amy,

I work with mothers and infants a lot. Often they get excited over saving money by making their own baby food. Baby food, however, is what sociologists term "an acquired need." While it may be the social custom to use it, or expectation to use it, it is entirely the fabrication of baby food companies and only serves to fill their pockets. It can certainly be done away with. A breast-fed infant can go directly to table food when ready. I always figured if a baby *needed* strained peas at three months, I'd have a third one for strained peas.

Patti Clark
Camden, Maine

READER POTPOURRI

Dear Amy,

My aunt used an adding machine in her business. She never tears the tape off until it is used up, and then she rewinds it inside out and uses it the second time.

Jean Roberts
Alton, New Hampshire

Dear Amy,

When I make a pot of coffee, I put the rest in a thermos. It sits on the counter until I want coffee later.

Diane Bull
Rockford, Illinois

Dear Amy,

My mother used to cut a roll of paper towels in half up to the cardboard tube so that a half sheet was used most of the time.

Karen Pence
West Baldwin, Maine

Dear Amy,

Use the cuffs from old worn socks as cuff protectors on children's shirt cuffs when they are doing crafts etc.

Anne Cutter
Westbrook, Maine

FREE NEWSPAPERS

Dear Amy,

Usually small local stores have copies of the Sunday paper left over. They only have to send in a portion of the paper for credit and are often willing to part with the excess parts, such as coupons. This works with the dailies, too. When folks shop as we do, coupons really help.

Charles Tanner
Falmouth, Maine

THE GLASS-TOP CANNING JAR DILEMMA

We have about 400 surplus quart glass-top wire-bail canning jars—people keep giving them to us. These are becoming obsolete as the rubber rings get harder to find.

There must be millions of surplus jars throughout the country in need of a new use. Aside from potential food storage containers I have pondered about what could be put in them to make gifts, such as soup, coffee mixes, or Epsom salts. I requested ideas for the soon-to-be-obsolete and abundant glass-top canning jar. Teresa Totaro of Powhatan, Virginia, suggests we rub it, polish it, talk to it, adore it, and say the magic words: "We think we found different uses for them now, unless a genie finds a new source of rubber canning rings." It must have worked. A reader sent an address for rubber rings with tabs:

Hershberger Country Store
50940 T.R. 220 Rt.1
Baltic, OH 43804

The Hershbergers are Amish, and do not have a phone. Their catalog is free with an order or costs $2. Regular jar rubbers cost 98¢ per dozen, and wide-mouth ones cost $1.25 per dozen, plus a fee for shipping and handling.

An alternative source costs about 40% more:

Vermont Country Store
Mail Order Office
P.O. Box 3000
Manchester, Ctr., VT 05255-3000
(802) 362-2400

Glass-top canning jars may not be as plentiful in different parts of the country as they are in New England, as several readers indicated. They are often thrown away here. I found many boxes of them on the curb during spring cleaning (sanctioned trash-picking) season. Older people often have jars in their cellars with

40-year-old contents, and they are often pleased to have a younger person express interest. However, even here jars can sell for $1 to $6 per jar depending on the type. The blue-tinted ones are valuable.

You might be able to find a free source (if you *aren't* overloaded with them) if you think about possible likely sources such as your glass recycling center. Because these jars are collectible, old-fashioned, and attractive they make visually pleasing containers.

Containers for Office Use: rubber bands that come around flyers, paper clips, pens, and pencils

Decorative Storage: Indian corn, buttons, marbles, sea shells, small pine cones, beads, stones

Containers for Kitchen Use: miniature canisters, wooden spoon holder, match holder, silverware holder for entertaining

Containers for Bathroom Use: cotton balls, cotton swabs, colored soaps, bubble bath, Epsom salts

Containers for Food: dried beans, pasta, candy, popcorn, dried fruits, bouillon cubes, hot chocolate mix, bulk-purchased foods that come in plastic bags or large containers

Containers for Homemade Gifts: croutons, marigold and sunflower seeds, potpourri, "play dough," bean soup, or coffee mixes

Containers for Kids: barrettes, ponytail holders, crayons, change

Terrariums: Make a miniature garden inside and seal closed. It will not need watering. If vapors cloud the inside of the jar remove the glass top for a day.

Honey-Do Jar: Inside is a list of repairs or fix-it jobs that need attention. Next to the Honey-Do Jar is a Honey-Thank-You Jar. Each time your spouse completes a honey-do he gets a honey-thank-you coupon, which is good for things like a back rub or a special meal. (Kevin and Callie Smith, Albany, Oregon)

Candleholder: Fill partway with sand and place a small candle in sand. Replace top to put candle out. Good for outdoor use.

Gag Gift: If you return from a trip, label an empty jar "warm air from Florida," "cold air from Colorado," or "winnings from Las Vegas." (LaDonna Jewson, Wasaba, Minnesota)

Scene Jar: Alexia Cripps of Fort Ripley, Minnesota, has a jar with a nest and artificial bird in it. The jar lies on its side on a small *U*-shaped frame.

Keepsake Jar: Save your child's small treasures. Give the jar to your grandchildren some day. (Darlene Black, Alexandria, Virginia)

MAILING OUT YOUR CHRISTMAS PACKAGES

HOW TO PACK YOUR BOX

The United States Postal Service and United Parcel Service suggest similar guidelines for mailing packages, and may reject parcels if not packaged to their specifications.

Both do not like twine, string, and masking and cellophane tape.

The string and twine can get caught in machinery. Masking and cellophane tape lose their tackiness if frozen. In each case, even if your package is accepted for mailing, you run greater risk that it will not arrive intact. UPS discourages the use of brown wrapping paper. If used for mail through the post office, write your name on the inside box, as well as the outside paper. Do not use brown paper bags. Stamps do not adhere to it as well.

Both services recommend using a sturdy cardboard (preferably corrugated) box sealed with packing, duct, or other strong tape. The outside of the box can have other markings, but any words should be crossed off with a marker. The size of the address is not important, but should be written with a marker that won't bleed when wet. For added protection you can include a second address inside the box. Clearly mark "To" and "From" as well. A label should not be adhered over a taped seam.

When you pack your gifts inside the box use crumpled newspaper or bubble wrap. "Foam peanuts" must be packed tightly because they can shift around when loose. Six inches all around packed items is recommended, and 2 inches between items in a box. Very delicate items can be double-boxed for added protection.

If you're mailing something small and unbreakable, consider a padded envelope . . . but not a new one from the post office. Any business receives a number of these, which can be reused by resealing with duct tape or staples. Businesses, especially ones that order supplies through the mail, may have a selection of boxes in various sizes, complete with packing material. The best source I ever found for clean, sturdy boxes was the Dumpster behind an office supply/copy shop. (I asked first.) I have also cut large boxes down to make smaller ones, to save on weight.

WHICH SERVICE SHOULD YOU USE?

I've always wondered, but had never researched, the cheapest way to mail packages. I obtained rates from the post office and UPS. I spent many bleary-eyed hours poring over rate charts and making color-coded graphs for UPS ground delivery, and the postal service's 4th class and priority mail. It was my hope to nail down clear guidelines; however, my findings indicate that there are too many variables to provide simple answers.

In the case of both services it is cheaper to mail one large package than two or more smaller ones that equal the weight of the larger one. If you are mailing to several households in the same town you might consider putting all your gifts in one package, especially if the households share a common Christmas.

Although the two services have some basic similarities they have the following differences:

Speed. UPS takes 6 days to ship a package cross-country, and fewer days when shipping to closer locations; 4th-class mail through the post office generally takes 8 days to get cross-country. UPS claims a 1-day delay during the holiday peak, whereas the post office admits that 4th class can require 7 to 14 days to get anywhere during this time. Priority mail takes 2 to 3 days to ship a package cross-country. If you mail early, speed should not be a factor.

Safety. UPS insures packages for $100 at no charge. The post office charges $1.60 for $100 worth of insurance and 75¢ for $50 worth of insurance. UPS also has a tracking service so that you can find out where your package is if delayed. Most people do not inquire with their relatives to learn if their package arrived on time, and so the tracking may be of no use. I have had only one gift break in transit in 15 years of mailing. I had packaged it poorly. Like most people, I am not very concerned about insuring Christmas gifts.

Convenience. The post office offers the advantage of more locations. We are 30 minutes from a UPS facility and would have to plan to drop off a package when we are doing other errands. Even so, the facility has an out-of-the-way location.

You can also mail UPS from a "storefront shipper," which is either a mailing business or a service operated by a local hardware or other store. These vendors charge a handling fee per package above the UPS rate. It might cost a few dollars extra, and may be worth it if you live very far from a UPS facility.

UPS will pick up for a $5 fee, and you must pay cash for the shipping charge and pickup. They charge $5 for the first time they pick up during a given week regardless of the number of packages, and the same $5 entitles you to an unlimited number of pickups during the same week.

If you know someone with an account, such as your employer or a friend with a business, you may be able to ship your personal package from their address without paying an additional pickup charge. The package must have the name and return address of the person the account belongs to. You can put your name inside the package so that the recipient knows it's from you. (I asked UPS point blank, and the service representative said that this was ethical.)

Economy. To compare rates let's set aside the issues of speed, safety, and convenience. And let's presume you don't have to pay a UPS pickup fee or storefront shipper fee.

In general, the heavier the package and the greater the distance, the more you will save by using UPS. The postal service is slightly cheaper when you mail under 2 lbs. UPS costs about the same or less than the post office on weights between 2 and 30 lbs.

Here's the tricky part. The cost savings can vary from only a few cents to many dollars per package. It's hard to make general rules because UPS's rates increase in a straight line, whereas 4th-class rates progress on a curve. Eventually the two rates cross over when you get to the heavier weights of 30 to 40 lbs. The further you mail a package the more exaggerated this curve is, and therefore the greater the cost

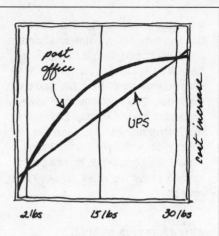

spread. Because of this curve, the UPS savings may be small on very light or very heavy packages, but significant on middle-range packages of 10 to 15 lbs.

But when mailing a package of any weight less than 1,500 miles the cost spread seldom exceeds $1, compared to an approximate $10 UPS savings for mailing a 10-lb package from Maine to California.

I also compared and charted the postal service's priority mail and 4th class. This chart was not without quirks. All the priority mail rates for mailing clear across country (or to what both services call "Zone 8") were only about 5¢ higher than 4th class until you get over 15 lbs. However, when mailing shorter distances the cost spread is far greater—$5 or more in some instances.

Have I lost you yet? The fact that this is so complex demonstrates why no one seems to have figured it out. And there are too many variables to give you cut-and-dried guidelines. Here's my conclusion:

Let your fingers do the walking. Consult the phone book for the UPS 800 number in your part of the country. Find the location of the nearest UPS facility or storefront shipper. Estimate the weight of your package, stand on a scale with and without it, and subtract the difference. Weigh it on a food scale or compare the weight to a 5-lb bag of flour. Call both the post office and UPS facility or storefront shipper for rates based on your weight estimate. Then figure out if the gasoline and hassle of using UPS is worth the savings in your situation.

If you are mailing several packages, a heavy package, or a package across country, it may be worthwhile to use UPS.

As a final note, choosing lightweight gifts is the best way to save on the cost of mailing. Don't do as I did one year . . . I mailed jars of homemade jam and pickles. The cost of the postage exceeded the value of the gifts.

THE TIME AND MONEY CHART

Many people think of their hourly worth in terms of their gross pay and presume that any effort that provides a smaller hourly yield isn't worth their time. On the other end of the spectrum, some people spend all their time doing things that provide very small economic yields (and that they dislike doing), while forgoing activities that save a greater amount of money.

The table on page 102 demonstrates the hourly worth of many tasks Jim and I have done. I often

IT ISN'T WORTH MY TIME TO...

time how many minutes a job requires to determine how many times I could, in theory, complete the job in an hour. I then calculate how much money a job saves. I multiply the times per hour by the savings per job to determine the hourly value. For example: A 10-minute task saves $2. The task could be done six times an hour. The hourly worth is $12 per hour.

Often the hourly savings appears to be deceptively small. You should also calculate your real hourly worth in the professional world. I could work as a graphic designer if I commuted an hour each way. Factoring in additional dressing and grooming time, dropping kids at a sitter's, the lost lunch hour, commuting and after-work-crash-from-exhaustion time, it really requires 60 hours for a 40-hour work week. I could earn $15 per hour. If I subtract taxes, the cost of child care, wardrobe, and transportation my $15 could become whittled down to $5 per hour. It would require 60 hours to earn $200 . . . or I would earn $3.33 per hour. (Hopefully your hourly rate is not so dismal.)

My chart includes two other columns that rate other reasons why I choose to do an activity.

MONEY-SAVING ACTIVITIES	HOURLY RATE	OTHER VALUES	ENJOY-MENT
Jim can make two cheese pizzas in 20 minutes including clean-up time (and not including rising and baking time). The cost of the homemade pizza is $2. It costs $18 to have two similar pizzas delivered.	$48	3	3
A couple of years ago my father-in-law gave me two bushels of small pears, which I canned with 40 hours of time. We estimate the savings was $40.	$1	4	2
If you change your oil and filter it might save you $7 for 15 minutes' effort including oil disposal at your convenience, as compared to having it done.	$28	1	1
I can hang a load of laundry and take it down in 15 minutes for a savings of 44¢ per load. (The savings increases when hanging heavy, large items.)	$1.76	5	3
It takes me 15 minutes to make two box lunches that cost about 45¢. A school lunch costs 95¢.	$2	3	2
Cloth diapers save about $7 per week when factoring in the cost of laundering. They require an hour of time per week.	$7	4	3
I spent 5 hours making a Halloween costume for my child. I could have purchased a similar one for $10.	$4	5	5
Jim made a 15-minute stop while on the way to do other errands, and bought three cases (72 jars) of sale peanut butter. He saved 60¢ per jar.	$86.40	1	2
I can cut a boy's head of hair in 30 minutes.	$12	3	3
Jim spent 20 hours shopping and negotiating for a new car, and saved $2,000 off the sticker price.	$100	1	4
We make jam from our own rhubarb. We can make 15 jars an hour at a cost of 40¢ per jar, or a savings of at least $1 per jar.	$15	4	4
It takes 5 seconds to save a clean but used piece of aluminum foil. (Yes, we actually timed this.) A 1' square of the store brand costs 2½¢.	$18	3	3
I could go to work as a graphic designer.	$3.33	1	1

"Other Values" might show that I do something because it is environmentally sound or healthier. I also do some things because I can combine the savings effort with family time. Kids learn from watching parents do-it-themselves, even if they are only passively involved.

The "Enjoyment" column rates how much personal satisfaction I derive from an activity. I am constantly amazed to discover that some people despise the very things I enjoy doing.

In the case of both these columns the higher the number the more I enjoy or feel I get other values from the activity. I also rated the enjoyment and value that I personally get from doing graphic design. Others, especially those in service professions, would rate their jobs much higher.

The purpose of having such a chart, if only mentally, is to help you decide which tasks to drop when your schedule fills up. Consider the hourly rate, the enjoyment factor, and other values that the task brings.

Everyone needs a source of income, but we also need a way to gauge if we should work additional hours away from home. People who work outside the home frequently forgo ways to save, which have higher economic yields, because they lack time.

If you have some financial flexibility you can choose an enjoyable task with a small financial yield. If both time and money are in short supply you might have to stick with tasks with the highest hourly yields, even if they provide little enjoyment. But there are so many ways to save money you should not have to do tasks that provide a small hourly yield, offer little enjoyment, and satisfy no other values.

Because we all possess different abilities, resources, likes, and values, no two tightwads would fill out this chart the same way. There is no "right way" to be a tightwad.

TIME SAVERS

You know you're tired when you're washing the pizza pan, and the last slice of pizza floats to the top of the dishwater. Or when you're putting a sleeper on a baby and for some reason the sleeves don't have holes for the hands, but the sleeper legs have holes for the feet.

I have redefined the concept of "no time"... which has not gone unnoticed by the readers. My most commonly requested article is "How *do* You Do It All?" Well...

1. I don't do anything as well as we would like.

2. I don't do it all. Jim has retired from the Navy and now runs our household full time.

However, so's not to disappoint those who wanted some ideas... here are some ideas that I use during crisis times.

Housework Division. Some types of housework are a form of organization, whereas some things are cleaning only. During my busiest of times I keep up with organizational tasks, but let the cleaning slide.

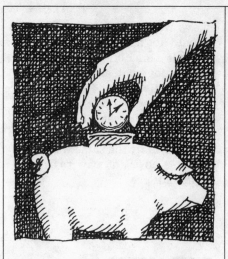

The most important organizational tasks are washing dishes and washing laundry. I place a priority on keeping up with these two things because they create a loss of time if I get behind. Dirty dishes take up space on the counter and make food preparation more time consuming. If I don't keep up with laundry I lose time "hunting for matched socks." In addition, these types of tasks accumulate if I don't keep up with them.

Tasks that are cleaning only tend to not accumulate. Vacuuming takes the same amount of time regardless of whether I do it every day or once a week. The work in washing windows is about getting out ladders and buckets.

But if I postpone dishes it's just going to require more time when I finally wash them. So to save time I try to do the noncumulative cleaning less frequently.

I like things to be clean, but it's not important to survival when I'm busiest.

The Container Principle. Use the container method to quick clean your home. Items in a loose pile are mess. Items in a container are neat. Dirty dishes on the counter are messy. Dirty dishes stacked in the sink are neat (or neater). Laundry on the floor is a mess. Laundry in a basket is neat. Miscellaneous junk in view is a mess. Miscellaneous junk in a junk drawer is neat.

I use two variations of this basic idea:

Use "intermediate containers" for temporary storage. You can sort them later when you have more time. For example, we have three kitchen junk drawers: the paper drawer, the tool drawer, and the real junk drawer. I can put things in these drawers to clean the kitchen quickly. Once every several months I might

clean out the paper drawer, throwing away or filing as needed. I have a basket in the living room to store kids' toys, shoes, books, etc. The first kid who wants to watch TV has to put the stuff away.

Use a "roving container" when the entire house is a mess with all types of things out of place. You have a laundry basket and a preplanned route in which you hit every room in your house without doubling your tracks. As you follow the route pick up the things that are out of place and drop them off in the appropriate place. By the time you complete the route twice, everything will be back in place.

Equipment Investment.

Most folks opt for time savers that provide a onetime benefit. TV dinners. Disposable diapers. Hiring a kid to mow the lawn. A long-distance call. The money is lost after a single use. To maintain the same level of free time they must continue to buy single-use time savers.

Equipment or tools represent money invested in permanent time savers. In a rural area there is a long list of necessary tools. We have had to acquire many (a computer, a garden tractor, a weed whacker, a utility trailer, a table saw), all of which were purchased used or at extremely good sale prices. We did not do this so we could watch TV, but rather so that we could sleep.

However, the wise purchase of tools does not include buying a Shopsmith, making one bookcase, and letting it gather dust in your garage.

The Federal Express System.

The guy that conceived Federal Express got the idea while a student in business school. If I remember correctly his paper got a failing grade. He persisted, and now several companies have copied his idea. Basically he saw that the postal service was inefficient in its method of delivery. He thought it would be quicker to take all packages to a central location to sort and send on to their destinations. Even when a package has to go only a few miles from origination to destination, it still goes through the central sorting location thousands of miles away. In the scheme of the big picture this is more efficient.

I have applied this idea to picking up children's rooms. All the dumped toys are swept to a central pile. I surround the pile with the various containers, and sort. Toys with further destinations are all taken at once. I have tried in vain to teach this idea to my children but they persist with the postal service method.

Mass-Production.

It is more efficient to repeat the same action several times rather than doing many individual tasks at random. In practical application I do things like make double and triple batches. I stand the kids in a line to comb hair and wash faces. When I read them a book everyone must be present. I mass-produce Christmas presents when I hit upon an idea that nearly everyone would like. I write a very good general family letter, reproduce it, and include a short personal note. Canning is a good example of this principle. In a day a year's supply of spaghetti sauce can be canned. This is more efficient than making from scratch every Wednesday night, and cheaper than store bought.

Employee Training. The best companies distinguish themselves by teaching their workers new skills. Even though this takes away from short-term productivity, in the long run it is more profitable. In the same way, you need to take the time to learn new skills. I know many women, who have been married for years, that claim they can't bake anything. Silly. They could learn to whip up a batch of muffins faster then a drive to the convenience store. I learned computer basics so that I could produce my newsletter quicker. Learning new skills often seems overwhelming. It is important to shut down production for a period, study, regroup, and then start up again.

SWAP SHOP

Dear Amy,

We have a large extended family and a family newsletter that goes out quarterly. "The 1st Annual Shryock Swap Shop" is an itemized list of all treasures taking up space in attics, garages, barns, sheds, and cabinets published for giveaway, trade, nominal fee, or Christmas gifts. I have wanted to do this for a long time. It wasn't until I read *The Tightwad Gazette* that I finally motivated myself to do it.

Bernadette Barber
Lusby, Maryland

TIN PUNCH

Dear Amy,

It cost my husband and me a measly $6 to install our look-alike "tin" punch cabinets. Newspapers discard the large aluminum sheets (known as "plates") they use for printing purposes. They are printed on one side and blank on the other. We bought a nice stack for $6, enough for a very large kitchen.

After a quick cleanup in the tub to remove excess printer's ink, we cut the metal with tin snips down to a size that would fit our kitchen cabinets. A crayon rubbing of our sister-in-law's pie safe provided us with an authentic antique design. We traced this to a sheet of paper and taped the paper to the metal panels, blank side up.

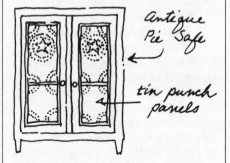

Antique Pie Safe

tin punch panels

With a hammer and nail, and a piece of wood underneath for protection, we hammered the design, right through the paper, dot by dot.

Derise Lohr-Stuckey
Beech Grove, Indiana

TIPS FOR BETTER GIFT GIVING

The flip side of the gift-giving question is the stress surrounding gift receiving. At one time or another most of us have had that sickening feeling of receiving things we don't want.

Gift giving is fun, and I am not going to suggest that we do without it. But aside from spending beyond our means, the biggest financial mistake we make is spending badly. So I am going to say for you all what you want to say to others, but don't have the nerve to. The following are a number of random thoughts based on the feelings expressed by readers and friends. There are always exceptions to these suggestions.

 Christmas gifts do not have to be a surprise. Most people would forgo the surprise element to assure that they will receive things they will genuinely appreciate. So if you are not sure your gift idea will be appreciated ask the recipient in advance. Give them that opportunity to decline. Or ask the recipient to make a list for you.

 If you don't know what to give, select an expendable gift—things such as food items, postage stamps, stationery, film, and gift certificates are always winners. These are especially good for elderly people, or people with limited space.

 Replace an item that is worn-out. If the recipient has a worn-out widget, chances are they want a widget in their home, but haven't gotten around to replacing their old one. Examples of things to replace include worn towels, an old wallet, holey socks, appliances that are acting up, etc.

 Avoid gifts that decorate people's homes for them, especially gifts that demand to be located in a prominent part of the home. Exceptions may include family photos and holiday decorations. One reader tells me: "I look around my house and everything I see that I don't like was given to me." It is not a matter of the thing being in poor taste but that the recipient would not have chosen it for his own home. This category would also include large appliances. If uncertain, ask!

 Consider giving modestly to the only child. These kids frequently become the entire holiday focus of a host of relatives, who swamp them with gifts. The parents have the chore of dealing with a temperamental overwhelmed child and a mountain of gifts they have no room to store. Consult the parents as to what and how much they feel might be appropriate for their child.

 If you are purchasing for a young relative ask for suggestions so you can target a void. "He has 14 good shirts but really needs pajamas." Children often have toys that can be added on to

. . . a few more tracks for the train set, or a set of Barbie clothes.

New presents appropriate for almost any child include art or "office" supplies. I like multipiece toys such as Tinker Toys and Legos, which have provided more entertainment than any other present my children received. If the child already has these, then "more is better." Choose durable toys, as any mother can testify to throwing away bushels of broken ones. Do not buy battery-operated toys for younger children, as they tend to lose the batteries.

 Give the recipient money to go toward a specific item that you do not feel knowledgeable enough to pick for them. One woman received a sewing machine. Although she wanted one, the model she received was too complex for her needs. Jim likes to fish, but I don't know enough about this hobby to buy for him. Instead I give him "permission" to buy. One year I taped a drafting compass to a toy boat, and wrapped it. After scratching his head a few minutes Jim deduced that I was granting him permission to purchase a boat compass.

 Give people presents that complete part of a set of something people already have. The most obvious example includes buying pieces to go with the recipient's open-stock china.

 Avoid the "domino principle" in gift giving. I look good in pink. Because I had a couple of pink shirts people kept giving me

pink shirts, often exactly the same style as the pink shirts I already have. Now I receive pink shirts with a note of explanation: "I saw this and thought it looked just like you."

 Often giving the same gift to someone year after year, regardless of the cost, will not be successful. Wouldn't it be dull if everyone gave everyone the same gift every year? Even a little variation from your theme will take the edge off predictability.

 Under certain circumstances giving used gifts can be appropriate . . . usually when you are giving to another tightwad who knows and appreciates the value of used items. This sort of activity could include the swap of an interesting puzzle (which you would only use one time anyway), a great sweater the style and condition fitting a Cosby (or Huxtable), a book, or a tool your spouse has had his eye on. In all cases the gift should be very special, uniquely appropriate for the recipient, and given to someone who will admire your resourcefulness, rather than think you are merely cheap. You could make it a family sport to see who can find the best used stuff for Christmas.

 Offer the recipient a service. You might offer a winter's worth of snow shoveling to an elderly person, or offer a night's babysitting to parents of young children. If you possess a specific skill offer that.

I love joke presents. They are cheap and entertaining.

I went to my uncle's first year wedding anniversary party. Being cheap as I am, and unsure if a gift was appropriate, I opted for a joke present. Previously I had found large rusty railroad square nuts while collecting aluminum cans. I bought two candles and matching paper napkins. Voila! I had a gift of matching candleholders and napkin rings. I wrapped the box in newspaper and spray painted it silver. I made a ribbon and bow of plastic wrap creating an iridescent elegant look.

When my uncle and his wife started to open the package they repeatedly gushed, "You really shouldn't have," and I repeatedly assured them, "It was really nothing." The wrapping and gift made us all laugh until we cried.

Make homemade gifts. Erma Bombeck tells of the Christmas when everyone decided to give only homemade presents. It was a disaster and they never tried it again. I think they started too big and gave up too soon.

A well-made and creative homemade gift has more value than a comparable store bought present. I try to settle on one idea that many people will like and then mass-produce.

Unfortunately some families do not appreciate these and regard them as cheap and inferior. If you are dealing with this, make their conversion your special mission and expect the process to take several years.

Gifts should be selected based on needs, internally generated desires and consistent with budgets. The fact that an advertiser has created a desire in your child by showing him a product scores of times does not mean you must succumb. During the holiday season, we are bombarded with ads for Isotoner gloves, Clappers, and Chia Pets. Consider avoiding these like the plague.

THE CASE OF THE LIGHTS LEFT ON

The computer hummed but the blank blue screen gave evidence of a silent keyboard. I stared through the window, focusing on the pale green lichen on a small sapling in the wooded area beyond. But my brain scanned the far corners of my consciousness for an idea to fill an empty page of *The Tightwad Gazette*.

The newsletter serves as a mere bread-and-butter sideline of a larger enterprise—FZ Private Investigation. Or F.Z.P.I. for short.

The phone rang, jolting me back into the present. I reached for the nearby almond-colored receiver, but paused before its smooth coolness filled my hand. With a stern drill sergeant tone I barked a command in the direction of nearby toddler mayhem. "OK, you guys, listen up, anyone makes a peep while I'm on the phone and you're in *big trouble*. Got it?" Instant silence.

I picked up the receiver on the third ring and answered in a calmer professional voice, "FZ Private Investigations."

"Frugal Zealot, Frugal Zealot!

I'm desperate; you gotta help me."

I recognized the frantic voice as belonging to a local subscriber. "Yes, Zelda, what can I do for you?"

"It's my husband...I...we've been arguing. It's driving us apart."

I broke in. "Hold on. This sounds like a job for a marriage counselor. I'm not qualified—"

"But," Zelda continued, "this *is* a job for FZ. It's about saving money. My husband, Zebulon, and I have been having this argument about the electric bill and we can't agree."

"What seems to be the problem?"

"Can you tell us if it's cheaper to turn out the lights if you leave the room, or to leave them on? Some people say that if you are

coming back in a few minutes it's cheaper just to leave them on."

"Wow, I never heard that one. I'll have to make an inquiry with my energy consultant and get back to you." I felt guilty. I knew she wanted some kind of answer now, so I offered what I could. "Zelda, I can tell you that the problem is not as big as it seems. Lighting makes up a small por-

tion of our electric bill. Do you know that it costs less than a penny to operate a 100-watt bulb for an hour? Here in Maine we pay 9 cents per kilowatt-hour. A kilowatt-hour is 1,000 watts of electricity per hour."

"Is that all?" Zelda exclaimed incredulously.

"Of course most of us don't use 100-watt bulbs, we use 60 or 75 watts, which cost even less. All those bits of pennies do add up, but not compared to other appliances like the dryer and water heater. Your dryer, for instance, uses 4,500 watts, so it costs about 44¢ per hour to run. It makes more sense to hang laundry instead of flicking lights on and off."

"Huh! That's pretty interesting, but could you still find out about turning the lights off when you leave the room for less than half an hour?" Zelda asked.

"Right, FZ Private Investigations is on the case. I'll call as soon as I learn anything." The receiver clicked back into position, signaling the resumption of toddler mayhem.

Two hours later my energy consultant arrived home from work. As he crossed the threshold I summoned him into the corporate headquarters. "Hey, guess what? FZ Private Investigations has a case you can help with. It has to do with electricity." As an interior communication specialist with the Navy for more than 20 years, Jim's qualifications were beyond dispute. I related the conversation I had with Zelda.

I knew the answer was not simple when he pulled up a thrift shop office chair. "Actually, it can be true that it's cheaper to leave the lights on if you are coming back within a few minutes."

"That doesn't make sense."

Jim continued, "Turning bulbs on and off wears them out. Since compact fluorescents are the most expensive type to replace, when leaving the room for less than half an hour, you should leave them on. When leaving for less than 15 minutes, leave tube fluorescents on, and when leaving for less than 5 minutes, leave incandescents on."

I was amazed at having been a tightwad so long without knowing this. I asked him, "Would you mind starting supper? I've got a marriage to save."

In rapid fashion I punched Zelda's number on the Touch-tone dial of the nearby almond-colored receiver, its smooth coolness again filling my hand. Zebulon answered. When he informed me that Zelda was out I related what I learned to him instead. As I spoke he finished all my sentences. Using my keen detective acumen I deduced which side of the argument he had taken.

Epilogue: Thanks to FZ Private Investigations, six months later Zelda and Zebulon remain happily married, no longer arguing about lighting. Their two sons, Zeke and Zeus, thrive in the contented bicker-free home life.

This story is based on events that actually occurred. The names have been changed to protect those who had no intention of becoming subject matter for *The Tightwad Gazette.* Some events have been changed or amplified for the purposes of clarity and enhanced humor.

FAST-FOOD COMBAT

Dear Amy,

Do you, or any of your readers, have strategies to combat "after game" stops to McDonald's and other fast-food joints? My 14-year-old daughter is involved in band and chorus. Many times she has gone with these groups to play or sing in various performances. She also runs cross-country, which means she meets away from school. Inevitably there is always a stop for supper or lunch. At times I feel like everytime I'm turning around, I'm handing her money for a meal. It adds up after a while. Has anyone you know of come up with a workable solution?

Kathy Closson
Wiscasset, Maine

In response to this letter I asked for help from readers. Suggestions came from parents, the wife of a coach, a bus driver, a 13-year-old boy, and many people who used to be teenagers. They suggested:

1. "Have her earn all or part of the money." (5 votes)

2. "Talk with other parents and adults who coordinate activities for a cooperative solution." (4 votes)

3. "Give her an allowance to cover expenses and have her budget." (4 votes)

4. "Suggest she brown-bag it." (3 votes)

5. "Educate her about the costs and health issues." (2 votes)

6. "Cut back on school activities." (1 vote)

Parents want the best for their children ... and sometimes they forget that adults have rights, too. After-school activities can require large amounts of chauffeur time, as well as expense. It may be worthwhile to figure out how much time the parents are giving, as well as money. Add up the monthly outlay of cash toward meals and calculate how many hours the parents are working to pay for the fast-food meals per month.

Second, it's hard to ask teens to earn some of the money to pay for the meals when they're busy with so many activities. I would suggest the daughter give up one activity and spend the free time doing extra chores, or an outside job. Fair is fair. If the teen wants Mom to give of her time and money there should be some equitable exchange. I do this all the time in the form of you-help-me-with-the-dishes-and-then-I'll-play-cards-with-you.

Some of the suggestions for parent cooperation were quite interesting. Peer pressure is fueled by the fact that parents tend to be too busy to get to know other parents. We don't want our kid to be the odd one out. But whenever I'm experiencing similar concerns I talk to other parents and learn my views are shared. It's just that there is no organized effort to bring about a change. And remember, there's no shame about admitting to your children or to other parents that you have budget constraints.

A school bus driver from Columbus, Ohio, wrote that they coordinate with a few other parents to make sandwiches, bring drinks, fruit, etc. Each child brings $1. If the groups are close to home Kate Lott of St. Louis, Missouri, suggests bringing them home.

Bonnie Click of Tucson, Arizona, suggests that you sit down with your kids and plan out all their financial needs for the year. Include clothing, shoes, entertainment, sports, and equipment fees, etc. Also include an untouchable 10% for savings, and another untouchable 10% for church giving, if that's part of your family values. Get their input and settle on something reasonable. The parent puts in 90% and the kids are expected to earn the other 10% (or whatever ratio you decide upon). Divide the money into 12 envelopes, one for each month. Teach them how to budget, and then stand firm and don't lend them a dime. "It's amazing, absolutely amazing, how unattractive their previously high-demand food can become when they have to pay for it."

As a final note about peer pressure, I must be out of touch. Seems to me that we ask our children to learn many hard lessons in life so that they will be fully equipped to deal with the adult world. For some reason we don't ask them to learn that it's OK to be different. Wouldn't it be a great victory if our children learned they could be different from their friends and still be liked?

THE CHEAPSKATE POSTAL SCALE

We've been hitting the used bookstores for books on saving money. I picked up a copy of *All-New*

Hints from Heloise. I cruised through it in rapid fashion and came upon one new idea that tickled me.

If you don't have a postal scale how do you make sure your letter is under one ounce? You need a 12" ruler, a pencil, and five quarters. Put the ruler on the pencil so that it is centered over the 6" mark, or in the center. Place the quarters (which weigh 1 oz) on the 3" mark. Center your sealed envelope on the 9" mark. (The 3" and 9" marks are the same distance from the ends of the ruler.) If the quarters don't move you know your letter is under 1 oz.

Aside from the fact that I think this is a very clever and astonishingly simple idea, it propelled me to further thought. The appeal of this postal scale idea is that it's made up of simple household items, that have another use. When you are finished, the pencil goes back in the cup, the ruler goes back in the drawer, and the quarters are returned to your pocket. You don't have an extra gadget on your desk taking up space.

I wondered what other gadgets do we think we need that could be conveniently replaced with simple household items? Since living in a small space is a great way to save on the cost of housing, learning to live with less stuff is crucial.

CHEAPSKATE WRAPPING

It's not that tightwads can't afford wrapping paper, but rather the thrill and the challenge to see how many years we can go without actually *buying* it. Five years have passed since our last purchase of a K mart special. Our success results from employing a variety of strategies.

Reusing Wrapping Paper. This idea must be as old as Christmas. We try to give smaller presents than our relatives give us, since clearly old paper must be cut down with every use. (If your relatives are also tightwads you'll be exchanging tie tacks and thimbles within five years.) Be creative and put a bow where old tape left a hole smack in the middle of an otherwise perfectly good chunk, or plan your ribbon placement to hide the old fold. Consider taping matching pieces together to make a larger sheet. Cover the seam with ribbon.

Alternative Wrapping. This includes comics from the Sunday paper, shelf paper, the paper from a bouquet of cut flowers, a piece of red-checkered paper tablecloth such as the type used for church dinners (we have a roll that came with the house), wallpaper, old maps, or the paper or plastic from a colored department store bag.

Tightwad Wrapping. This is when you capitalize on your reputation and use paper that is clearly old and very mangy. Or use common household materials like newspaper, duct tape, bailing twine, garbage bags, oatmeal cartons, etc. Plastic wrap pulled taut or twisted makes great ribbon. Do not use this for the actual wrapping, however.

Patchwork Wrapping. Say it's 11:00 P.M., Christmas Eve. You are faced with a very large box and small bits of paper remaining. Get busy and hope you've bought enough clear tape.

Scrounged Paper. We gleaned a box of 1960s wrap from a friend's house being cleaned out for sale. And we found three large rolls of Christmas paper in interesting-looking trash piles (OK, so my motorcyclist he-man brother-in-law wasn't thrilled about the Strawberry Shortcake paper.)

Angle Wrapping. As far as I know I invented this. It takes a bit of practice and doesn't look as good but uses far less paper. Instead of placing a box square on a sheet of paper place it on an angle. Fold sides of paper up one at a time. Practice with newspaper first.

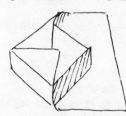

Permanent Wrapping. If you can imagine a Christmas tradition without frantic and wild tearing of paper, consider permanent wrapping solutions.

Make drawstring sacks that can be used from year to year. When wrapping a box use a larger square of fabric or a scarf from the thrift shop.

If you have the storage space you can also make present boxes —boxes with removable tops that are permanently decorated with paper or fabric.

Be resourceful in your acquisition of fabric. Use pinking shears to cut squares out of a dated garment. An old prom dress might be hopelessly out of fashion, but may yield several nice squares of fabric. The final hour of rummage sales often features one bag of clothes for $1. Try to pick articles that you can't imagine anyone would be caught dead wearing ... but also have new-looking decorative or shiny material. Something that is too gaudy to wear might make great wrapping.

Use permanent methods for ribbon alternatives as well. This might include rickrack, gold braid, strips of fabric cut with pinking shears, or elastic ties.

I read of one family that discovered other advantages to permanent wrapping solutions. The children enjoyed hauling their loot in the sacks and enjoyed replaying Christmas by reopening their sacks over and over. In addition, the living room did not have the usual litter of discarded wrapping paper.

As the tradition in this family continued from year to year, family members devised new usable gift containers. Some were appliquéd, embroidered, handwoven, or quilted. Someone even made a cedar box with the recipient's name woodburned on it. In their family the recipient's name and year are permanently marked on the wrapping, creating a family history after years of use.

Very large presents can be "wrapped in a closet" or other hiding place. Make a string trail or trail of paper clues.

Homemade Wrapping. I mention this last on purpose. Making wrapping paper is time consuming, and it also requires having a cheap source of large sheets of paper. Brown paper is commonly used. I have ironed out large sheets of packing paper left over from our move.

In addition, you need to have an easy way to make some type of repeat pattern. A shape cut into an art gum eraser makes a rubber stamp. You can make stencils from thin cardboard, like a margarine carton. Use crayon to feather in the design.

Or leave the paper plain and concentrate on decorating it with cut paper (such as snowflakes) or torn paper (to make a contem-

porary pattern). Adhere with white glue.

Marbled paper can be made by ironing crayon shavings between a piece of paper and a piece of wax paper. Instead of using tape seal the wrap with a warm iron.

Ribbons and Ties. Last year's ribbon can be gently ironed to look fresh again. If you have a variety of short pieces create a weave look as shown below, taping the underside.

One reader suggests one can macrame yarn and cheap ribbon into ribbon to wrap presents. Also cut fabric into strips to make ribbon.

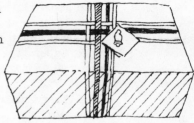

BEST ADDRESS

Jim and I are frequently amused by the variation of ways people address mail to us. Generally they either do not know how to spell "tightwad" or "gazette." Sometimes they write to the *Cheapskate Gazette* or *Penny Pincher Gazette.*

After a local television news spot, we received a postcard requesting information addressed in the following manner:

To That Woman Who Was on Channel 6 News, a "Gazette" About Cost-Cutting. Don't Know Her Name Nor the Gazette's Name . . . but Thank You. Leeds, Maine 04263

> **Bob White**
> **Litchfield, Maine**

PAPER CLIPPERY

Recently I repaired the rim of our laundry basket with paper-clip wire faster than I could have gone through a department store checkout line (which isn't saying a lot). As I "drilled" holes on either side of the break with the tip of an X-Acto blade and threaded through straightened paper-clip wire, I pondered the properties that make paper clips likely material for fix-it projects:

1. Everyone has more paper clips kicking around than things in need of clipping together.
2. They bend easily.
3. In a semi-unbent state the natural hook shape offers several possibilities.
4. Fully unbent, paper-clip wire has a handy length.

And I wondered how many repairable items had been thrown away for lack of a paper clip and a little resourcefulness.

For example, when I dropped my Dustbuster the plastic broke above the "catch" so that the cover and handle would no longer hold together, making the Dustbuster unusable. I repaired the Dustbuster in a manner similar to the way I repaired my laundry basket.

paper clips

One of my staff has used a paper-clip hook in place of a drapery hook. I have used paper-clip hooks to hang Christmas stockings. A sturdier hook, such as one that might be used for a pegboard, can be fashioned by doubling and twisting the wire from a large paper clip.

Jim keeps our three electric staplers working with paper clips. The cotter pins break and he makes new ones from paper clips.

The chain in a friend's toilet tank broke. He replaced it with a paper-clip chain. He found they worked well because he could adjust the length of the chain as needed. Because paper clips rust he will have to replace his chain in time. (A new toilet chain costs about $12). Or a paper-clip chain could replace a missing chain on a tea ball.

Paper clips in combination with rubber bands can be handy. You can make a miniature bungee cord with a fat rubber band and two paper clips. (As with real bungee cords, any hook attached to a snapping piece of elastic presents obvious dangers. Use with caution.)

You can replace the broken elastic on a child's Halloween mask with looped-together rubberbands and two paper clips.

You can use a small piece of paper-clip wire to temporarily fix the broken hinge

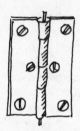

on a pair of glasses. Bend in such a way so there are no sharp ends sticking out.

If you have a small hinge with a pin, you can replace a broken or lost pin with a piece of paper-clip wire.

My grandmother gave me a fluted copper plate that I wanted to hang on the wall. I used two miniature bungee cords and a paper-clip hook. You might not

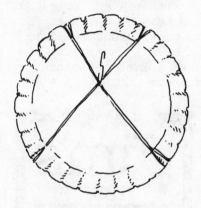

want to hang a $40 antique plate in this way, but the traction of the rubber band seems to make this more secure than the spring-type plate hangers.

Yes, the scope of possibilities of paper clippery is endless. I've always said you can fix just about anything with a paper clip, a hanger, twist tie, rubber bands and/or duct tape.

BEST FEEDBACK

Dear Amy,
   You are doing a wonderful job. You have helped me decide that I can retire at the earliest opportu-
nity and do what I think is necessary without regard to loss of marginal income.

   Ron Fisher
   Dixon, California

CHEAPER CHECKS

You can save money on the cost of printing checks if you order them by mail.

When you buy directly from a bank or savings institution, 200 plain ones can cost as much as $15.76—more for the fancy ones.

Checks printed by independent companies cost 40% to 65% less.

The article suggests two companies. Current Inc., a mail-order greeting card company in Colorado Springs, Colorado (800-426-0822), has a special introductory offer of 200 checks for $6.95 plus 70¢ shipping and handling.

The second company is Checks in the Mail, Irwin, California (800-733-4443). Its introductory offer is $4.95 for 200 checks.

Both companies offer wallet-type checks and a selection of a dozen or so designs. Current Inc. requests a check reorder form from your bank checks, a deposit slip, and a payment check. Each order takes about four weeks.

Advice for Seniors. Many banks offer free checking and checks with no minimum balance for seniors. Ask; they might not volunteer the information.

TAG IT

To enhance an otherwise ordinary homemade gift, I make an interesting or amusing tag to dress it up.

Since these tags are for mass produced presents, cheap reproduction is the first objective. Any black-and-white image can be produced well on a quality copy machine. You can paste up art and type, photocopy, white-out cut marks, and photocopy again for a clean copy. Combine hand lettering, typewriter type, any black-and-white printed drawing, original drawings, or left over press type.

If you have a computer with graphics capability, this will also produce a good tag. A few of my relatives without formal training are producing their own tags, labels, and cards with very respectable results.

Don't worry if your tags are not very professional looking. The most important element in any design is a good idea. I have a problem in that my tags can look so professional that recipients do not realize they are homemade. I have learned to customize (put their name or mine on it) or to not be too neat.

One year I made very successful potholders out of scrap blue jean material topstitched with gold thread. I cut up an old torn

quilted cowboy blanket that had been Jim's since he was young, to use as a filler. I included the following tag.

"Our products are made of naturally seasoned denim treated with an unpatented multistep process.

"First sewn into pants and worn by actual human beings, the material is exposed to sweat, grime, sunlight, and hundreds of washes to achieve an authentic fade and uniquely comfortable feel. Then using only select portions of unpatched, seamless, and pocket-free fabric we handcraft our original potholder design.

"THE BLUE JEAN POTHOLDER, a product already withstanding the test of time."

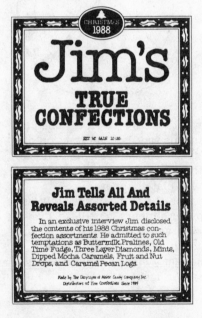

Jim has made candy for Christmas for the past few years. The acquisition of tins becomes the most expensive element of this gift. Three years ago we purchased plain red tins on sale in January and saved them for the

"HOW DO YOU MAKE BLUE JEAN POTHOLDERS?"

Following my mention of making potholders from blue jean material, readers asked for a set of instructions. They can be made in any shape, but mine were octagonal.

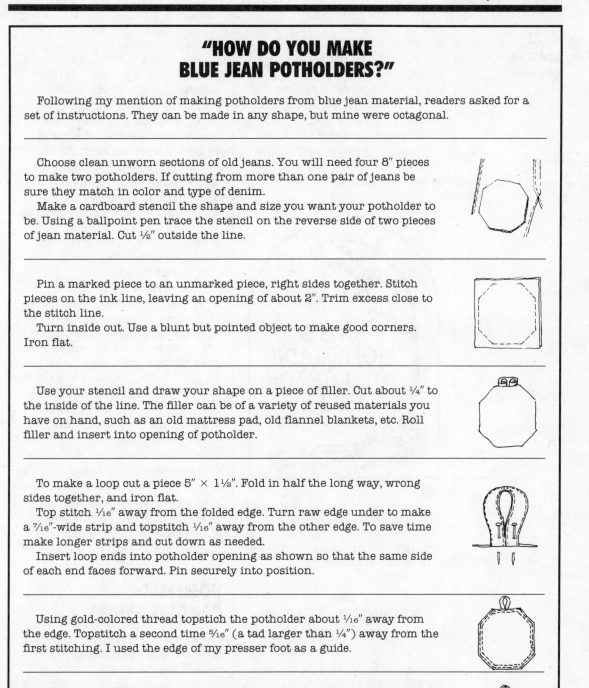

Choose clean unworn sections of old jeans. You will need four 8″ pieces to make two potholders. If cutting from more than one pair of jeans be sure they match in color and type of denim.

Make a cardboard stencil the shape and size you want your potholder to be. Using a ballpoint pen trace the stencil on the reverse side of two pieces of jean material. Cut ½″ outside the line.

Pin a marked piece to an unmarked piece, right sides together. Stitch pieces on the ink line, leaving an opening of about 2″. Trim excess close to the stitch line.

Turn inside out. Use a blunt but pointed object to make good corners. Iron flat.

Use your stencil and draw your shape on a piece of filler. Cut about ¼″ to the inside of the line. The filler can be of a variety of reused materials you have on hand, such as an old mattress pad, old flannel blankets, etc. Roll filler and insert into opening of potholder.

To make a loop cut a piece 5″ × 1½″. Fold in half the long way, wrong sides together, and iron flat.

Top stitch ¹⁄₁₆″ away from the folded edge. Turn raw edge under to make a ⁷⁄₁₆″-wide strip and topstitch ¹⁄₁₆″ away from the other edge. To save time make longer strips and cut down as needed.

Insert loop ends into potholder opening as shown so that the same side of each end faces forward. Pin securely into position.

Using gold-colored thread topstich the potholder about ¹⁄₁₆″ away from the edge. Topstitch a second time ⁵⁄₁₆″ (a tad larger than ¼″) away from the first stitching. I used the edge of my presser foot as a guide.

Using ballpoint pen, draw a light line from point to point of octagon as shown. Draw a second line ⁵⁄₁₆″ to the inside of the first. Topstitch on top of drawn lines.

I finished my potholders with an amusing gold colored tag.

following year. I made these (front and back) labels to glue on to the tins.

He produces six to eight varieties and mixes them to make an assortment.

We keep a few extras on hand for a spur-of-the-moment gift, but most go to tough-to-buy-for relatives.

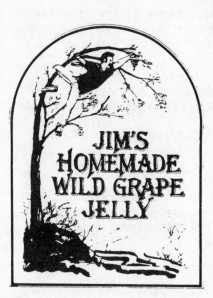

This tag was included on a jar of homemade jelly. The inside copy is a slightly overblown version of real events.

THE "JIM'S HOMEMADE WILD GRAPE JELLY" STORY

In September of 1986, while visiting the estate of his parents in Montague, Massachusetts, James Dacyczyn noted the pungent aroma of wild grapes in the wind. He remarked of it to his wife of nearly four years. Amy, a woman of enterprising character (and slightly pregnant condition) proposed a quest to harvest the fruit.

After careful preparation they entered the wood with bucket in hand. The terrain had grown fierce since his youth. Brambles, briars, swamps, and swarms of mosquitoes lay between the couple and their goal. Scratched, bitten, and muddied they finally came upon the grapes growing high atop slender saplings on an embankment that dropped sharply to the raging waters of the Sawmill River (1 foot deep and 10 feet wide).

Having come so far and braved such dangers James's determination was not lessened as he climbed the sapling to the upper branches to where the vines grew. Hanging far over the river he filled his bucket with the wild and elusive fruit. With each movement the sound of wild grapes could be heard plunking into the water 30 feet below.

To ensure maximum flavor the grapes were rushed to the kitchen of James's mother where they were transformed into the first jars of "Jim's Homemade Wild Grape Jelly."

HOMEMADE PANCAKE SYRUP

Three readers submitted recipes for homemade pancake syrup. We tested them all and priced them out. The most economical was one sent in by a nonsubscriber. It yielded 3¾ cups (30 oz) for 79¢. All recipes submitted tasted far better than the generic stuff we have been using. (Even the kids noticed.)

For the Maine readers . . . we purchased our maple extract at Meyer's Country Cupboard in Greene. It cost $2 for 8 oz, which is better than the supermarket price of $1.79 for 4 oz. However, if you have to pay supermarket prices it will increase the price of the recipe by about only 11¢.

Maple extract is not the same as maple flavoring. Truthfully, I was not able to find anyone who could tell me the precise difference; however, apparently the flavoring is not as concentrated. One of the recipes submitted, with a 16-oz yield, called for 1 Tbsp of flavoring . . . or half of a 1-oz $1.29 bottle. My teaspoon of maple extract cost just over 4¢.

Store bought syrup from generic to name brands cost between $1.59 to $3.19 for 24 oz. Since it takes only minutes to make a batch, the savings is worthwhile.

One of the differences between this recipe and the other that used extract is that the other did not call for butter flavoring. If you do not have it on hand try the recipe without.

Pancake Syrup

3 cups granulated sugar
1½ cups water
3 Tbsp molasses
1 tsp vanilla
2 tsp butter flavoring
1 tsp maple extract

Bring all to a boil, stirring until sugar dissolves (a good rolling boil). Turn off burner, but leave pot on burner until bubbling stops.

SLASHING YOUR GROCERY BILL

Our monthly food bill of $180 per month reflects the true cost of feeding our family. It includes all edible items, school lunches, the extremely rare meal out, canning supplies, and seeds. It does not include cleaning supplies, pet foods, toothpaste, etc. These items are often purchased in department or drug stores and may not be included in most people's grocery bills.

Although our oldest is only nine, most of my six children eat more than I do. But even compared to a family of four, we spend half of the national average for food.

There is no magic in our ability to do this but rather by using a variety of strategies. Not everyone wishes to do as we do. Some strategies only require better organization, but not a change in diet or more time. Obviously rural families have gardening options and suburban or urban families have greater shopping options.

1. Gardening (Families with limited space should look for books on urban gardening.)
2. Preservation of garden surplus (home canning, freezing, etc.)
3. A price book (or some system to keep track of prices between various stores)
4. Bulk buying (purchasing sale items, or good deals in stores you seldom shop, in quantities to get you through to the next sale)

5. Elimination of nonnutritious foods (soda, ice cream, candy . . . our remaining holdouts are coffee, tea, sugar, and cocoa)

6. Elimination of convenience foods (especially foods packaged in single-serving containers)

7. Choosing less expensive foods (the cheaper tuna, powdered milk, cheaper vegetables and fruits)

8. Buying store/generic brands

9. Buying marked-down damaged goods (also check deli for marked-down cheese and coldcut ends)

10. Coupons (we seldom use coupons as those products are generally more expensive than store brands or are for cold cereal. Also stores in our area do not offer double coupons. However, some people do very well with them.)

11. Vegetarianism (cut back on meat and substitute dried beans and whole grains.)

12. Portion comparison (Instead of comparing boxes of raisin bran, compare raisin bran to oatmeal or pancakes, or instead of buying steak when on sale compare portion price to that of chicken.)

13. Free food (garden surplus from neighbors, wild berries, food obtained through barter, groceries gotten free for buying $7.50 worth at some stores, etc.)

14. Preparing foods from scratch

15. Maintaining an optimum weight (Since your metabolism increases the more you eat, reducing your weight can make a significant difference on your food bill.)

16. Waste nothing (This includes making sure that children finish meals, cooking a turkey carcass for soup stock, and eating leftovers.)

17. Eat fewer meat and potato meals (Casseroles, soups, stews, stir-fry meals, etc. are generally less expensive.)

CHRISTMAS GIFT IDEAS FROM THE READERS

Make a "This Is Your Life" audio or videotape honoring a friend or relative. Include staged interviews with the honoree's family, friends, former teachers, and coworkers. Add narration as you tour places from their past—schools, former hangouts, etc. (Kim Frodelius, Solvay, New York)

Make a "beader" for a toddler using heavy-gauge wire, a block of hardwood, and non-toxic, brightly colored large beads. Drill a hole in the block the exact size of the wire, insert an end of wire and secure with epoxy. (Or secure from underneath with an electrical staple.) Bend the wire into curves and loops and secure at the opposite end. Tight loops can be made by wrapping around a clothes rod. Repeat with two more pieces of wire. Finish the wood with food-grade linseed oil. Make sure all edges are rounded and well sanded. (Susan Wiederhold, Austin, Texas)

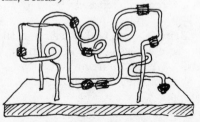

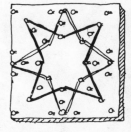

Buy magazines from antique stores dated the month and year of the birth date of the person you are buying for. Try to find magazines featuring their specific interests (such as an aviation magazine for a pilot). The average cost is about $3 per magazine. Recipients enjoy looking at ads of the new fangled gizmos of the year they were born. (Marsha Briggs, Placeville, California)

Make a "bandabout" (shown at right) for an older child from a sanded and finished 4½"-square block of wood about 1" thick. You also need 36 steel brads and a bag of colored rubber bands. With a light pencil divide the block horizontally, vertically, and diagonally. The brads are nailed into position as follows: begin nailing brads ½" away from the edge. Nail 4 brads on the diagonals allowing a ¾" space between. Nail 3 brads on each horizontal and vertical allowing a ½" space between. Nail another brad on each side of the outside brad of the horizontal and vertical line, allowing a ½" space between. The child can stretch the bands around to create designs. (Debra Posthumus Forbes, Portage, Michigan)

Make a clove-studded orange for an air freshener or moth deterrent. You need an orange and about 2 ounces of cloves. Use a small nail to make holes in the orange and push the cloves in, packing them tightly, using a thimble if needed. Allow the orange to dry for two weeks. The finished orange can be tied with a ribbon to hang in a closet, put in a drawstring bag for use in a drawer, or left plain for bathroom use. The total cost is about $6 with grocery store cloves or $1 with bulk-purchased cloves from a health food store. (Rebecca Hein, Casper, Wyoming)

Make cassette tapes of your child's favorite books. Record yourself reading the book and don't forget to say "Turn the page." (Elizabeth Gormley, Seguin, Texas)

Make up a price book for the "wannabe tightwad" in your life (see page 31). Credit for this idea goes to one of our staff workers who is making one for a relative.

Package your homemade jams and jellies in this unique manner: buy single wine goblets at the thrift store or yard sales. Put hot jam into goblets. Pour a thin coat of wax to seal. Take more melted wax and whip it with beaters until it reaches a foamlike consistency. Spoon the whipped wax on top of the sealed jam so that it looks like whipped cream. For easy wax removal don't use goblets that taper from a narrow top to a wider middle. Optional: decorate further with glitter, plastic flowers, and leaves.

If you are giving to a real tightwad they will appreciate a gift certificate to their favorite thrift or consignment shop for maximum value for dollars spent. Additionally, proceeds from thrift shops benefit needy individuals. (Elizabeth Roberts, Readfield, Maine)

Make designer placemats out of the fabric from sample books, which can be obtained by asking a home decor business for their old books. You would need twelve 3½" fabric squares to make one placemat three squares deep and four squares long. Sew to plain-colored backing. (Doris Ray, Harrison, Maine)

Give a gift certificate for a year's subscription to *The Tightwad Gazette* newsletter. Make copies of your subscription and hand deliver. (Tina Hoag, Alfred, Maine.)

Make pumpkin bread in coffee cans. Each batch makes four or five nice-sized loaves. After baking, cans can be wrapped in plastic leaving a pom-pom on top. Decorate with ribbon, or ornament. The recipe appears on page 127. (Kathy Haubner, Cincinnati, Ohio)

Make brightly colored wire jewelry from the wires in telephone cable. Scout around at construction sites or ask the phone company for scraps. Cut 12″ pieces with scissors. Make a loop on one end. Start wrapping the wire to build up in the middle. Make a second loop with the last ¾″, burying the end. Take another wire, make a loop, and attach to the first wire. Repeat previous steps. If final necklace is large

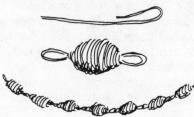

enough to fit over a head no clasp is needed. If you make a rainbow progression of colors the necklace can be shifted to complement different-colored outfits. Matching earrings can be made by attaching to earring findings.

Make up international coffee and tea mixes and give them

in Mason jars. The recipes appear on page 126. Ask around . . . Mason jars can usually be had for free.

Give an elderly person a roll of 100 stamps to pay bills and write letters. It costs $29.00, but it's practical. (Judy Kilmer, Byron Center, Michigan)

Make up a bean soup mix with different beans and spices layered attractively in a glass jar with a pretty lid. Include a copy of the directions. See recipe on page 127.

Make firestarters by dipping pine cones in hot wax. These work better than crumpled newspapers for starting fires. Put them in a decorative basket. (Marion Kuklewicz, Turners Falls, Massachusetts)

Purchase Epsom salts in a milk carton. Put about ½ cup each of salts in several small bowls. Add food coloring to make a variety of soft colors. Using a paper funnel put layers of colored salts in bottles or jars. Tip the bottles or jars at different angles to make designs that look like mountains, sunsets, and oceans.

Buy sale-priced sweatsuits (about $4) and decorate the tops. You can cut flowers out of fabric and adhere with Stitch Witchery (an iron-on adhesive used to fuse two pieces of fabric together) and finish the edges with fabric paint. Or make a splatter design for your teenager. (Anna Weisend, Cleveland, Ohio)

If you have someone on your list who has just recently married into your family make them an important-date calendar. Purchase an inexpensive calendar and mark birth dates and anniversaries of family members.

Also list family addresses on the back of the calendar for easy access. (Debbie Owens, Albuquerque, New Mexico)

Make hair bows. Look closely at how store bows are made and duplicate. Or make a simple bow from a 5″ × 9″ fabric scrap. Fold the 5″ edges to the center so that they slightly overlap. Fold the 9″ edges to the center so they slightly overlap. Flip over and fanfold the center. Secure with small rubber band or thread. Cut a 3″ × ¼″ piece of ribbon to cover the rubber band or thread. Secure with hot glue. Glue finished bow to a barrette or French clip. Decorate the center with ribbon rosebuds, pearl strings, colorful buttons, etc.

Make up gift baskets with baskets purchased at yard sales or craft outlet stores. For a teacher you might fill with decorative soaps and bath items. For a young girl you might fill with sewing notions to make her first sewing basket. Use your surplus notions to keep this inexpensive. This might also include directions for a project and a coupon for free lessons from you. (Susan Pugh, Statesville, North Carolina)

If you can do calligraphy you can letter favorite Bible verses or sayings. Put in yard sale frames. Or purchase a kit and practice for next year. You can also press flowers for decoration.

(Susie Finley, Albuquerque, New Mexico)

Make spice hot mats. You need cinnamon sticks, whole cloves, rice, and fabric scraps. Crush 4 cinnamon sticks and 2 Tbsp. whole cloves. Mix with one cup of rice. Cut a 7″ × 7″ square of denim and printed fabric. Hem all raw edges. Sew the two squares together on three sides (wrong sides together). Sew three even slots toward the open end. Fill with rice mix and sew the opening closed. A spicy aroma will fill the room when a hot dish or pot is placed on mat. Store in Ziploc bags to preserve the scent. (Penny McCauley, Hurley, New Mexico)

fill slots here and sew to close.

Make gag family portraits by cutting humorous or interesting photos of people out of magazines. Cut out the faces of family members from surplus snapshots. Glue snapshot faces over the faces in the photos. You and your husband can become Fred and Ethel. Uncle Hubert can have the physique of a body builder, etc. These can be given as cards or put into yard sale frames. (Doreen Gulley, Silver Spring, Maryland)

Make a tooth fairy pillowcase for a family with many small children. Buy or make a pillowcase and sew on a small pocket to hold the tooth. Decorate creatively with rickrack, lace, or gold braid. Or paint a fairy design with tube paints. (Ruth Palmer, Glendale, Utah)

CHRISTMAS GIFT RECIPES

Cafe Vienna

½ cup instant coffee
⅔ cup sugar
⅔ cup nonfat dry milk solids
½ tsp cinnamon

Stir ingredients together. Process in a blender until powdered. Use 2 teaspoons to one cup of hot water. 35 calories each.

Italian Mocha Espresso

1 cup instant coffee
1 cup sugar
4½ cups nonfat dry milk solids
½ cup cocoa

Stir ingredients together, Process in a blender until powdered. Use 2 tablespoons to one small cup of hot water. Serve in demitasse cups. 60 calories each.

Swiss Mocha

½ cup instant coffee
½ cup sugar
1 cup nonfat dry milk solids
2 Tbsp cocoa

Stir ingredients together. Process in a blender until powdered. Use 2 tablespoons for each 4 oz cup of hot water. 40 calories each.

Cafe Cappuccino

½ cup instant coffee
¾ cup sugar
1 cup nonfat dry milk solids
½ tsp dried orange peel mashed in a mortar and pestle

Stir ingredients together. Process in a blender until powdered. Use 2 tablespoons for each cup of hot water. 40 calories each.

Spiced Tea

2 cups water
1 cup Tang or orange drink
1 cup instant tea
1 tsp each cloves and cinnamon

Combine and mix with hot water to taste.

The recipes below were sent in by a second reader. She suggests making up a basket with mugs (yard sale), cookies, and these two mixes.

Orange Cinnamon Coffee

⅓ cup ground coffee
1½ tsp grated orange peel
½ tsp vanilla extract
½ tsp cinnamon

Butter, Nut & Rum Coffee

⅓ cup ground coffee
½ tsp nutmeg
butter, nut, and rum flavoring

Blend coffee and dry ingredients in a blender. Blend in flavoring and extracts. Scrape sides and blend 15 seconds more. Each recipe makes one 8-cup pot.

Place each coffee mix in a filter. Place filter on a square of plastic wrap. Draw together with a ribbon.

Bean Soup Mix

¼ cup white beans
¼ cup kidney beans
¼ cup split peas
¼ cup pinto beans
2 Tbsp pot barley

Layer these beans in a jar with a lid.

2 Tbsp parsley
2 Tbsp dried onions
1 bay leaf
2 Tbsp powdered beef broth

Wrap these spices in plastic wrap and place on top of bean layers.

Cooking directions: wash beans and soak overnight. Drain and top with 6 cups of water and simmer until done. Add one can of tomato soup. Also add one pound of fried and drained hamburger. Simmer a few more minutes.

Do not add salt of any kind until the last five minutes. It toughens the beans and the cooking time will be twice as long.

Pumpkin Bread

3 eggs
4 cups sugar
1 cup oil
1 16-oz can of pumpkin
5 cups flour
2 tsp soda
1 tsp salt

1½ Tbsp cinnamon
1 tsp allspice
½ Tbsp cloves or nutmeg
1 cup applesauce
½ to 1 cup chopped nuts
1 cup dates or raisins

Beat eggs. Mix in sugar. Mix in oil and pumpkin. Combine dry ingredients and add to moist batter. Mix in applesauce, nuts, and raisins.

Grease and flour five 1-lb coffee cans. Fill with batter over ½ full. Bake at 350° for 1 hour.

25 HOMEMADE PRESENTS FOR KIDS

Unless your children have been brainwashed extremely well they will not appreciate receiving *only* homemade presents for Christmas, but I like to give each child at least one.

Store bought toys must meet safety guidelines. Likewise when making homemade presents also consider age appropriateness and durability for safety reasons.

Most of the December women's magazines will offer homemade present ideas. These usually require that you buy kits, ready-made components, or materials from craft shops. Instead I suggest you first look to materials you already have—things that could be reused or recycled. Then, if necessary, purchase inexpensive new materials, and save any leftovers for future projects. Here are a few ideas:

1. Bean Bags (Use durable material scraps and dried beans left over from your unsuccessful ven-

ALEC'S SCRAPBOOK

ture into vegetarianism. Decorate with rick-rack, gold braid, and other remnants in your sewing basket. Try shapes such as hearts or stars.)

2. A Scrap Book (Reuse an old check binder, notebook, or make traditional tie type. Construction paper can be bought all one color for $2.50 per 50 sheets. If you have the ability, custom design a cover or first page with the child's name.)

3. A Hobby or Rocking Horse

4. A Dress-Up Box (Fill with yard sale finds or items donated by Great-Aunt Ethel.)

5. A Treasure Box (Make from scrounged and durable wooden box with lid, add hinges and a padlock.)

6. Play Food (Fisher-Price is too expensive. Save all small food containers like spice cans and plastic containers. Also look for plastic fruit—not grapes—at yard sales. Cardboard containers, such as pudding boxes, can be filled with solid styrofoam and covered with clear contact paper. Look for possibilities in scraps of raw material you have. I made kid-size play bread cut out of ⅜" foam rubber and colored the edges with brown marker.)

7. A Lady's Pocketbook (For the young child who likes to empty Mom's. Fill a thrift shop purse with a ring of old keys, wallet with play paper money, pictures, old credit cards, empty compact, etc.)

8. Play Dough (Recipe on page 194.)

9. Doll Blankets and Pillow (I have made them from dog-chewed pink satin-trimmed blanket.)

10. Denim Vest (Use scrap denim, especially stone-washed, and decorate with patches or embroidery.)

11. Gingerbread Cookies (Make large and decorative with frosting and silver balls. Customize with child's name.)

12. Drawstring Bag (Large or small depending on loot to be stored.)

13. A Work Bench (Build boy-size, utilizing scrap building materials.)

14. Child's Room Accessories (such as small and colorful braided rug, wall hanging, fanciful throw pillows, or sign with his name).

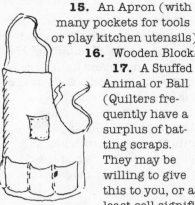

15. An Apron (with many pockets for tools or play kitchen utensils).

16. Wooden Blocks

17. A Stuffed Animal or Ball (Quilters frequently have a surplus of batting scraps. They may be willing to give this to you, or at least sell significantly cheaper than a craft store.)

18. An Invention Box (A collection of gears, nuts and bolts, nails, wood, etc. that your inventor can create from. It might also include things she can take apart such as an old alarm clock.)

19. A Picture Album (Make using surplus pictures of the child's family with acetate pages. Tape completely on all edges.)

20. Sock Puppets (Use any odd sock you have saved for more than five years.)

21. Doll Clothing (This is another way to use up little scraps in your sewing basket. Make new outfits for the special doll.)

22. Coupons (Good for not picking up room on one occasion, a batch of favorite cookies, staying up late, an afternoon outing of their choice, getting Dad to make time to help with a special project, etc.)

23. Bulletin Board (Adhesive cork tile on a scrap of plywood with thin wood frame, decorate with pictures of favorite things and child's name.)

24. Large Floor Pillow (for watching TV).

25. A New Paint Job (Instead of purchasing a new bike or wagon, surprise your child by giving the old bike a facelift. Aside from new paint, replace worn accessories, steel wool any rust, and clean off dirt and grease. Below is a way I devised to make streamers. They aren't as durable as the store kind but provide thrills for a month or so.)

To make bike streamers (shown at right) choose a durable plastic bag at least the weight of a bread bag. Cut many long strips ¼" wide. Twist paper clip as shown to secure strips. Add electrical or adhesive tape. Paper clip pops into the small hole of the handle grips.

HOMEMADE BRUSHES

Dear Amy,

I make disposable, foam paint brushes. Cut plastic from a milk jug, fold and staple to a popsicle stick as shown. If your staples won't penetrate, soak the wood in warm water until it softens. Cut carpet padding (if you don't have any, you may be able to get scraps from a local carpet installer) as shown: the beveled edge can be cut with scissors, the split down the center is cut with an X-Acto knife. Slip the padding over the plastic and add a few more staples to hold in place. Adjust the size according to the paint job.

Jay Patterson
New Albany, Indiana

staples

stick

plastic folded in half

padding side view

STOCK UP

Dear Amy,

Buying even a single share of stock in some companies can get you discounts. Tandy shareholders get discounts at Radio Shack. Marriott shareholders get discounts at the company's hotels. General Mills shareholders get a price break at Red Lobster restaurants. And stock in Disneyland/World makes you a member of the Magic Kingdom Club, which entitles you to discounts in the parks, hotels, etc.

Linda G. Bukvic
Williamsburg, Ohio

USE YOUR NOODLE

Dear Amy,

Did you know that to cook pasta you don't need to boil the water for 10 minutes or whatever the directions state? My neighbor from India taught me that you bring the water to a boil (covered), add noodles, bring it back to a boil and then turn it off. Leave it covered for about 20 minutes, stirring once or twice to keep the noodles from sticking. It really works!

P.S. After following your instructions and making a price book, I was amazed at the outrageous prices my "favorite" market was charging. What an eye-opener that book is!

Mary Leggewie
Placentia, California

BLADE TIP

Dear Amy,

You can extend the life of the blade of a utility knife by carefully (using pliers) breaking the blade at the dotted line when it gets dull.

I. Appel
Ft. Lauderdale, Florida

(There is a special kind of utility knife available that makes this easy ... its blade-inserts are scored, and one insert can be snapped off 12 times. These cost about the same as regular blades but may not be quite as rugged as regular utility blades.

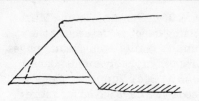

However, the same basic idea can be used for other types of blades. You can snap off or grind down the tip of an X-Acto blade from the back side to get a new tip. FZ)

DUELING DEALS

Dear Amy,

At least two major chains in this area, Wal-Mart and Eckerds Drug Stores, will match the current sales prices of other stores on the products they carry. You simply bring in the other store's advertisement and they will match the price. This is a real timesaver since I don't have to shop five stores for the best buys. I have found that other stores, such as Kmart, that don't advertise the policy, will match competitors' sale prices.

Teresa H. Morris
Garner, North Carolina

BREAD-CRUMB COOKIES

(a genuine tightwad recipe)

1¼ cups flour
1¼ cups sugar
½ tsp salt
½ tsp baking powder
⅓ cup cocoa
½ cup milk
1 egg
1½ tsp vanilla
⅔ cup melted shortening
2 cups bread crumbs

Sift together dry ingredients. Combine wet ingredients and add to dry mixture. Add melted shortening and bread crumbs. Drop by spoonfuls onto an ungreased cookie sheet. Bake at 350° for 15 minutes or until done.

This recipe works with the soy-flour-for-egg substitution (a heaping tablespoon of soy flour and one tablespoon of water substitutes for an egg). I have also had good success substituting ⅓ cup applesauce for ⅓ cup of the shortening.
Contributed by Ruth Palmer, Glendale, Utah

THE ART OF LEFTOVER WIZARDRY

We know it's time to use up leftovers when one of two things occurs: we run out of yard sale Tupperware and (donated) Cool Whip containers, or the freezer door no longer closes. More often than not Jim prepares meals, but he steps aside on leftover night to let me perform leftover wizardry.

Our house rule dictates that all leftovers go directly into the freezer, as any leftovers that go into the refrigerator may become forgotten and fertile territory for future growths.

I would prefer to report that we mark all our leftovers for date and content. In reality, the morning preceding leftover night I probe through the motley collection of containers, make educated guesses as to the probability of the frozen contents, and remove 20% more than I think I will need to implement my plan of action. (The extra 20% is in case I guess wrong.)

All tightwads have their preferred methods for dealing with leftovers, most of which fall into one of seven basic categories:

1. The Menu Management Method. There are no leftovers. This generally occurs when:
  a. You have a family that devours everything regardless of how much you cook.
  b. You're psychic and can accurately predict the appetite of all family members.
  c. You live alone and possess a rare intuition that enables you to monitor internal signals indicating the size relationship between your eyes and your stomach.
If you fall into one of these three groups skip to the next article.

2. The Leftover Lunch. Always eat supper leftovers for lunch. Before Jim retired from the Navy he kept our leftovers in check by taking them for lunch to heat up in a microwave at work. Since his retirement, leftover management has become critical.

3. The Perpetual Soup Container. Leftover remnants, like sauces, bits of meat and vegetables, soups, etc., go into a large

container, such as a 5-lb peanut butter bucket, which occupies a permanent spot in the freezer. When the bucket is full, cross your fingers and thaw. The result can be surprisingly good, especially if you avoid combining conflicting spices.

A potpie variation of this theme was sent in by one reader. She saves leftovers in a plastic container, rinsing vegetables first, but not rinsing meats (to preserve the good flavor). When the container is full she heats up the leftovers, and then spoons them into a crust, vegetables first, then meat, and finally enough broth to cover vegetables and meat. If the leftovers don't yield enough broth, make more from bouillon and water. Cover with a second crust and bake at 350° until done.

4. Smorgasbord Night. Thaw a variety of leftovers, line up the family and let them choose what they want on their plate. Then warm in the microwave. Our kids love this, as it's the only time they can escape my "you-get-what-you-get-and-you're-lucky-to-get-it" philosophy passed on to me by a wiser soul (my mom).

A single woman told me she regularly holds get-togethers with others for a meal of exchanged leftovers. To her way of thinking, someone else's leftovers are new to her. To avoid "leftover glut" some families designate one night a week for a smorgasbord.

5. The TV Dinner Method. Obtain TV dinner trays or microwave dinner plates from spendthrifts. Fill these with leftovers and freeze. Use when the family cook has a night out and the other adult in the household

persists in a claim of kitchen incompetence.

6. Serial Leftovers. You deliberately make too much of something because you have a repertoire of recipes that use this item as an ingredient. For example, leftover ham gets packaged in portions specifically for future meals. Ham slices go in one package, smaller pieces are saved for a casserole, and the bone is saved for soup.

7. Leftover Wizardry. You perform a feat of magic, transforming leftovers into a completely new dish. The more skilled you become at this craft, the more types of leftovers you combine to make a single culinary sensation.

If you have a working knowledge of cooking you know there are few hard-and-fast rules. Look up any one recipe in as many cookbooks as you can lay your hands on—muffins, for example. You'll see that each recipe is different. Many ingredients are interchangeable. Leftover hot cereals and fruits, as well as some vegetables, can be used in making muffins, pancakes, waffles, and cakes.

Quiche makes a great leftover disguise, especially for mushy vegetables. The following is my version of quiche, which may not be as tasty as richer counterparts, but healthier and economical. I make a rice crust from 1½ to 2 cups of leftover rice, 1 egg and 1 oz of grated cheese for an 8-inch pie plate. This mixture is patted into the plate and baked at 425° until firm. Put 1 cup of chopped leftover vegetables and 2 oz of grated cheese in the bottom of the crust. You can use any hard cheese for a quiche, although cheddar and Swiss are best. Use this opportunity to use up any dried-out pieces of cheese. Combine 2 beaten eggs, ⅔ cup dry milk powder, and 1 cup vegetable broth (saved water vegetables were cooked in) and a pinch of salt, pepper, and nutmeg. Cover the vegetables and cheese with egg mixture. Bake at 350° for 45 minutes or until solid.

To create casseroles you need only to combine meat and/or vegetables, a binder such as a white sauce, and a topping like bread crumbs or cheese.

Any basic cookbook tells you how to make a white (or béchamel) sauce and other variations. I save all bread crusts in a bag in

my freezer to make crumbs for topping.

You can make a soup from casserole leftovers by adding liquid, and make a casserole from soup leftovers by removing liquid. For example, a soup that contains rice can be combined with more rice and baked with a cheese topping to make a casserole. Or a stew can be put in a shallow baking pan and topped with dumpling batter. The batter absorbs the excess liquid to make a casserole. Watery soup creations can be thickened either by topping with dumplings or by putting a portion of the soup in a blender, and mixing it back in.

When we make chicken cacciatore (chicken parts cooked in spaghetti sauce with onions and peppers) we always have leftover chicken-flavored sauce and vegetables. This can be combined with leftover rice and leftover baked chicken cut off the bone and chopped, and topped with cheese.

Be persistent in your use of leftovers. One summer we had an abundance of rhubarb and strawberries. Jim made strawberry shortcake, but he overbaked the biscuits. Then he made rhubarb jam, but misread the directions, resulting in a batch of runny rhubarb jam. He decided to make rhubarb betty (like apple betty) with ground, overbaked biscuits instead of bread cubes. The result was very dry. However, when we topped the betty with our rhubarb "syrup" it was . . . well . . . good enough to save it from the compost pile.

I would like to suggest a terrific book on leftover use. It is organized alphabetically by leftover—everything from apples to zucchini.

The Use-It-Up Cookbook
By Lois Carlson Willard
Practical Cookbooks
145 Malcolm Ave. SE
Minneapolis, MN 55414

It costs $9.95 per copy, including shipping.

MISSION (NOT QUITE) IMPOSSIBLE

(As you read imagine the *Mission Impossible* theme music played on Christmas bells.)

Objective: Your mission, should you choose to accept it, is to accomplish the scaling down of Christmas.

The Adversaries: This is a large and powerful syndicate made up of family members within your household including young children, teenagers, and yes, even your spouse. Other key players include relatives, friends, and friends of your children.

Your Partners: Anyone from the above group that you can possibly convert.

Prior History: Although the origins of the Christmas holiday date back to the birth of Christ, in recent generations it has become an event infiltrated by high levels of commercialism.

Tactic Suggestions: Depending on your adversaries and partners (and their respective ages) you may need to employ several of the following strategies.

1. Advertising Interception. Hide all incoming sale flyers and discourage Saturday morning cartoon watching. Avoid trips to the mall and toy store.

2. Create Diversions. Develop inexpensive family traditions such as attending the local church play, drives to see the gaudiest light display in town, stringing popcorn and cranberry garland, and involve even the youngest family members in gift giving.

3. Intelligence Gathering. Attempt to determine what other relatives intend to give to your children. Intercept incoming mailed gifts and determine contents by feel or carefully opening and resealing so that your activity is undetectable. This can prevent duplication. The exchanging of lists will discourage a shotgun approach to gift giving.

4. Alternative Excellence. In an effort to encourage adversary defection and win support, give superb scrounged and homemade gifts. Be creative in your acquisition of these items. Barter your gift-making skills with a parent who possesses another. Or barter with another family for used but very good outgrown toys.

5. The Family Council. Call a meeting of adversaries and partners. Provide facts and figures such as how long it took to pay off last year's Visa bill. Offer alternatives such as a present spending limit among adults. Couples can agree to purchase a single house present together or to simply spend the limited budget on the children. Try to help young children understand the importance of larger financial goals.

6. The Long-Range Plan. Accomplishing the scaling down from a Smuckster to a tightwad-style Christmas in one year may be unrealistic and should not be attempted unless your circumstances are dire. Instead work toward a gentle transition over a period of a few years.

THE TIN ANGEL ORNAMENT

I couldn't resist including this idea, which has to be the ultimate tightwad tree ornament. You'll need a tin can lid, a paper clip, a birthday candle, an ornament hanger and a tiny glass ball ornament.

Cut the tin can lid as shown at the right. Then bend the lid to shape the angel. Make a halo out of the paper clip and attach glass ball, halo and candle.

THE SPENDTHRIFT CHRISTMAS DEBT CHART

Knowing that a few well-intentioned spendthrifts are reading I have included the handy-dandy credit card debt chart shown below. Simply choose the figure closest to the amount you estimate you will charge this Christ-

mas and follow the column down to the number of months you think it will take to pay it off. If you plan to make the minimum payment, it will take 36 months to pay off. Using this chart you can roughly figure what this Christmas will *really* cost.

BREAD DOUGH RECIPES

The Flour and Salt Recipe

4 cups flour
1 cup salt
1½ cups water

Bake your completed designs in a 350° oven for at least 1 hour. Paint and when dry dip in polyurethane, shellac, or clear nail polish.

This recipe is used in many applications but most commonly for Christmas ornaments. One year I made one for everyone on my Christmas list. The most expensive aspect of this gift was the boxes to put them in. At that time Woolworth's was the only source of small boxes I could find.

	$250	$500	$750	$1000	$1250	$1500
4 mos.	$259.44	$518.89	$778.33	$1,037.78	$1,297.22	$1,556.67
8 mos.	267.17	534.34	801.50	1,068.67	1,335.84	1,603.01
12 mos.	275.04	550.08	825.12	1,100.16	1,375.20	1,650.24
16 mos.	283.06	566.12	849.18	1,132.24	1,415.30	1,698.36
20 mos.	291.23	582.46	873.69	1,164.91	1,456.14	1,747.37
24 mos.	299.54	599.09	898.63	1,198.18	1,497.72	1,797.27
28 mos.	308.01	616.02	924.02	1,232.03	1,540.04	1,848.05
32 mos.	316.62	633.23	949.85	1,266.47	1,583.08	1,899.70
36 mos.	325.37	650.74	976.11	1,301.49	1,626.86	1,952.23

If you are not artistic, consider letting your kids make these for Christmas gifts. When my oldest was only three I helped him make abstract design ornaments. I provided Alec with 1-inch flattened balls that had an ornament hanger stuck in the back, and an assortment of household items with textures or designs, such as screws, bolts, a comb, spools, etc. He used a cookie sheet as a work surface, so that I could pop his creations into the oven when completed. I hovered about to make sure he designed enough, but not too much, and then moved him along as he reached the precise point of design perfection.

After baking the ornaments I gave him a brush and water-base red paint, again moving him along as he added the right amount of swishes. The next day he dabbed green paint. The last day he dipped them in polyurethane.

On Christmas morning Alec was hardly able to contain himself as grandmas opened the treasures. (This highlight by far superseded his interest in the presents given to him.)

The White Bread and Glue Recipe

(Possibly the only good use for white bread)

6 slices white bread
½ cup white glue

Remove the crusts from the bread and discard (i.e., save for bread crumbs). Tear bread into small pieces. Mix with glue and knead. This is quite messy. Persist and continue kneading until it makes a nice smooth consistency. You can mix food coloring into it. This dough does not need to be baked but dries hard as a rock in several days. (The color darkens and lightens to original color after dried for a week.)

This recipe will work for some projects where the flour and salt dough will not. It makes very nice jewelry for older children. When making beads, the holes should be at least ¹⁄₁₆″ as they become smaller when they dry. If you can find a source of pin backs you can epoxy them to dried dough.

JIM'S BEST CANDY RECIPE

Fruit and Nut Candy Bars

⅓ cup sugar
¼ cup light cream
¼ cup butter or margarine
1 3-ounce package cream cheese, softened
2 cups sifted powdered sugar
1 cup chopped mixed dried fruits
½ cup chopped nuts
½ tsp vanilla
1½ lbs white dipping chocolate

Line an 8″ × 8″ × 2″ baking pan with foil, extending foil over the edges of the pan. Butter the foil and set the pan aside.

In a heavy 2-quart saucepan combine the sugar, light cream, and the ¼ cup butter or margarine. Cook over medium heat to boiling, stirring constantly to dissolve the sugar. This should take about 8 minutes.

Cook over medium heat stirring

occasionally for 3 minutes. Mixture should boil at a moderate, steady rate over the entire surface. Remove pan from heat. Add cream cheese; stir until smooth. Add powdered sugar, dried fruits, nuts and vanilla; stir until well combined. Spread mixture into prepared pan. Chill about 1 hour, or until firm. When firm, lift foil to remove candy from pan; cut candy into 2″ × 1″ rectangles.

Melt the dipping chocolate. Carefully dip the rectangles, one at a time, into the melted chocolate. Let excess coating drip off rectangles. Place dipped rectangles on a baking sheet lined with waxed paper until dry. Store tightly covered in the refrigerator. Makes 32 candy bars.

DEBTS AND DOWN PAYMENTS

Since I wrote the premiere issue of *The Tightwad Gazette* newsletter I have come to understand the tremendous confusion about why "young people can't buy houses nowadays."

First-time home buyers see that they earn twice what their parents earn and assume they should be able to buy a house of the same value. But frequently a couple with a joint income of $50,000 fails to qualify for a $25,000 loan.

Couples that bought more than 10 years ago often do not understand the current value of their own homes or the income required to buy a similar home in today's market. If they were just starting out today many older couples would not be able to afford their own homes.

If you fall into one of these groups, an interesting exercise would be to take your income figures and debt figures (other than mortgage) to a bank and see how much you could borrow. Next go to a real estate office and get listings of houses you could afford based on the bank mortgage only. Actually drive to see what these homes look like. Pictures are deceiving.

For a young couple hoping to buy within a few years this exercise is imperative. For the older established couple it is merely entertainment.

Supposedly real estate has risen faster than the average wage. I don't know if this is true, as I look at the homes of our parents and their incomes at the time of purchase the figures are roughly proportional to today's market. Realtors I spoke with told me that houses appreciate about the same rate as inflation or 3% to 5% per year.

I can say that of the 177 houses we saw in our price range fewer than ten compare to a house my father bought without a down payment when he was in his early twenties. At the time we bought our house Jim was 40 and earning more proportionally, and we had more than $49,000 saved.

Double-digit interest rates stand out as the one glaring difference between today's economy and the old days. At the top of page 138 is a chart that shows roughly what a couple earning $30,000 could buy with different interest rates. Estimated taxes and insurance have been factored in.

Second, today's consumer debt

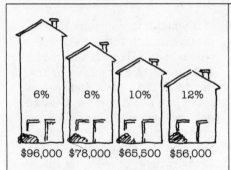

6%	8%	10%	12%
$96,000	$78,000	$65,500	$56,000

tends to be much higher. Some people blame TV for giving us an inaccurate picture of American life. Young couples tend to believe that they will live at the same standard of living that their parents gradually achieved over a period of years and the same standard of living as typical TV families.

In essence both sides are true. It is harder to buy a house today, but couples tend to wipe out their only real chance with high consumer debt. Banks still lend money the same way they always did. The mortgage, insurance, and property taxes cannot exceed 28% of the gross income, and that combined with other debts cannot exceed 36% of the gross income. Few banks will break away from these guidelines as they resell the loans to other institutions who insist on these figures. The chart below demonstrates buying power as impacted by consumer debt and down payments. (Based on 10% interest and a $30,000 income.)

$600 monthly debt	$20,000
$300 monthly debt	$54,000
$0 debt & $0 down	$65,500
$20,000 down	$85,500
$40,000 down	$105,500

There are several ways to buy more house than you can techni-cally afford. (1) Trade up. Buy a starter home and resell it after five or so years. (2) Buy a duplex and rent half to help pay the mortgage. (3) Save up a large down payment. (4) Buy a fixer-upper if you have the skills, extra cash, and determination to actually do the work.

Many combinations of these methods work well. A question remains as how long to rent and save a down payment. There are several factors to determine which way—the trade-up method or the down payment method—is best. If you save up a big down payment you have to pay rent for those years. When you finally buy, your payments and total purchase price will be much less since you are financing less. But it will take several years to make up for the loss of the rent money. If you opt to trade up you must keep the home long enough to make a profit to make up for the realtor fees and the thousands in the process of purchasing a new home. (Points, lawyer fees, inspections, moving costs, etc.) And you have to buy in a buyer's market and sell in a seller's market. If you try to sell in a buyer's market you may not profit enough.

Clearly, it is very complex to weigh all the factors. We did one thing that gave us a tremendous economic boost. The first 18 months we were married, 8 of which I worked full time, we worked extremely hard to save. We lived in a dirt-cheap crummy third-floor three-and-a-half room apartment. During that period we saved half of all we were able to save in seven years.

Once children enter the picture, families need to rent larger spaces with yards, as we did. Child-care costs severely compromise a couple's ability to earn. As a general rule parenthood slows (or stalls altogether) the climb up the economic mountain.

Whatever the market factors clearly the critical economic period in any marriage is the years before children. Typically couples tend to see this time as the final opportunity to have the fun "they deserve," squandering a valuable chance.

Instead they should live in the cheapest place possible for a short period of time—one to three years. Using this time to the maximum, earning and saving more, while not acquiring debt, couples can propel themselves into a higher standard of living they will enjoy the remainder of their lives.

GIFT GIVING THROUGH THE AGES

I am chatting with a friend in my kitchen, relating some of the Christmas ideas I am planning to include in the *Tightwad Gazette* newsletter. My friend sighs and says, "All this talk about Christmas is making me feel depressed."

In one sentence she expressed what a great many people feel about the holiday. Will I have enough money? Will I have enough time? How will I handle the conflicting family values about Christmas spending? What will I buy to thrill my husband, or wife, or child? Will people give me gifts I don't like?

My own personal Christmas stress tends to be about, Will I be able to pull another rabbit out of the hat this year? How will I solve the problem of finding wonderful *and* inexpensive gift ideas? Some years my gift giving has been brilliant, but other years I dug deep and found no rabbit.

So how is it that Christmas, a holiday about joy, peace, and festivity, has gotten to this point where we feel so overwhelmed and harried? Traditional gift giving, as we know it today, has only been a part of the holiday for less than 100 years.

Christmas was first celebrated in the fourth century. Prior to that time the early church frowned upon celebrating the birth of Christ. Roman pagans celebrated the winter solstice on December 17 and 25. St. Nicholas died on December 6 about A.D. 350. December 6 became the feast of St. Nicholas. January 6, the feast of the Epiphany, was celebrated as the date that the Magi

came. These four days eventually fused to become Christmas.

Each of these festivals brought its own tradition of gift giving. The participants in Roman festivals gave twigs from a sacred grove, and later gave candles, food, trinkets, and statues of gods. St. Nicholas was revered for his generosity, and it became the custom to give gifts on December 6 as well as on Christmas. The Magi brought gold, frankincense and myrrh to the Christ child.

In all cases gift giving was only a small part of the tradition. Participants decorated houses with evergreens, danced, sang, lit bonfires, ate, played games, made music, and told riddles.

Throughout history, with exception of the most wealthy families, people generally only gave gifts to young children and to the poor. Literature provides us with a few images from early Christmases in this country. The Laura Wilder *Little House* series depicts gifts for children of a tin cup and candy, or a hair comb. In the book she wrote of her husband's childhood, Almanzo Wilder received a jacknife and a hat in his stocking. Almanzo grew up in a relatively prosperous family. My own in-laws, who grew up in immigrant farm families during the Depression, tell of receiving nuts, an orange, and cookies in their stockings.

Jo Robinson and Jean Coppock Staeheli, authors of *Unplug the Christmas Machine* researched the commercialization of Christmas. They found that turn-of-the-century Christmas advertising featured toys for children and a few adult gifts called "notions." Adults might have exchanged a

pouch of tobacco, a hat pin, or a handkerchief.

Robinson and Staeheli began to find ads that depicted more elaborate gifts in the early part of the century. The industrial revolution had made goods less expensive, and in the process, accelerated gift giving.

The fire was again fueled after World War I. It was feared that the prosperity brought about by the war would become a sluggish economy in peacetime. Advertisers fought back with a stepped-up campaign. In some cases, according to the authors, the ads were unconscionable, implying that more money spent on gifts showed how much you cared, and even assured domestic tranquillity. The ads played on people's insecurities about themselves as parents, spouses, and providers.

The ads worked, and people bought into the commercialism. Giving expensive gifts became a sign of their own prosperity.

The "Have a Natural Christmas 1987" publication by Rodale Press also outlines gift giving in the U.S. during this century. Although sales for toys were going full force, adult gift giving grew in fits and starts. Gifts remained practical, especially during the Depression. In the '40s small appliances made their entry as appropriate gifts, as well as the then-new board game Scrabble.

However, it wasn't until the prosperity of the '50s that more expensive gifts, such as we give today, became prevalent—jewelry, clothes, furniture, and liquor. This trend continues into the '90s, especially with the high percentage of double-income households. We don't have time to be thoughtful . . . instead we throw money at the problem.

Today's holiday revolves around the gift giving. In most households, present opening is the climax of the day. Families may go on to visit extended family members, share a meal, or watch a ball game. After the paper and ribbon explosion subsides we are left with the Is-that-all-there-is? feeling. But from the years 400 until 1900, or the first 1,500 years of Christmas celebrations, gift giving played a minor role. The opening of presents was the beginning, not the end.

Although I have focused on the topic of gift giving, I could similarly question dozens of aspects of what we believe to be tradition surrounding Christmas—writing cards, traveling long distances, helping with school or church activities, holiday baking. . . . Most of these traditions came about when the majority of families lived on one income. Today's Christmas remains the holiday largely orchestrated by women. They want to continue the same traditions as their mothers, who did not work outside the home.

The stress surrounding giving could be summed up simply. You feel unable to do as much as you want to do or feel you are supposed to do. This stress robs you of some of the joy you should be experiencing.

The solution is simple. Give yourself license to do less. Lower your self-expectation to a minimum level. If necessary, let your family know you feel a need to scale back so that you can enjoy the holiday more. You can do more if it happens that you find more time, energy, inspiration.

Whatever you can do beyond your minimum will feel more joyful.

I could write pages on the topic of how to forge new Christmas attitudes, but someone already has. *Unplug the Christmas Machine* contains a few recipe and craft ideas, but the bulk of material covered is on the subject of changing attitudes. They offer several exercises to help the reader rethink through exactly what they find to be satisfying and unsatisfying about the holidays. The authors answer many commonly asked questions about how to deal with Christmas issues. Many readers would feel greatly liberated with a cruise through the chapters of this book.

If you can't find a copy at a bookstore, write to:

William Morrow & Co.
Special Sales
1350 Avenue of the Americas
New York, NY 10019
(212) 261-6500

The suggested retail price is $9 plus postage. They offer a 40% discount if you buy 10 or more. If you find a copy, and feel strongly about it, you (or a group of friends) could purchase several as gifts for family members as reading material for the coming year.

GIFT IDEA

Dear Amy,

  If you are stumped for a gift for a couple who has everything (my parents, for instance), I've often found that they have sets of china, crystal and silver that

have been discontinued. They also have pieces missing from these sets. A unique and much-appreciated gift is to fill in these missing pieces. Two of the best places to find these things are:

Replacements Ltd.
1089 Knox Road
P.O. Box 26029
Greensboro, NC 27420-6029
(919) 668-2064

Walter Drake & Sons
Drake Building
Colorado Springs, CO 80940
(800) 525-9291

Susan Garrett
Webster, Texas

(Both companies accept phone orders and take credit cards. Delivery time varies from 10 days to 6 weeks. FZ)

GOOD WOOD

Dear Amy,

One day recently I went to a nearby high school to have the industrial education metals teacher do some metal work for me. He was busy at the time and I had to wait a few minutes. I walked to the woodworking lab and saw a truck bed about half full of wood scraps. I asked the woodworking teacher what they did with the wood scraps and he told me they sold them all for $5. I asked if I could buy $1 worth from him and he said, "Sure." I selected 50 pieces of hardwood . . . oak, walnut, cedar, and maple. They ranged from 12 to 48 inches in length and ¾ to 5 inches wide. I will use them for breadboards, and a variety of other projects.

Ken Cannon
Provo, Utah

CHARCOAL STARTER

Dear Amy,

We cut up Christmas trees and store them in boxes or bags for later use as a charcoal starter when grilling out-of-doors. The boughs burn great and have a more pleasant scent than commercially marketed chemical products.

C. Rieck
Forest Park, Illinois

FREE WOOD

Dear Amy,

Many of us heat, or supplement house heat with wood. Living on a suburban house lot creates a problem. We have no woodlot.

For the past several years I've gotten all of my wood "free." People around town take trees down from time to time. Generally the tree "experts" take the wood "to get it out of the way." But not always! So I've left notes in mailboxes and called neighborhood people.

The note simply says "I'll split your wood for you if you'll 'split it' with me."

It works! Many people are delighted to have their wood prepared for their fireplace. And this system has kept us warm just for the cost of our exercise.

> Dave Shaub
> Lake Bluff, Illinois

TIGHTWADDING

Dear Amy,

My 13-year-old son sat down to lunch in the school cafeteria. He took out his sandwich (in a washable container), other homemade items (also in washable containers), and finally a cloth napkin.

He turned to his friend next to him and sadly said, "My mom's tightwadding." The other boy replied, "Yours, too?"

It's an epidemic!

> Cindy Kay
> Topsham, Maine

THE MERITS OF COLD MEDICINES

Americans spend more than $900 million a year on cold and cough remedies. Amazingly, it has been known for some time that there is no evidence to prove that a great many have any effect at all.

Modern science knows of no substance to prevent the cold. This includes vitamin C, which has been extensively studied and may be as effective as a placebo. (Vitamin C and placebos often work because people believe they do.) Although it won't prevent a cold, recent studies indicate that vitamin C may shorten the duration of colds. But remember, megadoses can be harmful.

Colds are spread by sneezing, coughing, shaking hands, and handling contaminated articles. Therefore the best prevention is to avoid people with colds. I have found that once you have a school age child, colds are an inevitable aspect of life for all family members.

The primary reason why the cold continues to be an enigma is that there are more than 120 viral strains. Additionally we all bring a host of factors to the problem such as individual resistance and emotional well-being.

Most of the remedies we buy are actually directed toward suppressing symptoms rather than prevention or cure.

The over-the-counter cold remedies such as Dristan, NyQuil, and Contac combine several ingredients in a fixed combination. This "shotgun" approach forces the patient to take medications he might not need for his particular symptoms.

Most of these cold remedies contain similar ingredients. Antihistamines were developed originally for hay fever. Their use in cold remedies is unwarranted since there is no evidence to show

that they affect the cold. They do have side effects, the most common of which is drowsiness. People who feel they are getting some relief may have a cold and allergic reaction in combination, or may feel better because they are somewhat sedated.

Cold remedies contain small dosages of aspirin or acetaminophen, which is helpful in reducing muscle aches and fever. However, the dose is generally too small, and plain aspirin or Tylenol is cheaper and more effective.

The decongestants in cold remedies are also useful, but again the dose is too small. A decongestant is important for the child who is prone to ear infections since it can help prevent blockage of the eustachian tubes.

The time-release aspect of some cold medications is nothing more than a marketing ploy because, again, the dosage of the ingredients is too small to be effective. NyQuil does aid sleep because it contains an antihistamine and alcohol, both substances that produce drowsiness but are ineffective in symptom control.

If you want an oral decongestant look for a product that contains pseudoephedrine or phenylpropanolamine, or a combination. Sudafed and Sinutab-II are examples.

Decongestants in the form of nose drops or sprays are generally considered to be more effective than the oral type, but they can also be addictive if taken for more than two or three days.

In the same manner that cold medicines do, many cough medicines also use a shotgun approach by combining a number of ingredients in the hope that at least one will work.

The FDA has approved three substances as safe and effective. Of those dextromethorphan is the best. Romilar is an example. The downside of this particular drug is that taken in large doses it can produce a high. There have been reported deaths of teenagers who have overdosed.

Cough drops are no more effective than any piece of hard candy. A hot drink can also be helpful.

Vaporizers can also relieve cold symptoms; however, products such as VapoSteam or VapoRub provide little additional relief. *Consumer Reports* recently said that there is some evidence that breathing steam from a vaporizer may shorten the duration of the cold, but the particular vaporizer that worked cost about $100, and was probably not worth the cost. Breathing steam from a teakettle may cause burns and should not be done.

There is some disagreement among doctors if symptom relief is actually in our best interests. Some authorities believe you may actually prolong your cold by preventing your body from doing what it wants to do naturally to rid itself of respiratory infection. Coughing, for example, is an important function of your body to prevent infected mucus from entering your lungs. The supression of symptoms may be an act of postponement.

The best thing to do for a cold is to have a good diet, drink plenty of fluids, and *rest*. If your symptoms are severe enough to prevent rest some doctors would suggest you take some medication. If you do that, at least treat the specific symptoms with pain reliever, a decongestant, or a cough medicine with dextromethorphan. To save money, seek out the generic or store brands that contain the specific drug you desire.

All the shotgun medications are clearly a waste of money. Even the medications that are known to work are expensive. Taking medications to make us feel better, even though we are going to get better anyway, is unnecessary in the majority of cases.

As a general rule the best approach to a cold is patience. It will probably last a week or two regardless. You should limit your contact with other people to try to avoid infecting others.

Your emotional well-being will also play a role in determining the length of your cold. Therefore give yourself a few days off to relax and to be "self-centered."

CHRISTMAS IDEAS

Dear Amy,

Ever since my children were small we have had an outing in the fall to gather fallen birch bark, small pine cones, and small pieces of spruce bush. From these three items one can make "to" and "from" cards one can purchase in a department store or card shop for approximately $1.99. By cutting the bark into pieces of 2″ × 3″ and gluing pieces of spruce and pine cones to the smooth side we have a festive card for our Christmas packages. You can write what you wish on the smooth side of the bark.

Karen B. Allen
Ellsworth, Maine

Dear Amy,

Cut circles of the same size out of Christmas cards. (A small juice can or silver dollar makes a nice size.) It takes eight circles to make one decorative ball for the Christmas tree or to hang in the window.

Fold one and use as a model. Make a triangle in the middle. Use this one to trace and fold other circles.

Glue four circles together using side folds to make the top and do the same to make the bottom. Then glue top and bottom together using the middle fold. To hang attach ribbon, string, or hook.

Carol Ordway
South Portland, Maine

Dear Amy,

Make your own vanilla to give away for Christmas presents. It is much cheaper than store-bought and we prefer real vanilla to imitation.

Here's how: Buy vanilla beans at your local health food store. Split the bean lengthwise without cutting it in half, and place in a tall narrow jar filled with white liquor such as vodka. It needs to age several weeks before you can use it. Also it will not be as dark as commercial vanilla. Just add more liquor as you use up the vanilla. Be creative with jar shapes and packaging.

Holly Moulton
Bath, Maine

THE SNOWBALL PRINCIPLE

Living paycheck to paycheck, or spending your final dollar, leaves no money to reinvest and no money to take advantage of bargains.

But when a portion of savings is reinvested in tools and skills which will save money or earn money the savings will compound, or snowball.

To demonstrate this concept I have created a simplified scenario that compares the spending habits of two couples over a five-year period.

The first couple, depicted in the column to the right, believes they deserve an occasional splurge. In contrast, the couple on the opposite page carefully reinvests surplus dollars. The first figure in each equation of the second scenario shows that this couple repeats the same saving effort from the previous year.

Year 1. Clyde and Bunni Smuckster have no long-term goals. At the end of the year they have $100.

$100 total savings

Year 2. Clyde and Bunni spend the $100 on a night on the town of dinner and dancing. At the end of the year they have saved another $100.

$100 total savings

Year 3. Clyde and Bunni spend the $100 to buy a small TV for the kitchen so that Bunni can catch all the soaps and get her housework done. At the end of the year they have another $100 saved.

$100 total savings

Year 4. Clyde and Bunni have a friend who needs to sell his entire Nintendo game setup to raise cash. They spend their $100 to pick up this "bargain." At the end of the year they have saved another $100.

$100 total savings

Year 5. Clyde and Bunni spend the $100 on a hotel weekend getaway. At the end of the year they have saved another $100.

$100 total savings

Clyde and Bunni live next door to the Albrights. They think "some folks get all the breaks."

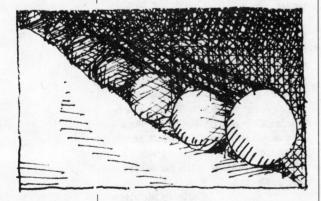

Year 1. Craig and Susan Albright have goaled
themselves to save up a down payment to purchase a house in five years.
But Craig's income is modest and at the end of the first year they have
saved only $100.

$100 total savings

Year 2. Craig and Susan put $50 in savings and spend $50 on cloth diapers.
The weekly savings of $6 enables them to begin bulk purchasing sale items at
the grocery store. The cloth diapers save the family $312 and the bulk-sale pur-
chasing saves them $600.

$$\$100 + \$312 + \$600 = \$1,112 \text{ this year's savings}$$
$$\$50 + \$3 = \$53 \text{ last year's savings + interest}$$
$$\$1,165 \text{ total savings}$$

Year 3. Craig and Susan put $600 into a three-year CD. The remaining $565
is used to purchase a used sewing machine, a used freezer, and a used chainsaw.
By freezing bulk-purchased day-old bread and sale meats, as well
as their garden surplus, they are able to save an additional $600 on their food
bill. Susan uses her sewing machine to repair clothing and to make handcrafted
Christmas gifts to save $200. Craig uses his chainsaw to cut up delivered logs
and deadfall to save $300 on their heating bill.

$$\$1,112 + \$600 + \$200 + \$300 = \$2,112 \text{ this year's savings}$$
$$\$600 + \$54 = \$654 \text{ last year's savings + interest}$$
$$\$2,766 \text{ total savings}$$

Year 4. Craig and Susan keep their CD and put an additional $1,000 into
savings. The remaining $1,166 is used to purchase a newer used car in excel-
lent condition. The old beater car is sold for $200. This saves them $200 on gas
and $500 on maintenance annually. Susan's sewing skills improve and she is
able to earn an additional $900 by selling her handcrafted items and doing
alterations.

$$\$2,112 + \$200 + \$500 + \$900 = \$3,912 \text{ this year's savings}$$
$$\$600 + \$54 + \$1000 + \$60 = \$1,714 \text{ last year's savings + interest}$$
$$\$5,626 \text{ total savings}$$

Year 5. Craig and Susan keep their $600 CD and leave $4,614 in savings.
Craig uses $400 to purchase and fix up a utility trailer. With this he is able to
haul home wood already cut and split for the same price as the delivered logs.
With this time savings he hires out to clean garages and haul the contents to
the dump. He gleans the "good stuff" and holds a yard sale. This effort earns
$1,700. In a brilliant stroke of financial genius they spend the remaining $12 to
subscribe to *The Tightwad Gazette* newsletter. The ideas they learn save $800.

$$\$3,912 + \$1,700 + \$800 = \$6,412 \text{ this year's savings}$$
$$\$600 + \$54 + \$4614 + \$276 = \$5,544 \text{ last year's savings + interest}$$
$$\$11,956 \text{ total savings}$$

GIFT IDEAS

Dear Amy,

Make a glass cover for cookbooks to keep them clean while in use. You need a piece of glass about 8″ × 10″ and electrical tape (preferably red or green if making for Christmas gifts). Tape all four edges neatly. You can add holly and berry designs cut from the electrical tape in one corner.

Ann Davis
Andrews, North Carolina

Dear Amy,

The great story about your aunt giving you aluminum foil for Christmas gave me an idea. Why not purchase this year's Christmas gifts at the grocery store? I would be overjoyed to receive a month's worth of toilet paper rather than some useless item that will sit on my shelf or in a closet for the rest of my natural life. Most grocery stores have a gourmet or sugar-free candy section. Even an expensive sort of meat ready for the freezer to be enjoyed in the lean months of February when everybody will be cutting back to pay the fuel bills.

Chris Gernhart
Richmond, Texas

(I have two ideas along the line of practical Christmas gifts. One [different] aunt has given us a food basket for the past several years. It usually contains goodies that she knows I appreciate but am too cheap to buy. A ham, nuts, chocolate chips, etc.

The second idea I did for a grandmother who bakes hermits for us each time we visit. I made her a "Hermit Kit." This included nuts, raisins, a half gallon of molasses, brown sugar, flour, etc. I decorated the box, which

weighed a ton, as if it were real packaging with the list of contents on the outside. FZ)

CALENDAR STRETCHER

Dear Amy,

Some friends of mine have a lovely summer home on the coast of Maine. On one of my visits a few years ago, I noticed that their kitchen calendar was odd. It had the word "November" crossed out and the word "August" written beside it. I asked about the calendar, and was informed that last year's September, October and November correspond on the calendar to this year's June, July, and August. Just cross out the old months and write in the new ones, adding also the 31st day to the new August. When they told me this I laughed. Now I pass along this fine idea that extends the life of a calendar by 25%.

David Westerberg
Chicago, Illinois

CALENDAR REUSE

Dear Amy,

Our calendar system (based on the Gregorian calendar) has 14 variations. If one were to save old calendars, just check the World Almanac's Perpetual Calendar listing to determine the years for which that outdated calendar would suffice.

T. Morse
Greenbelt, Maryland

TURNING DOWN THE DOOR-TO-DOOR SALES KID

I must admit I have not had to deal with this plague since I moved to rural Maine. Well, I bought one box of Girl Scout cookies because our local troop leader is a mother of five and I give her credit for filling an important niche. The story was something different living in a suburban area where there is a steady stream of short doorbell ringers selling overpriced goods. If you succumbed to your sense of civic guilt you might as well hang a flashing neon sign reading "Soft Touch." When a kid came selling $5 Christmas bobbles I decided enough was enough.

To deal effectively with the door-to-door sales kid you will need to have a convincing list of excuses. Make up a crib sheet and post it in an easily visible adult eye-level position just inside the door. This way you will be prepared if you are caught by surprise.

SALES KID CRIB SHEET

1. "I just bought one of those from the red-headed kid down the street . . . you know the one with braces?" (There is no such kid but details are convincing.)

2. "Sorry, we're on a diet." (Use this excuse only if they are selling something edible.)

3. Fumble in your wallet for a few minutes and then say "Gee, kid, sorry. I only have $100 bill. Maybe next time."

4. "Boy what rotten timing. My dog just ate my wallet." (This will click with her as she just that day told her teacher that *her* dog ate her homework.)

5. "I'm sorry. We are trying to save to buy a house." (This is fairly effective. I have found that even children will respect adults when they express a need to implement personal discipline.)

THE DOOR-TO-DOOR SALES KID UPDATE

I wrote a humorous article suggesting that it is acceptable not to buy items that kids are sent home from school to sell. Since then I have been on the other side of the door for the first time. Both my kindergartner and first grader brought home glossy flyers depicting goodies in fancy tins and wrapping paper . . . and they were overpriced. I read, pondered, and in the end finally decided that there was genuinely nothing I wanted.

In all fairness, schools raise funds in this manner because it happens to be a very effective method of involving every family, therefore probably raising a larger sum of money.

Since the fund-raiser was for the parents' group that sponsors many worthy events, why should I be a stick-in-the-mud over this?

First, it is consumerism—buying for the sake of buying and sometimes because we feel a little coerced. We feel that we cannot send our child back to school without at least one order. We also don't want our kids knocking on our neighbors' doors pressing them to buy and I don't want my husband peddling them at work.

The manufacturing of most goods harms the environment in one way or another. The culprit is not the factory, but it is we who buy what it produces. Therefore we should think carefully about items we purchase.

Second, a portion of the money that we spend to help a worthy cause leaves the community. And I am concerned about those people who buy and can't afford to.

The parents' group in our community offers a few excellent alternatives. In the fall there is a potluck supper and auction. People who attend bring crafts, baked goods, and garden surplus. In this way you have the option to donate or bid for something. Our pumpkin brought $10. They also run a carnival in the springtime. Our church youth group "auctions" teenagers to do house and yard work. These types of events foster community spirit, keep all the money within the community, and are not consumer driven.

It was interesting that as I asked around I found several teachers and parents who shared my views. And, frankly, I didn't want to make waves any more than anyone else. I finally arrived at what I felt was my best choice. I simply donated money without buying anything.

NEWSPAPER KINDLING

If your town has a recycling program you will want to dispose of surplus newspaper in that manner. However, if you cannot recycle, or if you have a shortage of kindling and a surplus of newspaper, this is a terrific idea.

Starting with one corner roll a single sheet of newspaper into a long tube less than 1″ in diameter. Fold the tube into a V. Continue by alternating and folding over the underneath side until you have only 1″ ends left. Tuck these under so they are secure.

This type of newspaper kindling is so dense you will need to use crushed paper to start them burning. They burn hot enough to start a log burning without the use of wood kindling. About 10 will be enough.

If we do not pick up small sticks around our property, gen-

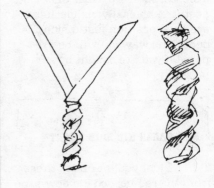

erally we make kindling by chopping scrap wood into smaller pieces, thereby reducing the heat value. If we make kindling from newspaper we increase the heat value.

TIGHTWAD VALENTINES

Over the years Jim has been the lucky recipient of creative and artistic valentines that relied heavily on my graphic art background, including a pop-up valentine and a most impressive animated one.

These things provide interesting reading but lack applicability to those of average abilities. In truth, creativity and thoughtfulness supersede artistic ability. If your middle name is not da Vinci try one of the following.

♥ Bake a pie with strawberry or cherry filling. Cut a heart design in the crust.

♥ Make a very simple card with a meaningful or funny poem. Your middle name doesn't have to be Browning either. I was pregnant our first Valentine's day. I included a poem in a simple card:

> *Roses are red.*
> *Violets are blue.*
> *Within me beat*
> *Two hearts for you.*

(Maybe I should stick to art?)

♥ Why not complete the procrastinated task that has most annoyed your spouse, and then leave a valentine conspicuously in the area? I have a friend who papered the bathroom for his wife as a birthday present.

♥ Make a heart-shaped pizza, topped primarily with red items such as pepperoni or red peppers.

♥ Give your spouse a coupon for a massage.

♥ Make a heart-shaped cake by baking a round cake and a square cake. One side of the square cake must be of an equal length to the diameter of the round cake. Cut the round cake in half and combine with the square to make a heart. Frost to hide seams.

♥ Ambush your spouse as he or she comes home with a booby trap plastic bucket filled with small paper hearts, attached over the door, in such a way as to dump when the door is opened (see page 290).

♥ If nature cooperates, stomp out a valentine in a large area of snow. I tried this one year but was far too ambitious. We have a great view of our cornfield from the third-floor attic. My 50-foot valentine was not visible until I had stomped around it about 20 times. Every few laps I would run back to the house, across a distance of foot deep snow, up to the third-floor attic, to see if the valentine was visible yet. I exhausted myself and I am sure passersby thought the new neighbor was loony tunes. Before Jim arrived home, late afternoon shadows obliterated my creation.

I suggest you try something no larger than 20 feet and be sure it

will be seen when your spouse arrives.

❤ Pick a bouquet of pussy willows or other winter growth, and tie it with a large red bow.

❤ Rent a romantic classic movie, especially one that you might have seen together when you were first dating.

❤ One year Jim (a fellow of less than average artistic abilities) made a card for me. He cut a heart design into an art gum eraser and stamped the entire cover of the card. This is a simple idea for kids to make their own cards for school also.

❤ Bake a batch of heart-shaped cookies (make a cutter from a tuna can).

EVERYTHING I ALWAYS WANTED TO WRITE ABOUT DATING, BUT WAS AFRAID TO SQUEEZE INTO ONE ARTICLE

In the 10 years I have known Jim we have had only one real argument. A few hours later he apologized and admitted that he had been dead wrong about the croquet rule.

Aside from this single shouting match we have had the occasional "stressful conversation" or "agreement to disagree," but generally we enjoy remarkable compatibility.

I have always believed that teamwork has been our greatest economic asset. It is about more than simply agreeing on how to handle money. We do not need to expend energy "working on our marriage," whatever that means. As a result we have maximum energy to devote to our common goals.

It is much like the biblical analogy of a team of oxen that is "unequally yoked." If the oxen work against each other they are ineffective. But pulling together they accomplish more than they would individually.

Compatibility is more likely to be found than created. A psychologist told me that whatever a relationship is in the beginning is what it will always be. In other words, people can modify their behavior to a degree, but sweeping changes are rare. While they may occur, they should not be banked on.

Since money is the most common marital problem, it occurs to me that people must be running amok in the selection process. Historically, we most commonly selected our soul mates through an economic bait-and-switch dating style.

Traditional dating has its roots in the Neanderthal era. The man demonstrated his ability to provide by bringing the desired mate (or her parents) gifts of furs, food, and other valuables. This tradition has continued until recently. The smitten spender (the man) demonstrated his economic prowess by paying for food, entertainment, jewelry, and other gifts.

He "baited" by sending the message that he could provide security and that he expressed love through money. It followed that if someone baited a mate with extravagant spending he was likely to attract a spouse who appreciated it. The "switch" occurred after marriage, when he or she balanced the joint checking account for the first time. If they were lucky they learned they were both tightwads, as Jim and I did. If they found they were both spendthrifts, they might be equally yoked but blissfully plowing off into the sunset . . . together but in the wrong direction. The third common scenario occurred when people found themselves in a "mixed marriage," or they discovered they had different economic styles.

In the past 10 years, the financial responsibility of the date has become more equitable, at least once couples get beyond the initial courtship. However, even when couples live together they tend to retain separate budgets, and the money never becomes

"our money." In some cases after marriage couples may still keep separate accounts. It isn't until the state of "our money" occurs that couples develop a heightened awareness of economic incompatibility. When couples learn they have to make choices they may discover they wouldn't choose the same things.

The financial problems in marriage can involve more than a lack of sufficient funds, but also a difference in spending style. Even when there might be enough money, it can still drive a tightwad to the brink of insanity to see his spouse get little value for the dollar.

The issue of economic incompatibility may not come up until long after the couple has become emotionally hooked. But the signals are present from the beginning. They're just ignored or not looked for.

Our culture seems to frown upon the concept that we "choose" our marriage partners. Romance, we are told, is something that just happens. Early attempts to weed out a potential mate on the basis of incompatibility is "too cold and calculating," especially in relationship to money.

In reality, we fall in love with people we spend time with. It makes sense to look for the signals of all sorts of incompatibility during the first dates, before the emotional hook occurs, and not spend time with people who appear to have dissimilar values and goals.

Ignore social pressure to spend extravagantly on dates, and thereby send out the wrong message. If you want to attract a tightwad soulmate put out "frugal date bait." Instead of sending roses, give a flowering plant that you potted from your cuttings. Make your own chocolates. Invite her to dinner. Even if the meal is substandard, the right woman will love it.

What's the difference between putting out frugal date bait and being cheap? Lu Bauer, a CPA in Falmouth, Maine, who teaches courses on money and relationships, suggests that your dating style should be consistent with a whole life pattern. If you spend lots of money partying with your friends, and little on dates, you might rightfully be labeled "cheap." Largely it is a matter of thoughtfulness and style. Whipping out your two-for-one coupon at a cafeteria-style chain steak house may lack a certain class. Instead plan a modest but elegant picnic at your special private spot. If you really want to separate the wheat from the chaff, plan a

characteristically tightwad date, something that you enjoy and is a regular part of your life. It might be a date to go yard saling. You plan the route, and bring the homemade muffins and thermos of coffee.

While you are putting out your tasteful but frugal date bait, look closely at the reactions it brings. Look for it in the eyes. A spendthrift will appear to not "get it," and have a furrowed quizzical look. A tightwad will twinkle with delight.

When you are dating, don't worry about making a good impression. Make an accurate impression. Spend in a way that is consistent with your income and values. In doing so you increase your chances of attracting someone with whom you are most compatible.

Compatibility in all areas, not just spending, is a tremendous economic advantage.

THE KISS GIFT

Dear Amy,

Make a "kiss gift." Take a cardboard circle that is larger than the gift. Place tissue around the base to give it body and wrap the gift in tissue paper. Wrap the circle, tissue paper and gift in aluminum foil so that it looks like a

Homemade Chocolates

Hershey's Kiss. Run a piece of
paper out of the top for a nametag
and tape securely.

Mildred James
Greensboro, North Carolina

PHOTO VALENTINE

Dear Amy,

Last year I made my husband a
card that is still on his desk at
work. I made big letters out of
construction paper for the words
"I love you" and took a picture of
our son holding each letter. I put
them all together on a long cardboard card and underneath each
picture wrote a short sentiment.
L is for the lovely songs you sing,
etc.

Jill Boyd
Seattle, Washington

A.M. VALENTINE

Dear Amy,

Get up before the family and
write your Valentine's message
on the bathroom mirror with lipstick.

Ruth Palmer
Glendale, Utah

SMOOCH CARD

Dear Amy,

Have Mom and all the children
put on red lipstick. Take a plain
piece of paper and have each person kiss it. Sign it if desired and
frame.

Beverly Huff
Nashville, Tennessee

STUFFED HEART

Dear Amy,

I'll always cherish a red stuffed
heart my mother gave each of her
girls for Valentine's Day. The material probably came from a fancy
gown or remnant. It is about 8″ at
the widest part and can be stuffed
with whatever you have. Mom
sewed lace around and made a red
tab with which to hang it. I have
it in my bedroom with a fancy pin
collection in it.

Lois Funke
Ontonagon, Michigan

(Or make a hanging from three
hearts with different red-patterned
material. Stuffing possibilities include
cup-up nylons or the filling from an
old baby quilt. FZ)

A SWEET HEART PACKAGE

When it comes to valentine ex-
changes at school, packages of
20 for $1 (on sale) are hard to
beat, even though it seems un-
creative. The problem with making your own is figuring out a
way to make a lot cheaply and
easily, and trying to do something
that's at least as good as store

bought. It's a pretty tall order.

This little idea was sent in to me by a reader who made a heart package from an old greeting card. As I experimented with different cards I found many unlikely designs worked, such as Christmas cards. You see a small section of the original picture on the heart so it creates an abstract design. Trace the pattern onto lightweight paper. Make a template by transferring the tracing onto a lightweight piece of cardboard, such as a margarine box. An inexpensive way of making an erasable "carbon" is to cover a piece of paper with graphite, using the side of a No. 2 pencil. A template will save time if you are planning to make several hearts.

Fold up the cut-out heart package as shown. Glue the flaps where indicated. Secure with a ribbon.

As a suggestion for something to put in your heart try making these easy mints.

1 cup granulated sugar
4 Tbsp water
peppermint flavoring
red or pink food coloring
1 cup powdered sugar

Combine granulated sugar and water. Bring to a boil. Add flavoring, food coloring, and powdered sugar. Drop on wax paper quickly. (The first mints will be round, and as the mixture cools they become lumpier.)

By using different colors this recipe works for other holidays.

A BAKED BEAN HERITAGE

When Jim was a boy living in western Massachusetts, his fam-

cut on
solid line →

fold on dotted line → ← glue

ily visited friends in Maine. During that trip they experienced a "bean hole supper" in which beans were cooked in pots buried in the ground along with hot ashes. The beans used at that supper were Jacob's Cattle beans. These attractive beans, appropriately named for their brown-and-white markings, look much like a dairy cow.

Jim's parents bought a package of Jacob's Cattle beans and brought them home. They planted the beans, and have eaten and replanted the surplus year after year for 30 years. When we moved to Maine, my father-in-law gave us some Jacob's Cattle beans, and now we grow them.

Dried beans are an excellent protein source, are nearly always less expensive than meat, and should be considered a staple of the tightwad diet. Because most of us are familiar with baked beans, they make a great dinner for the entry-level vegetarian.

When I married Jim I ate these scratch-baked beans for the first time, and loved them for their character and rich, dark flavor. You can use most types of dried beans in this recipe.

Maine Baked Beans

2 lbs dried beans (4 cups)
1 tsp. baking soda
1 medium onion
½ lb bacon or salt pork
¼ cup brown sugar
½ to ⅔ cup molasses
2 tsp dry mustard
½ tsp salt

Soak the beans overnight in cold water. In the morning pour off the soaking water and parboil beans with baking soda in fresh water until the skins crack when blown upon. Cut onion in quarters and put in the bottom of a bean pot or large casserole. Add parboiled beans. Put cut-up bacon or salt pork on top of the beans. Mix brown sugar, molasses, dry mustard, and salt with a pint of water. If necessary add more boiling water while baking. Bake at 300° for 6 hours or more.

This recipe makes the equivalent of six 28-oz. cans of B&M baked beans at $1.28 per can. The ingredients of the scratch beans (if you buy the beans) cost about $2 versus $7.68 for store bought. Even allowing a generous figure for electricity, scratch beans will cost well under half the cost of B&M beans.

We make this recipe in our two bean pots. It's hard to find old bean pots complete with lids, as the lids break easily. We've solved the problem with a little ingenuity. My grandmother gave us a bean pot without a lid. Shortly thereafter I found a smaller bean pot with a same-sized lid at a yard sale for 50¢. I bought the bean pot, saved the lid and resold the pot at my yard sale for 50¢. We now have a second bean pot that also lacks its original lid. Sometime earlier I broke my glass coffee perker. I must possess tightwad ESP, because I saved the seemingly useless glass top. We later found the glass top makes a nice bean pot lid if used upside down. (You didn't need to know this, but I think it's funny.)

We freeze the leftover beans in 1-cup size margarine containers to use in other recipes.

Although I recall eating mostly store bought baked beans, my own childhood is not without a baked bean tradition. My mother made two recipes that used baked bean leftovers:

Dunkin' Soup

2 cups baked beans
1 8-oz can of stewed or canned tomatoes
1 large celery stalk with leaves
1 chopped onion
salt and pepper to taste

Process all the ingredients in a blender. Heat to boiling and simmer 20 minutes.

We called this Dunkin' Soup because it was our tradition to eat it by dipping (dunkin') bread into the soup. As an adult, I no longer need all the carbohydrates I would get from eating the soup with bread, so I now enjoy it with a spoon. This recipe has become a favorite of my children.

Corn Pone

1 lb hamburger, browned and drained
⅓ cup chopped onion

1 Tbsp shortening
¾ tsp salt
1 tsp worcestershire sauce
2 cups canned tomatoes
1 cup baked beans

Sauté onion in shortening. Combine the remaining ingredients and place in a large casserole (we use a large cast-iron frying pan). Top with ½-inch layer of cornbread batter (recipe available in any basic cookbook). Bake at 425° for 30 minutes. Bake any remaining cornbread batter in muffin tins.

As with any good marriage, elements of Jim's family traditions have blended with elements of mine. But we experiment and add to our repertoire, thereby forging new food traditions. This is a soup recipe we have discovered and grown fond of:

Bean-Bacon Chowder

6 slices bacon, cut up
1 cup chopped onion
2 Tbsp flour
3 cups milk
2 medium potatoes, peeled
¼ tsp crushed dried thyme
1, 22-oz jar of baked beans (substitute homemade here)
¼ cup snipped parsley

Cook bacon and onion in a saucepan until bacon is lightly browned and onion is tender. Blend in flour. Add milk; cook and stir until bubbly. Dice potatoes; add with thyme, 1 tsp salt and ⅛ tsp pepper. Cover and simmer 12 to 15 minutes or till the potatoes are done. Stir in beans and heat through. Top with parsley. Serves six.

Spring

EASTER IDEAS

The commercialism surrounding Easter bothers me more than that which surrounds Christmas. Despite this a few foil covered bunnies have crossed our threshold.

I have worked out a few less expensive alternatives to the enormous pink plastic-wrapped baskets that crowd store shelves at this time of year.

Give smaller baskets. The smaller the basket the less needed to fill.

I have resorted to ridiculous lengths to create homemade baskets from recycled materials. Sane mothers reuse the same baskets from year to year.

Fill baskets with homemade edible items and inexpensive treasures. One year I made necklaces out of Froot Loops (purchased with coupons back when we lived in double-coupon territory) and marshmallow bunnies. I also collected all the freebies with coupons given to me by the Welcome Wagon lady. Many items ended up in Easter baskets.

Or do not fill the Easter baskets. Instead hide jelly beans for kids to find to fill their own baskets. A bag of jelly beans is comparatively inexpensive. The degree of difficulty will control the rate of sugar consumption. Do not do as my mother did. She would toss many beans in the toy box. The thrill of the hunt diminished when we were forced to clean out our toy box.

It is not necessary to purchase egg decorating kits. A cup of boiling water, a teaspoon of vinegar, and food coloring works as well. Professional paste food coloring produces better color.

My final thought is my most radical. Focus on the spiritual significance of the holiday.

HOW TO MAKE MARSHMALLOW BUNNIES

Clip the marshmallow as shown by the dotted line using a pair of scissors. Sprinkle confectionery sugar in cut places so it does not stick. To make eyes dot with a toothpick that has been dipped in red food coloring.

HOP, SKIMP, & JUMP

Dear Amy,

Sometimes by going through Las Vegas you can get cheaper fares when flying cross-country. For example, buy a round trip from San Diego to Las Vegas, and then a round trip from Las Vegas to your final destination. This is because Las Vegas is always having specials when the rest of the country isn't.

Jeannie Coulson
San Diego, California

LAS VEGAS

FIX-IT LADY

Dear Amy,

My husband is not mechanical and so I am left to fix things or to have them fixed. I have repaired hundreds of things by trial and error. I fixed a Coleman lantern that would not stay lit. (It only had cobwebs in the air flow tube.) I also put a new belt and heating element in my Whirlpool dryer.

Most companies have 800 numbers you can call to talk to a serviceperson. Call 1-800-555-1212 for information or send a 19¢ postcard for more information.

I always order replacement parts for toys or to fix something cheap I got at a yard sale. All you need is the company name, toy name, or model number of the toy.

Fisher-Price offers a free Bits and Pieces Catalog of Replacement Parts:

Fisher-Price
636 Girard Ave.
East Aurora, NY 14052

Rachel Wiegand
Stanley, Virginia

50% SHAMPOO SAVINGS

Dear Amy,

Most shampoo instructions tell you to "lather, rinse, repeat." I've stopped "repeating" years ago and never noticed any difference in how clean my hair gets.

Eileen Mierski
Pittsburgh, Pennsylvania

JELL-O EGGS

Dear Amy,

Every Easter my mother takes a couple-dozen eggs and with a needle breaks a ¼-inch hole in the top of the eggs. She drains the eggs and rinses the shells before submersing them in boiling water for a few seconds. She then fills them with this mixture:

1 cup water
1 large box gelatin mixture
1 pkg. Knox gelatin
2 cups cold water

Dissolve the gelatin powders in one cup boiling water, then add the 2 cups cold water.

My mother sometimes lets this jell a bit, then pours in different colors to get striped eggs. She leaves them in the fridge till morning and we usually help her crack the eggs, which she serves with dinner. This turns out to be fun and exciting for grandchildren, who don't know her secret and wonder how Grandma got Jell-O eggs. She saves the drained eggs and makes omelets or scrambled eggs.

Robin Lively
Idaho Falls, Idaho

DESPERATE MEASURES

Dear Amy,

When Ron and I were first married, March 1970, we had an income of $258/month; rent was $145. Those were extremely lean times. I kept track of all expenses as a matter of pure survival. We had a strict limit of $17 for food every two weeks. We wrote prices down as we went through the commissary, and if the total went up to $17.01 we put something back.

I sat in the dark (Ron worked nights) in order to save on electricity. We didn't buy magazines, newspapers, or clothes. We used our car only for him to go to work and to get food. We walked a lot. We gladly would have done without a phone but the Air Force insisted we have one.

Our apartment was furnished, so we asked if we could give the furniture back and drop the rent to $95. The landlord agreed to it and we made the eight-hour trip to Illinois to get my bed and a couple of chairs. To save money while we were gone we totally emptied the fridge, freezer, turned it off, and unplugged everything electric.

I was raised to use a towel once and throw it in the laundry, but when we got married, it quickly (1 week) became apparent this was nuts! We simply couldn't af-

ford that luxury! And, even though I'd lived that way for three weeks short of 22 years, suddenly using a towel once, then washing it, seemed awfully wasteful, so I stopped and started using a towel for a week.

We lived in a tiny, rundown apartment—no balcony—but I strung lines over the bathtub to dry some things and would drape things over the outside back steps railing to dry while I read on the steps (to prevent them from being stolen). I've also been known to hand wash our laundry to save on water and electricity.

There are all sorts of measures you can take when you're financially desperate.

Pat Wagner
Columbus, Ohio

THREE PRINCIPLES OF USED ACQUISITION

A prerequisite for our dream home was the existence of at least one wood stove hookup, preferably in the kitchen. My great-grandmother's house had one of those black monster cookstoves with warming ovens, and my grandmothers both have small wood stoves in their kitchens. So in keeping with my "matriarch complex," I wanted one, too.

As it happened our kitchen had one such hookup and an empty space that cried out for a large cookstove. After several months of diligence we found a Glenwood F cookstove at the right price.

The location of the wood stove resulted from a strategy that I call "putting out the word." If you're looking for something, casually mention your search to every soul you run into. Very often someone you know, or someone they know, has the very thing you want and would be willing to give it to you, or sell it for a reasonable price.

Putting out the word should not be confused with mooching. You are not asking for the shirt off someone's back. Instead you say, "I am looking for another good shirt. If you know someone who has one they might sell at a reasonable price, let me know." (Do not stare at their shirt while saying this.)

If someone has an item they are not using, such as a tool buried in a garage, or a piece of old furniture in the attic with at least 40 years of dust on it, let them know that you'd be willing to buy it for a reasonable price. You might also suggest a barter arrangement. Whatever the deal, always pay a fair price for a used item—though they'll often let you have it for free.

When you put out the word be sure to speak to the best scrounger you know. (In our case, it's my father-in-law. When you hit pawn shops and flea markets, speak up. And if your swap magazine runs ads for free, place a "wanted" ad.

In the case of our stove, Jim learned of it through speaking with a woman who ran the thrift shop. She had it stored in her garage in (rusted) pieces and would let us have it for $100, or $75 if we gave her dog a home, too.

We took the stove, but not the dog. I spent a few hours cleaning it with a wire brush, and applied stove blacking, and Jim replaced the fire brick. The stove is worth at least $500 today.

When we set the stove up we realized that,

even though the price was right, it was a smaller version than what we wanted. We still want a larger stove—a Glenwood E with warming ovens. Our plan includes a strategy called "trading up."

Most people know someone who has traded-up in housing. I know a man who acquired a handsome antique gun collection the same way. He bought a rifle in poor condition, restored it, and sold it. He used the profit to buy two more guns that needed work, restored those and so on.

We figure that if we bought a stove for $100 and sell it for $500, perhaps we could buy a larger stove for $500 in need of elbow grease. Ideally we could eventually own a stove worth $800 or more for an initial investment of $100, plus the cost of fire brick and stove blacking. If you need an item for a short period of time, or if you can't find exactly what you want but need something to tide you over, you can get free use of an item by using a method I call "temporary ownership."

A new thing depreciates rapidly with its first ownership. A young couple might buy a new crib for $200 and sell it in two years for $50. The two-year-use of the crib cost $150. It depreciated by 75% of its value even though it's still functional and good-looking. (Multiply that cost by all the other short-term-use equipment and clothes you need for a child and you can needlessly spend many hundreds of dollars.)

As you become familiar with the used-stuff market you'll find a significant price range. That same crib might sell for $25 to $75. Shop around and buy items at the low end of the range—in other words, buy the $25 crib. After you've used it for your tribe, resell the crib. Even though the crib will be more worn, you'll be able to recoup your $25 because you bought on the low end of the price range. The use of the crib becomes free to you.

We've used the put-out-the-word strategy to acquire our first cookstove, which we plan to temporarily own until we can trade up when we find a black iron Glenwood E (or similar stove) with warming ovens. Using this example to illustrate ideas in my newsletter must be the ultimate example of putting out the word.

P.S. I used the hand-me-down crib as an example in this article. Before purchasing used baby equipment you should learn about current safety guidelines. You can receive free pamphlets on crib safety and tips for baby safety by writing to:

Consumer Products Safety
    Commission
Washington, DC 20207

PUT OUT THE WORD

Dear Amy,

I recently tried your "put-out-the-word" strategy (as mentioned in the *Parade* article) and asked a friend where I might find an engine for my rototiller. He offered a complete tiller if I would just come and get it. It turned out to be a Craftsman 5 HP rear tine, self-propelled model! It needed a 50¢ flywheel key and now runs great. My friend did have a mower in need of a tune-up so I made his mower look and run like new in exchange for the tiller. Now we are both happy and I'm planning to do more small-engine repair for friends and neighbors after my initial success.

Lyle Merril
Logan, Utah

A GOLF TIP

Dear Amy,

Golf balls are getting more expensive each season, ranging from $16 per dozen for in-line balls on sale to as much as $30 per dozen for top-of-the-line tour balls. Many manufacturers of golf balls brag about their balls being durable, and several go to the trouble to print a guarantee on the packaging of the balls (sleeve of three) stating they guarantee their ball will not cut or split during the ball's lifetime. If they should, the company will replace the bad ball with three free balls.

Problem is, many golfers don't read the fine print on the package and never learn what a great guarantee they are offered. This season I have had six balls cut during play and have sent in all six using the guarantee. Now I have eighteen new balls.

> Kevin Brown
> Sheboygan, Wisconsin

QUICKIE CALL

Dear Amy,

I would like to point out a cost-effective procedure—the 1-minute phone call. Such calls are rare but on my recent phone bill 31 of the 58 calls cost less than a 1st-class letter. Some were calls to leave or pick up answering machine messages, but others had real-live participants who simply got to the point and said goodbye.

Try this exercise: Write down before the call what you really need to say on the phone. Time yourself reading it back. Can you stretch it to one minute? Probably not. Most of our phone talk is casual conversation that could be put into a letter.

There are many times when talk could not or should not be cut to the minimum, but you can be pointed and polite in one minute if necessary.

> Ken Lundeen
> New York, New York

KIDS' CAR SEATS

Dear Amy,

If anyone is planning to buy a child car seat at a yard sale or already has one that was handed down, they can write to the following address and request a current copy of "The Recommended Child Seats and Recalls." Enclose an SASE.

Center for Auto Safety
2001 S Street, NW
Suite 410
Washington, DC 20009

I purchased a car seat at a yard sale for $15. Upon checking the list I found the seat was listed under recalls. When I called the toll-free number they took my name and address and sent me a new redesigned one free of charge.

> Dorothy L. Johns
> Woodbury, Connecticut

STEEL WOOL PADS

Dear Amy,

After using a soapy steel wool pad, pop it in the freezer. It will thaw quickly for the next use and won't be a pile of rust next to your sink!

> Susan Abbott
> Windsor, Connecticut

Dear Amy,

You asked for time-saving helps. My neighbor and I exchange meals once a week. She cooks for me on Tuesday and I cook for her Thursday. We just do the main dish, adding the salad or whatever. Since she lives right next door, delivery is simple. We both enjoy our night off.

Lucy Scholand
Ypsilanti, Michigan

CONVERTING YOUR SPOUSE

I have hesitated to write this article because I cannot draw from personal experience. Although I might have implied it, I did not convert Jim. We were both spendthrifts with underlying tightwad tendencies . . . my tendencies being a bit stronger than his. Therefore, changing gears was a natural process for both of us.

I have observed many tightwad spouses who have struggled for years, or even decades, to change their spendthrift partners without success. In some cases they tried all the suggestions I have. The truth is that you cannot .change your spouse.

Genuine change results from an inner willingness and cannot be imposed by others. I suspect that if a change runs completely against someone's character, the best you can hope for is a small degree of behavior modification.

As dismal as this sounds, consider spouse conversion to be a worthy pursuit. Many of my suggestions are proven sales or relationship strategies. Some are pure theory. With the exception of the first two, my suggestions are presented in random order.

In my experience men and women are equally as likely to be spendthrifts. My use of the gender-neutral "he" is for simplicity only.

1. Establish a financial goal that you both can agree on. Without a goal, saving money has no meaning, but with one you have a beginning point for encouraging change. The goal should be very specific and have a time period attached. By choosing a goal you show him how *he* can benefit by change.

2. Gather evidence. Know how much money you have coming in and where it goes. Record your spending habits meticulously. If your spouse will not participate, then you can at least show him how much is unaccounted for. Put together as comprehensive a proposal as possible before you call a meeting. Graphs and charts are not too extreme.

3. Always confront your spouse at a "good time." He should be relaxed and in a good mood. You may have to schedule a specific time. Do not confront in the heat of an argument.

4. When you discuss the problem stick with the facts. Do not label, accuse, or blame. Say something such as:

a. "We agreed that we would try to pay off our credit cards."

b. "This month you bought a $75 fishing reel."

c. "We only made an interest payment on our Visa card this time."

He may not agree that he is a spendthrift, but he cannot deny the facts.

The objective is to discuss the problem in a way that is easiest for him to hear. You want to maximize your chances to sell tightwaddery . . . not to be "right."

5. Be the leader. Your record of spending should show that you didn't spend on anything that could possibly be considered nonessential. If cutting on the food bill requires more cooking from scratch, and your spouse doesn't want to do it, then *you* need to learn to cook.

6. Request small changes rather than sweeping reforms. For example, request a waiting period of a month between when he tells you he wants to buy something and when he makes the purchase. Or convince the meat-and-potatoes spouse to have one meatless meal per month. When these changes have been accepted, increase the waiting time, number of meatless meals, or ask for new changes.

7. Give your spouse some freedom. Agree to a small amount of money that your spouse can spend on anything wanted . . . say $5, $10, or $25 per week. Determine a sum of money that fits into your budget. That discretionary fund is to be spent without comment or criticism from you. Give yourself a discretionary fund as well. Naturally, you will put yours into a savings account.

8. Show him. If an item goes on sale for which he paid full price a week earlier, point it out in a tactful way. If you discover something that works and saves money, show him. The gentle and regular sharing of information over time may win him.

9. Sometimes the person your spouse is least likely to hear information from is you. If this is the case in your marriage, get him to think it is *his* idea. Say to him "What do you think about . . . ?" Repeat this every few days. With any luck in time he will tell you about *his* new idea.

10. Be patient. Pushing too hard for change may cause your spouse to reject your wishes. My mother's favorite saying is, "You catch more flies with honey than with vinegar." Real behavior modification takes time. Hopefully you will be married for several decades. In the light of that, a transition that requires a few years may not be too long.

11. Leave copies of *The Tightwad Gazette* within the pages of his well-worn bathroom copy of the Sears, Roebuck catalog.

If you are single and think this is yet another article for married people that doesn't pertain to you, you're wrong. The very fact that large numbers of married tightwads have requested this article should be a red flag to you. Continue to weed out the candidates until you find one whose fiscal philosophy matches yours. Every good tightwad knows that an ounce of prevention is worth a pound of cure.

CONVERTING YOUR SPOUSE UPDATE

As a follow-up on my article "Converting Your Spouse," readers sent in the following suggestions. Contributors' names have been withheld to ensure future domestic tranquillity.

Single tightwads should note that fewer than half a dozen people shared success with conversions.

"In order to have any success in converting a die-hard spendthrift you first must understand the mental dynamics behind one:

1. They do not understand the concept of money. Period.

2. Like small children, they need instant gratification.

3. They are slow to realize that their money must be used to pay for life's necessities.

4. They don't understand that control over their money, in the long run, will give them more freedom and peace of mind.

5. Any attempt to make them responsible for money is perceived as punishment or an attempt to control their lives, and may backfire into another spending binge.

Coping suggestions:

1. Accept the things you cannot change, and change the things you can. Know the difference between the two.

2. Agree that purchases of over x-amount must be discussed.

3. Post your income and outgo in a place where it can be seen ... either weekly or monthly.

4. Take care of necessities first, before discretionary funds are distributed. This seems like common sense to most, but spendthrifts get it backward. They buy 'wants' before 'needs.'

5. If you know a major expense is coming up, let them know well in advance there will be less discretionary funds available and ask for cooperation.

6. Make it clear that a savings account is not a discretionary fund and must be 'paid' like a bill. If necessary, set it up so that the spendthrift spouse cannot access it. Do not discuss how much is there, as it is frustrating for them to know that funds are available that cannot be spent without proving true need.

7. When there has been a spending binge do not retaliate with one of your own. This only proves to your spouse that the money was available all along, and your efforts to convert your spouse will go right down the tubes."

"I think it is an awareness process, so for phase one I tried to convince my husband that those little things such as stopping at the market for a drink and a snack on the way home add up. I started casually asking about his day and if he stopped at the market. If he did I put the same amount as was spent in a jar. A month to 45 days later he wanted to buy some large purchases. I brought out the jar, explained what I had done, and had him count it. There was $80 in the jar. Phase one completed."

"I did not change my husband overnight. He came to our marriage with the idea that the key to financial solvency was to earn more money. He spent the first two years of our marriage pressuring me to get a better job, while many of our careless habits were eating away at our savings. Words were of no use because he felt it was beneath him to examine the food bill or live in a cheaper apartment. I slowly began to take control of areas I knew best, without discussion, as previous attempts made him angry and defensive.

"First I found a larger apartment with a savings of $100 per month. Then I began keeping track of our grocery bill and was able to show him how costs could go down.

"I didn't confront him with any 'I told you so's' and reminders of previous wastefulness, and soon he did internalize many of my money-saving ways. Now I have a quiet laugh when he expounds his thrifty principles, nearly all of which he learned from me!"

"My husband would never consider anything used. 'Someone else's junk' he called it. He had al-

ways been a stickler for 'if you're going to get it, get the best' philosophy. So I can't tell you how many top-of-the-line things we have lying around the house, which have since become obsolete, vastly decreased in value, or just plain useless.

"He hated mowing our 100′ × 100′ patch of lawn because it took so long with a push mower. Yet, the only riding mower he would consider was a 16 HP beast that mulched, vacuumed, plowed earth and snow, and tuned the car. New, they cost over $2,500, a bit beyond our budget. One weekend, after several summers of knee-high weeds, I looked in the classifieds, drove out with our pick-up, and returned with a used, reconditioned 8 HP riding mower for $350. It didn't look like much, but it got the job done. For the first few weeks he would have nothing to do with it and I took over mowing the lawn. Gradually his resistance faded, and now he even changes the oil in it.

"Next we wanted a Vermont Castings 'Vigilant,' a stove that burns coal and wood and costs $1,600 new. We found a classified that advertised one with considerable equipment for half the price. My husband, who was initially cynical, did the bargaining. After that I saw a subtle, but undeniable change in his attitude.

"Just recently, it was he who suggested we advertise in the wanted column to buy a used travel trailer. We found just what we wanted in excellent condition for a fraction of what they cost new."

CHEAP THRILL

Dear Amy,

I thought you might enjoy reading about how my husband and I entertained our daughter and her overnight guest. We created an elegant private dinner for two in a "rustic country inn" (our home).

We discussed the concept with the girls in the afternoon. We gave them an outline of the evening and reviewed table settings and helped them develop a menu based upon available foodstuffs suggesting traditionally appropriate relishes. We set a few ground rules as to the scope of services that could be requested (these had to be in line with what one would normally require of a restaurant staff). We explained that a distant relative had provided the dinner at no charge to the girls so that money was not the issue (no making menu selections based upon price). We also explained that the basis of all good manners is respect for the other party as a human being so that condescending behavior was nipped in its potential bud.

The girls dressed in an assortment of "dress-up" clothes, consisting mainly of cast-off lingerie and plastic beads, bracelets, and large hair ribbons. As maître d', Erik dressed in a tux with an outrageous multicolored tie, and I, as waitress, dressed in an evening gown and loaded up with every rhinestone I could find (earrings, necklace, rings, bracelets, hairclips, pins).

We set a table in Anna's upstairs room and provided:

a "linen" tablecloth (a white
    sheet) and napkins
candlestick (with a hurricane
    shade)
flowers (silk) with ribbon
    streamers across the table
an ice bucket on a stand (plant
    stand)
water in crystal goblets
a service table (also with cloth)
a handbell for service (this was
    a highlight)
music by Vivaldi

The arrival: a knock on the door, the maître d' opens the door, and welcomes the diners, exclaiming over the honor of welcoming them to the country inn and promising them an extraordinary evening. He introduces his wife, the cook and waitress. They are escorted to their table where the evening menu is presented in an embossed leather folder with each course described and listed in order (the girls prepared the menu inserts during the afternoon after the selections had been made, refined, and agreed upon).

The maître d' arrives with a towel over his arm and pours water and presents fresh hot rolls with maple butter; he assists the young ladies by using a pair of tongs and places the roll on the bread plate so the evening begins smoothly with no initial blunders (the individual butter knife is across the top of the plate).

When the girls are ready for the next course they signal by

using the handbell and a great flurry is created in answering their call along with some sort of anecdotal tale relating to the freshness or preparation of the next course. There is also a gushing of compliments.

Each course is served on an individual plate, and the main course is served at the table from service bowls. The silver platters and bowls are amazing in the candlelight (most of them are foil-covered pie plates with a ruffled edge).

Dessert arrives as a choice between a huge uncut chocolate cake and an assortment of cookies. Herb tea is served in the cups (liberally assisted by sugar and milk) and the maitre d' and waitress regale the guests with amusing stories of previous escapades at the country inn. The ladies are given a tour of the rest of the facilities and are chauffeur-driven home. (They take a ride down our long driveway and back up). The spell is not broken by any requests for dishwashing or cleaning up, but a timely bedtime is required. They awake the next morning to find the table, flowers, and menu still resplendent in the corner of the room.

This one evening showed up in the story writing of both girls in school and became quite a subject for discussion among the teachers. We did it for fun, but it was the teachers who pointed out the value of role-model learning of basic social graces.

Erik and I relearned a lot of the small points, and the entire evening paid off in a big way this summer when my parents treated us to an elegant seven-course dinner at a lakeshore resort. Our

daughter, Anna, never skipped a beat.

Susan Davis
Bristol, Vermont

THE $64,000 QUESTION

Since the first page, you've been dying to know: How *do* you recycle a vacuum cleaner bag?

After extensive experimentation I have hit upon a method to get extra use out of a used bag. I unroll the glued bottom to open it. After it's emptied I reroll the end and staple it closed about 10 times to make an airtight seal. (Do not recycle a bag several times. A weakened bag could develop a hole and escaping dirt might damage the motor.)

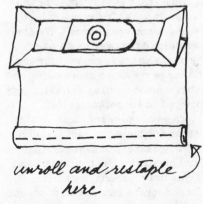

unroll and restaple here

Is this nitpicky money-saving idea worth your time? I can recycle a bag in under five minutes including refilling the stapler. In theory I could recycle 12 bags per hour. The last time I bought bags they cost 85¢ each. So this effort is worth $10.20 per hour.

For me to net $10.20 per hour by working outside the home I would have to earn close to $20 per hour (figuring in child care, gas, taxes, etc.).

Granted, I do not spend my days recycling vacuum cleaner bags, but I do fill them with many ways to economize.

By learning how to optimize my time and resources I can create a tax-free income. I can elevate the standard of living of our family without working more hours outside the home.

It *is* worth doing. Not just the vacuum cleaner bags, but all the thousands of ways to save money. It *does* all add up.

THE $64,000 QUESTION UPDATE

I have recently learned that Kenmore makes a reusable cloth vacuum cleaner bag that fits our model. It sells for $9.99 through Sears. It only fits some models.

To learn if the manufacturer of your vacuum cleaner makes a reusable cloth bag call 1-800-555-1212 to see if they have a toll-free number.

A SUCCESS STORY

Dear Amy,

Last year my husband and I realized our dream. We purchased a rural home on 9 acres and were completely debt free. This was accomplished on my husband's income of less than $30,000.

After five years of marriage, my husband and I had buried ourselves in debt with the purchase of a second home. We soon came to the realization that there must

be a better way to live. So we sold our home and moved into a one-bedroom duplex with two daughters.

After a year of saving all we could, we bought our third home. This time we had decided to set the unreachable goal of paying off our mortgage early.

We taped an amortization chart on the wall to show the progress each extra payment made. Raises, overtime, Christmas bonuses, and tax checks were all dumped on the principal as the years melted off our mortgage.

I began using coupons, mailing in rebates, packing lunches, and shopping at garage sales. We rarely ate out. Jeff and I agreed not to buy each other gifts. Jeff miraculously kept our junk vehicles running.

In four short years, despite skepticism of friends and family, we had paid off our $30,000 mortgage.

Some remodeling we did to the home increased its value from $48,000 to $62,000.

Just weeks after we paid off the house, we came across a home on nine acres that had been foreclosed on and was about to be sold at auction.

We immediately put our house on the market and it sold before the auction.

Never did we imagine we would be highest bidder at the auction with a $43,000 bid. The market value was almost twice that.

We were recently blessed with our fourth daughter, and look forward to many happy years on our "mini farm." We thank God for the opportunities he has made available to us.

Monica Stahlhut
Danville, Indiana

THREE INCOME TAX MYTHS

1. An income tax return is a good thing. Some people declare fewer allowances on their W-4 form, so that more money will get withheld so they will get a bigger tax refund. Part of the argument people use is they don't have the discipline to save on their own.

The problem with this is that the government gets the use of your money, interest-free. I know of one case where a couple's tax refund was delayed, and they didn't get their $1,500 until July. In this case some of the extra withheld money was in the possession of the IRS for 18 months.

2. It's foolish to earn more money because you'll be in a higher tax bracket. Some people think if they move up to a higher tax bracket all their income is taxed at the higher rate. Not so. If you are married filing jointly you pay 15% if your adjusted gross income is under $34,000. If your adjusted gross income is $35,000 only $1,000 gets taxed at the next higher rate of 28%. Earn to your heart's content.

3. You should not pay off your mortgage because you will lose your tax deduction.

The standard deduction for a couple is $5,700. In other words, you will take the standard deduction unless you have deductible expenses over $5,700. Aside from mortgage interest, itemized deductions include charitable gifts, medical and dental expenses, other taxes, moving expenses, losses from theft, etc.

Say your taxable income is under $34,000 and you are in the 15% bracket. You might think this means you could save 15% of your mortgage interest. But if your other deductions are below the $5,700 standard deduction, you only benefit from the 15% of the mortgage interest deduction that is above the $5,700.

And even then, you are still shelling out 85% of your mortgage interest. Conclusion: prepaying your mortgage principal remains one of the best "investment" strategies for the average homeowner.

If readers need last-minute tax advice, here are two sources:

1. Free tax clinics are held in many communities. Sponsored by the IRS, they are staffed by law school and graduate accounting students, who work under the direction of their professors. Call (202) 566-6352 for information.

2. If you want advice direct from the experts, call them at the IRS in Washington, D.C., at (800) 829-1040, or call your local IRS office.

ENVELOPE REUSE

Dear Amy,

I have a recycling method for business reply envelopes. Just insert table knife or other thin object, separate where it's glued, turn inside out, and reglue. To seal just lick the flap, tuck inside, and press down well.

John Etter
Hood River, Oregon

(John sent this idea in and it tickled me as the essence of tightwad ingenuity. I now look forward to junk mail

so I can reuse business reply envelopes. I have also used this idea to reuse 9" x 12" envelopes, closing with tape. FZ)

"I WAS A DISPOSABLE DIAPER MOM."

In the more than 20 years since the introduction of disposable diapers in the American scene they have become an unquestioned aspect of motherhood. However, researchers now believe that seven out of eight users suffer from "Disposable Diaper Parent Syndrome." The common symptoms include various types of distortion in perception. Users often have a mistaken sense of the amount of work involved in the cloth diapers (the archaic method) and an inability to grasp the cost both personally and to the community.

And is it a wonder? Our team of roving investigative reporters has uncovered a conspiracy by disposable diaper manufacturers to lure unsuspecting parents into their clutches. They provide large quantities of samples to new parents in hospitals. Coupons litter parenting magazines. Rebates and point systems further lure parents. Cloth diapers are promoted as unsanitary and are therefore against code in daycare centers.

Few parents have gone down the disposable diaper path and returned to tell their story. After an exhaustive search we have found one such parent. This former disposable diaper mom has granted an interview with *The Tightwad Gazette*. She has requested that her identity be concealed. She appears in silhouette and her voice has been electronically altered.

FZ: I would like to start by thanking you for agreeing to share your story with us. I appreciate how difficult this is for you to talk about. How long were you a disposable diaper user?

Ex—Disposable Diaper Mom: I used them for nearly three years.

FZ: Can you tell us how you first became involved with disposable diaper use?

XDDM: It was a combination of many things. Our washer was old and cranky and we did not have a dryer. I began working nights when our son was three months old, and my husband did not want to use cloth diapers. Later, when the baby was six months old I returned to daytime work. Most child care providers will only accept babies with disposables.

FZ: Do you recall how much you were spending on disposables every week?

XDDM: I spent a minimum of $10.50. The cheapest generic diaper is $8.47 a box. The infant size has 64. Most infants need to be changed 12 to 14 times a day, so I used more than one box a week.

FZ: And how much trash did the disposables generate?

XDDM: I filled a couple tall kitchen bags every week.

FZ: Wow! That much? But you can see why our nation spends over a billion dollars a year to landfill them. They make up a staggering 5% of our trash.

XDDM: Yes, that is why I switched . . . well, at first I switched to save money. When our twin girls were born I gave up daytime work. The cost of a toddler and two infants in day-care was prohibitive. At that point we also bought a new washer and dryer, so giving up disposables made sense. I couldn't see spending over $20 on disposables every week. Later I got to thinking about the environment . . . what I was passing on to my children. I hate using them now.

FZ: When you switched, how much did you spend on cloth diapers?

XDDM: I paid $6.00 to $9.50 a dozen for the prefolded Curity diapers. I bought eight dozen for the twins. So a mother with one baby would spend less than $50.

FZ: How long have the cloth diapers lasted?

XDDM: My girls are 18 months old now. Only two of the diapers have gone to the rag bag.

FZ: Since you are washing diapers for twins do you find this to create a lot of work?

XDDM: Hah! Mothers with one baby ask me this all the time. Actually, I don't feel it requires much more work than disposables.

FZ: I understand you have an unconventional method of cleaning your diapers.

XDDM: Yes, I soak them in the warm soapy water that comes out of my portable dishwasher. The way I see it any food particles in the water are basically the same as the material in the babies' diapers.

FZ: Dishwashing detergent is strong stuff. Doesn't it bother the babies?

XDDM: I am a nurse, as well as a mother of twins. If it caused a problem I wouldn't do it. I do add ¼ cup of vinegar to the wash to neutralize it. I wash them in Tide with bleach with cold water. I only run them through the washer's precycle. I have found it is not necessary to put them through the entire cycle.

FZ: My own method is also un-conventional. It is recommended that cloth diapers be soaked in a disinfectant like bleach, Borax, or Lysol. I just soak the soiled ones in plain water and rely on a hot water wash and dryer to help kill germs. I do this because my husband is sensitive to bleach and I am also sensitive to certain detergents. Each parent eventually settles on the method of least work that suits their child's tolerance. How frequently do you wash?

XDDM: I wash a load every day; however, I wash that often because our apartment is small and we don't have room for laundry to sit around. Other cloth diaper moms I know with one baby wash only once or twice a week. I usually don't get around to folding them before they are used again.

FZ: What misconceptions did you have about cloth diapers?

XDDM: I thought they would be smelly but they aren't any worse than a bag of used disposables. If you add a tablespoon of baking soda to the soaking water it also helps.

FZ: How about diaper rashes?

XDDM: Much less, especially in girls. Disposables used to give my girls yeast infections. I have heard other mothers say that disposables gave their babies severe sores and they had to switch.

FZ: One final question. As a nurse, can you think of any reason that cloth diapers are less sanitary in daycare centers?

XDDM: Well, with a cloth diaper you have more contact with handling something wet. Since you also wipe the baby off I can't see that it makes any difference. Also the manufacturer recommends that you rinse disposables. Read the box. At any rate you should wash your hands after every diaper change. Then the centers claim it is unsanitary to store them. But disposables sit around in a trash bag. Why can't a soiled diaper be returned to a plastic bag in the diaper bag for the mom to deal with?

FZ: Thank you for sharing your story with us.

XDDM: I wanted to do this. If, through hearing my story, I can prevent at least one other mom the suffering of Disposable Diaper Parent Syndrome it was worth doing.

A few final notes.

In the years since I have been a cloth diaper user I have had difficulty determining even a rough figure of the savings in cloth diapers because factors widely differ . . . how frequently parents change their babies, which brands they purchase, and if they use coupons and rebates. They appear to be packaged in a volume to last about a week, regardless of the size of the baby. Bigger babies are changed less but their diapers cost more.

One also has to subtract the energy and detergent with cloth diapers. Even at a dollar per load twice a week I come up with a savings of $7.00 per week ($8.47 plus tax and cost of garbage bags minus $2.00 for laundering) or $364 annually. If it is made known that an expectant mother plans to use cloth diapers, she will receive them as shower gifts, as I did. Therefore, the purchase cost need not be a factor.

To "earn" that $7 tax-free savings a cloth diaper user will expend less than one hour weekly. The $1,000 or more savings by the time each child is trained can become capital for reinvestment.

NO SHAME

Dear Amy,

What is most important, I realize after reading your first issue, is that I need not, cannot and will not be ashamed or apologetic about my change in lifestyle. I have chosen this for our family and my husband will go along. How else can we achieve our dream of an outstanding education for our daughter?

Karen Richards
Solon, Maine

PLANT YOUR BIRDHOUSE

If you are better at gardening than carpentry—and you are a bird lover—grow gourds to use as purple martin houses.

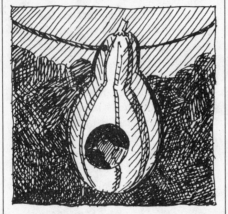

Grow large, round gourds that have short necks. Let them dry on the vine until midwinter. Pick, and cut a hole about 2 inches in diameter on one side. Let dry for another day, then sand the doorway's edges smooth. Clean the inside with a spoon. Drill holes in the bottom for drainage. Cut two more holes in the neck so that you can run a nylon cord through them.

Putting a teaspoon of sulfur in each birdhouse will help keep mites away and will not bother the birds. Sulfur can be purchased from Agway for $4.99 lb. Obviously, you would have to make a lot of birdhouses or have another use for the sulfur to make this purchase worthwhile.

Martins are colonial nesters, so in early spring, hang at least two or more gourd birdhouses at least one foot apart on wooden crosspieces fastened to a pole that is 12 to 20 feet high. The pole should be at least 40 feet away from trees or buildings, but not more than 90 feet from your home . . . martins like to be near human beings. Martins live in all states east of the Mississippi River and in several western states.

While writing this, I received the following information from reader M. Huckle of Tonganoxie, Kansas: to obtain a package of 15 to 20 gourd seeds, plus a 12-page book about growing and preparing gourds for purple martin houses, send $2 and a long SASE with two 29¢ stamps to: The Purple Martin Conservation Association, Edinboro University of Pennsylvania, Edinboro, PA 16444.

BUSINESS WEAR

Dear Amy,

In answer to a reader who requested ideas for saving on business clothes, I have a couple of suggestion. L'eggs and Hanes both sell "irregular" pantyhose through a catalog at about 60% less than discount stores. I have never found anything wrong with them.

She should be able to find beautiful, perfect designer suits, skirts, and tops for practically

nothing at secondhand or "consignment" stores. I frequented one store where I found several like-new Evan Picone women's suits for $20 each. My best buy was a beaded cashmere sweater for $10. The key is to find a store in a nice neighborhood that has the kind of clothes you like. Get friendly with the sales staff. They will call to let you know when something in your size has come in.

Katherine Kenward
Homewood, Illinois

SHEDDING LIGHT ON FLUORESCENTS

After I printed the address of a mail-order source for fluorescent bulbs in my newsletter, I received a few letters concerning their downside.

Common complaints about fluorescents include: they don't fit many residential light fixtures, they cost a lot, they don't give enough light, they don't provide instant light, and they "look funny." In fact, they are environmentally and economically sound. By understanding the limitations and the different options, most homeowners could find ways to use at least a few.

In researching this article I spoke with Owen Garner, an energy-lighting specialist from Conservation Lighting in Portland, Maine.

The average price for a quality fluorescent bulb is about $20. You should look for brands such as Osram, Sylvania, General Electric, Panasonic, or Philips.

Mr. Garner told me the bulbs sold by discount stores for about $8 are generally considered to be inferior. These bulbs do not last as long as they are supposed to, can cause radio and television interference, and light up slowly. When the quality $20-bulbs are sold for less by clubs, they probably have been donated for sale and can be sold cheaply.

Many on tight budgets will be hard pressed to fork over $20 for a single fluorescent bulb. But for every $20 investment you will save an average of $40 (and come out $20 ahead) in electricity and bulb replacements. Fluorescents used 2 hours per day will last for 7 to 10 years, and pay for themselves in 3 to 5 years.

The residential fluorescent industry is still in its infancy. For this reason, right now fluorescents are hard to find and have limited applications for home use.

Unless you know which bulbs you can use, purchasing bulbs in quantity through the mail is less than ideal. If possible, find a distributor who will show you the variety of options, and even lend you one to take home and try. This way you will learn how many and which bulbs you can use.

Each fluorescent is composed of a bulb (or lamp) and a ballast. The basic combinations include:
- All-in-one units (ballasts and bulbs are one piece).
- Screw-base adapters with replaceable bulbs.

(Separate ballast and bulbs. The replacement bulbs cost between $3 and $8.)

- Hard-wire conversions. (Ballasts are permanently wired into existing fixtures, allowing them to accommodate larger bulbs.)
- Fluorescent fixtures (permanent ceiling or wall fixtures specifically designed to accommodate fluorescents).
- Lamp conversion kits. (The kits have a ballast that plugs into the wall. A plug from a table or floor fixture plugs into that. The fluorescent fits into a small screw-in adapter in the socket.)

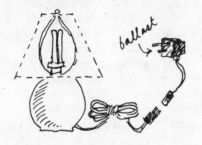

Compact fluorescents have two basic styles: either a twin tube (a design with two tubes) or a quad (a design with four tubes). Sometimes the tubes are encased in glass, making the bulb look like a large incandescent.

A 13-watt quad produces the same light as a 60-watt incandescent but has twice the length. It also has the bulky ballast near the bottom. These two factors make the lamps hard to use in many residential fixtures. To get more light you need an even longer bulb. They also take a few seconds to come on and a few minutes to give complete light.

The early compacts had the same bright cool light as industrial lighting. The newer soft white or daylight bulbs produce light that is very similar to an incandescent.

What about the "funny look"? It is true that fluorescents look different than incandescents. They look funny to us because we aren't accustomed to this bulb style. However, they are accepted in other parts of the world, where they have been used for some time.

Fluorescents do not work well in freezing temperatures, and cannot be used with dimmers.

Given all the limitations, fluorescent bulbs can be best used where instant or very bright light is not needed and the size or look of the bulb is not an issue. Because of the long payback time, look for uses where you have the greatest energy consumption, such as kitchens and hallways. For example, they work in a mounted ceiling fixture when the globe is at least 9 inches in diameter. If the fixture will accommodate two bulbs you can get ample light.

Fluorescents do not produce heat, so they will cut the energy consumed by air-conditioning (although incandescents help heat in the winter).

By far the most appealing aspect of the fluorescent is its positive environmental impact. Depending on the method of energy production in your part of the country, a single fluorescent bulb over the course of its life can prevent as much as 1,000 pounds of carbon dioxide and 20 pounds of sulfur dioxide from being released into the atmosphere.

After learning more we decided that we could use fluorescents in our home. We have a lamp conversion kit that will work with our living-room floor lamp. We can use two quads in our kitchen fixture. We are using one in our bathroom ceiling light, which we leave on for a night light. We can also use them in our office, where aesthetics are less important.

If you can't find a local source for fluorescents you can mail order them from Seventh Generation. They'll sell just one. Including shipping, you can get a 15-watt quad for just over $20. Call: (800) 456-1197.

SHELL MAGNETS

Dear Amy,

I went on the theory "spend to save" and purchased a hot-glue gun and have started making gifts. People love my wreaths, but the best gifts are my seashell magnets.

I purchase the shells at a local craft store. The average price is 35¢ for the unique ones. A package of six small magnets costs under $1.

Take the shell and, using the hot-glue gun, place a small amount of glue on the shell and then place the magnet on the glue. Hold the magnet for a few seconds until it sticks completely to the shell. The whole process takes only seconds to make and the cost for a beautiful gift is minimal.

Judy McAtee
Dallas, Texas

RECYCLED GROUNDS

Dear Amy,

Recycle your coffee grounds by making the first pot of coffee the usual way. Then to make the sec-ond pot add only ½ the amount of grounds already in the filter. This allows me to have two pots of coffee at 1½ the amount of grounds. This has worked for me in all types of coffee pots.**

Eileen Wells
Knoxville, Tennessee

SENIOR RESOURCES

If you are a senior citizen you have a wide range of discounts available from restaurants, schools, banks, clubs, etc. You should routinely ask for senior citizen discounts. The answer might be no, but it doesn't hurt to ask. Most of the time the answer will be yes.

In addition to these discounts you should investigate the benefits of organizations and services specifically for senior citizens. Here are only a few:

The American Association of Retired Persons
601 E St. NW
Washington, DC 20049

This has to be the best deal around for folks over 50. For a $5 annual membership fee you can get a variety of services.

The membership includes an annual subscription (6 issues) to *Modern Maturity*. The magazine features articles such as financial planning, retirement living, and travel. You also receive a bimonthly bulletin to keep you up-to-date on legislation that affects retired persons and contains information on AARP activities. They also offer a wide selection of information guides on a variety of topics.

In addition, the AARP offers the following services:

- The pharmacy service has wholesale prices on prescription drugs, over-the-counter drugs, and medical supplies. Members mail in their prescription. It takes 8 to 10 days to receive the prescription. Their prices may not always beat your local pharmacy, so compare.
- Group travel programs are reasonably priced.
- The Automobile and Home-owners Insurance Program (from Hartford) is considered by some to be the best and most economical available.
- Their motoring plan offers low-cost road service from Amoco. This includes nationwide road service, free maps, and trip routing. They also offer sizable discounts for some major hotels and rental cars.
- The Crime Prevention Program helps seniors protect themselves from crime.
- The Consumer Affairs Program educates seniors about consumer goods and services.
- Income Tax Preparation Assistance is done by IRS trained volunteers.
- The Widowed Persons Service offers counseling.
- The Medicare Assistance Program helps seniors fill out Medicare forms and assists with related problems.

- The Driver Refresher Course could help you get a discount on your auto insurance.

The AARP has more than 32 million members and 4,000 chapters.

The National Council for Senior
  Citizens
1331 F St. NW
Washington, DC 20004-1171

This organization offers many similar services to the AARP. Their annual membership fee is $12 and they have a monthly newspaper for seniors.

The Golden Age Passport. If you are 62 or older and going to a federally operated national park, monument, historic site, wildlife refuge, or recreation area you can get in free with proof of age. This benefit extends to all persons traveling in the car with you.

Meals-on-Wheels. Good nutrition is your best strategy to combat rising medical costs. If you are having difficulty preparing meals, call your local Area Agency on Aging for information and to learn if you qualify.

Personal Emergency Response System. This is a small wireless alert system that must be kept in reach at all times. In emergencies the hospital or other help is alerted. Private companies charge a lot, but sometimes the service is offered as low as $15 by nonprofit organizations. Contact your Area Agency on Aging for more information.

In the front of most phone books there is a section for seniors that lists local resources. And don't forget to check with nearby colleges. Some offer free tuition for seniors.

TEENAGERS ARE SO EXPENSIVE NOWADAYS

MY TEENAGER PLAN

One reporter wrote a generally favorable article, except he seemed to express some cynicism that I would not be able to pull off tightwad parenting in 10 years or so, when I would have a handful of teenagers to deal with.

Guess what? I have a teenager plan currently being implemented.

I have heard the legends concerning the amazing amount of food they can consume. If their only option is the less expensive healthier foods this problem can be curtailed somewhat. Chips, soda, and cookies are expensive. Garden produce, potatoes, and oatmeal are not. The teenage metabolism speeds at a phenomenal pace. Allowing unlimited consumption of snack foods is like trying to fill a bottomless pit. The more you feed the metabolism the faster it goes. Therefore, limiting their options to cheaper, healthier (and less tempting) foods will help in cutting the expense.

The cost of food consumption is secondary to the teenager's lust for consumer goods, much of which results from peer pressure. We have taken a giant step to avoid peer pressure by moving to a rural area with few close neighbors. The pressures here are less than in an affluent community.

So far the "peer pressure monster" has only reared its ugly head when the kids take something for lunch and a classmate expresses a dislike for that item (such as pumpkin pudding or homemade dill pickles). I have given my best "march to your own drummer" speeches, but I still can't put pudding and pickles in their lunch boxes. Still, I have not given in to the expensive lunch box items that other children bring.

Dealing with their "externally generated desires" is different from their internal ones. In other words, sometimes their wants are not a result of peer pressure or commercials. Sometimes we are in a store and they see something they desperately want. I deal with this by asking, "Where is your money?" Usually they have none.

In our home any kid can do a job for a quarter at any time. Usually this is a 10-minute job. They do not get an allowance. By doing this they never get the idea that it is the duty of their parents to buy them more than the basics of food and clothing.

We start this policy as the kids reach the age of five or so. Although we are not within striking distance of businesses where they might get jobs when they are older, we will always have a long list of tasks for them around here. Even if the money eventually goes for something that I consider to be worthless, in exchange I get the value of having them understand money.

Current child psychologist wisdom says that children should do household tasks for no pay and also get an allowance so that they can learn how to handle money.

But if the money is not tied to a specific task, they miss the most important concept behind it. One must trade effort to acquire money.

Our children do tasks for no money on a daily basis. But I think it is important that they understand that a $5 plastic toy is equal to 20 jobs. They need a gauge to determine the value of money.

Surprisingly often, children are not willing to trade the effort to get the $5. They decide the hunk of plastic isn't worth the 20 jobs. And even though my first grader has money in his treasure box he is not willing to spend it on the more glamorous school lunches.

If your teenager wants the $75 sneakers and you want to buy the $15 pair, offer to chip in your $15 if he'll come up with the other $60.

Right about now all you parents of teens are laughing yourselves silly. I am aware that I am not going to be able to pull this off without rough moments. I don't imagine it will work perfectly. But my ideas are not untried theory. It is basically the same method my parents used.

Look for my teenager plan update in about 10 years.

GOOD GADGETS

THE WATER HEATER TIMER

These cost between $30 and $75. The cost difference reflects amperage capacity. Some are also digital. With an amperage of 4800 (about average) we bought a timer at the lower end of the price range on sale for $20. The installation requires a short length of wire and an hour's worth of time by someone handy. We have set ours to go on between 4:00 to 9:00 A.M. and 4:00 to 9:00 P.M. We haven't noticed any inconvenience. Friends who have installed them report a monthly savings on the electric bill of $10 to $15.

THE BATTERY RECHARGER

Is there anyone who doesn't have one of these yet? The cost runs between $11 and $20. The manufacturer claims rechargeable batteries equal between 65 to 150 regular batteries, depending on the size of the battery. Recharging takes 2 to 6 hours. Based on our own unscientific observation the charge seems to last about half the time as a disposable.

Rechargeables cost roughly 150% to 300% more than disposables. This initial investment deters many people, although the long-term savings are clearly substantial. The cost of the recharger and a pair of D rechargeables equals the cost of about eight pairs of disposable D batteries.

Keep separate containers for "dead" and recharged batteries near your recharger. The batteries need to be recharged in pairs, so recharge as soon as you have enough.

THE FUZZ AWAY

Remington manufacturers this gadget, which resembles an electric shaver. We broke down and bought one when the cost dropped to $7. It removes the "pills" especially common to synthetic fabrics. Used in combination with my stain recipe, many a yard sale find has regained respectability.

"SPUDGATE" OR THE GREAT POTATO CONSPIRACY

An eternal mission of *The Tightwad Gazette* is to single-handedly wipe out the convenience food industry. In accordance with this we continue our series of investigative reports exposing the practice of the food industry to make inexpensive and healthful foods more expensive and less nutritious.

The focus of this article is the potato. Infinitely versatile, this humble food is completely natural, good-tasting and loaded with fiber.

The potato can lay claim to being the perfect tightwad food, because it is also very inexpensive. Depending on the season, area of the country, and type of potato a 10-pound bag of potatoes can be purchased for around $2.29, or 23¢ per pound. We buy

50-pound sacks for $3.90 each, or 8¢ a pound. A large potato the size and shape of a squashed baseball weighs about 8 ounces.

I sent Jim on a fact-finding mission to a large chain supermarket. Cleverly disguised, the potato spy posed as a regular guy just getting off work. His tools of espionage included state-of-the-art pen and pad of paper. (He felt his bow tie camera might be too conspicuous.) Other than arousing the suspicions of a clerk stocking shelves, Jim's activity went unnoticed. He obtained prices for instant potatoes, potato chips, potato sticks, and frozen fries.

Acting on his own initiative Jim also made note of the high sodium content of these products.

An element of the conspiracy is the deceptive "standard serving size" on the nutrition panel. This is common to cold cereals and other convenience foods also. Many of the potato products list 3 ounces as a serving size. A 3-ounce potato is a tad larger than a squashed golf ball.

For purposes of comparison we will assume a 5-ounce potato (squashed tennis ball size) equals the suggested 3 to 3½ ounces of the frozen potato products, to account for any possible dehydration. We are also assuming the ½-cup serving size of mashed potato equals our 5-ounce potato.

Many of the potato products, such as au gratin mixes, contain elements other than pure potato —preservatives, salt, milk, or cheese, etc. Some are more expensive and some are less, but you have to add your own milk and butter. One prepared serving size does equal 5 ounces. We are giving the food industry the benefit of the doubt and call it equal.

Undoubtedly some will argue that it is unfair to compare potato chips and sticks to potatoes, since they are really a snack food (entertainment). Within the tight-wad frame of reference, grocery shopping means expending money for nutrition. Besides it makes for more interesting reading.

To compare the chips we calculated how many $\frac{1}{16}$-inch slices we could get from a 5-ounce potato and compared it to the weight of an equal number of chips. Potato slices get thinner as they are made into chips.

A plain uncompromised 5-ounce potato, purchased in a 1-pound sack costs about 7¢. The chart below indicates what this potato would cost after the convenience-food industry repackages it into the potato products we've researched.

We do use instant mashed potatoes in a pinch, because they are inexpensive. However, they lack the fiber of the real thing.

Oven-Fried Potatoes
A SUPERIOR ALTERNATIVE

Wash, but do not peel, one potato per person. Slice into $\frac{1}{4}$-inch slices and soak in cold water for at least 20 minutes.

Melt four tablespoons of margarine on a cookie sheet. Drain potatoes and pat dry. Place potatoes on cookie sheet in a single layer, coating both sides with margarine. Salt and pepper to taste.

Place in a 425° oven and bake 20 minutes (or until lightly browned) on each side.

Save the surplus margarine on the cookie sheet for other uses. To save energy, prepare this when you are using your oven to cook something else for dinner.

Product	Cost
Bulk Potato	2.5¢
Store Brand Mashed	6¢
Sack Potato	6.7¢
Betty Crocker Mashed	8¢
Crinkle Cut Fries	11¢
Taters	13¢
Alphabet Fries	15¢
Store Brand Fries	18¢
Betty Crocker Au Gratin	19¢
Store Brand Chips	20¢
Tom's Chips	27¢
Durkee Potato Sticks	30¢
Ruffles Chips	32¢

THRIFT SHOP THOUGHTS

1. There are four basic sources of used clothes:

a. Someone gives them to you. The selection is limited but the price is right. Always express thanks and keep what you can use.

b. Garage sales. These are the cheapest places where you can *buy* clothes—usually about half the price of thrift shops.

c. Thrift shops. They charge more for clothes, but they have a greater selection. Ask about specials. Some charge half price on colored-tag days. I have seen slacks as high as $5, but would plan to return if I knew the item would be half price another day.

d. Consignment shops. They offer the greatest selection, but the highest price. Items might be priced twice as high as a thrift shop. At $8 for a pair of kids' pants, one might do as well shopping sales at retail stores. However, consignment stores are a great source for adult business clothes. If you develop a relationship with the owner, he or she might help you find specific items.

2. Change your method of shopping. If you're used to retail you expect to find clothes in your size and your color wherever you shop. If you bring that attitude into the thrift shop you will be disappointed.

Instead of thinking about what a shop doesn't have, look at what it does have. You might really be looking for slacks but instead find a great blouse you can use.

3. Develop a notebook for your needs, especially if you are shopping for a large family. Record sizes and measurements for each family member. More than sizes, measurements are important because used clothing may no longer have the tag indicating size. If, for instance, you have a pants size, also write in the measurement of the waist and length of the inseam. Armed with a measuring tape and a notebook you won't need to bring along your child to try on clothes.

If shopping for an adult, you might also want to include color chips for clothes you hope to match. I have heard of someone who gets paint chips from a hardware store for this purpose. This practice falls into the "fuzzy-ethical" area for me. Instead I would suggest cutting a small square from the pages of a Sears catalog. If the match with the original garment isn't perfect indicate "lighter" or "darker."

4. Examine all clothing carefully for defects. Don't be put off by flaws. If an item is cheap enough it might be worthwhile to restitch a seam.

5. Don't be discouraged by poor-quality clothing you find. Look to the positive side. If something made it to the thrift shop and still looks respectable, it is likely to be a garment that will hold up well. New clothing is a greater gamble. Who hasn't had a new garment hopelessly pill, shrink, or fall apart after two or three washings? Even if a used item doesn't hold up, at least you didn't pay full price.

6. When you look at a used item, think of it as a new thing that's been washed 10 times. My

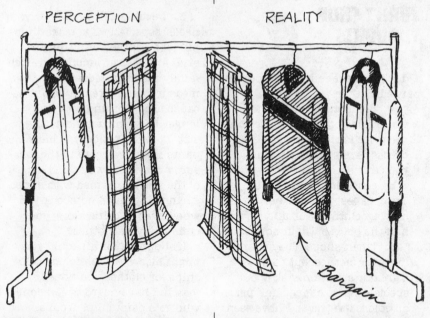

PERCEPTION   REALITY

Bargain

kids have had new clothes given to them. I would challenge anyone to go through their closets and pick out what they received new and what they received used.

7. Many of the same rules apply to used-clothing purchases as new: Buy classic styles. Know what colors and styles look good on you. Learn the signs of quality clothes. Learn which brand names hold up well.

8. When buying for kids, buy a few years in advance, and develop a storage system. It's unlikely that you will find everything you would need at one yard sale.

9. Know that there might be some things you won't find at a thrift shop. We've never been able to find tall men's shirts for Jim at thrift shops. We buy used clothing whenever we can, and expect to fill in around the edges with new stuff.

10. If you're trying to find things for a picky teenager, try to tune in to the subtleties of current trends. Hopefully you have

successfully educated them since they were young. If not, you are going to have to make a case for the change.

There's good used stuff out there, and it ain't all plaid, polyester bell-bottomed pants and shirts with pointy collars.

THE (NOT SO) COMPLETE GUIDE TO TRASH PICKING

I do not have a lengthy and colorful career as a trash picker as some experts who have devoted decades to this calling. In fact prior to a year and a half ago my background was rather skimpy and I can recall only a few times that I gave in to the lure of the interesting-looking trash pile.

Fifteen years ago I lived in the Boston area. I strolled in the vicinity of the gates of Harvard University with a visiting aunt. She had been a veteran city dweller of a more bohemian era. We passed a pile of what appeared to be discarded building materials from a remodeling project. My eyes strayed to a pair of old decorative iron shelf brackets still attached to a worthless chunk of board. My aunt, noting my hesitation, said "You want that? I'll get it for you." And she did. It was my first inkling that this sort of scavenging could be OK.

I don't recall committing the act again until a few years ago. At the time, Jim and I were living in a suburban area near Norfolk, Virginia. Our neighbor had spent the day cleaning out her garage and sheds, creating a huge pile in front of her house. It appeared to be the first time she had done so in recent decades. Pleased with her accomplishment she treated herself to a dinner out. Jim and I took note of her departure and decided that it was time to take our evening walk. It was a short one. We came home with a cooler, a few toys, two dozen canning jars, and our long-lost basketball.

Shortly thereafter Jim received choice orders to the Brunswick Naval Air Station, and we were lucky enough to get a government house while we looked for a home to buy. One evening as I read the Brunswick paper I came upon a remarkable ad for the "Spring Cleaning Season." (In other words, sanctioned trash picking).

Every year many towns in Maine, as well as a few other parts of the country, offer a week or two when residents can put out good, repairable, or very large items. These are left on the curb for about a week so that others might pick items they may have a use for. This effort helps to alleviate the problem of overburdened landfills. Additionally, when items are reused fewer goods are produced to replace that which is thrown away. World resources are conserved and less pollution results.

Naturally, I felt an obligation to do my part for the environment.

On opening day, as I revved the car engine in the driveway, Jim came out and pointed to our half-filled garage. We had moved from a larger home to a smaller one, and many things had never been unpacked. He cautioned me about getting too carried away. (Having known me for half a dozen years I am sure he understood the futility of his request.)

The Brunswick season got off to a dismal start. The first day I came home with only a small suitcase. But every few days I went out again and I sensed a building momentum. In the beginning I heeded my husband's words and brought home only very useful items. But my increasing success softened his stance. I began to bring home broken items that appeared to be repairable and discovered Jim possessed a wonderful ability to fix almost anything. Later I would scavenge more challenging projects for him. Little was thrown out again.

When the Brunswick season overlapped with the Bath season, a neighboring town, Jim was fully converted. Unlike Brunswick,

Bath's season started with a bang. You had to be out there the first weekend to get the good stuff. Jim came along for the first time. On the return trip our fully loaded Suburban resembled the Beverly Hillbillies on the move.

Aside from picking up enough items to jam our garage to capacity I learned a great deal.

We felt it a bit odd to hear our preschool cherubs exclaim "Yeah! We're going trash picking today." We quickly learned to substitute the more acceptable term "treasure hunting."

"When in doubt, throw it in" became our motto. If we were unsure we took it anyway. Later if we decided not to keep the item putting it out in our trash was a simple matter. On one occasion we came across a large oriental rug neatly folded in a trash bag. Rather than inspecting it on the spot to see if it had any salvageable parts we took it home. At home we spread it on the lawn to discover it was completely useless. We folded it up, put it back in the bag, and set it on the curb. Twenty minutes later a pickup stopped. A man got out, looked briefly at the rug, and then threw it in the back of the truck before speeding away. I wondered how many times that rug would hopscotch around town.

There was a great variety of types of people involved in picking up items. There were poor families driving 15-year-old beaters and yuppies in Volvos.

As the people varied, so did the items they collected. One man told us he only collected old motors. Another man had a buyer for any complete bicycles and lawn mowers. I saw an ancient Jeep so fully loaded inside and on top with small pieces of scrap wood that the passenger had to ride on the running board clinging for dear life. We collected a little of everything for a future yard sale.

Trash varies from town to town, neighborhood to neighborhood. The spring cleaning season in a community with older homes is more likely to yield antiques whereas a suburban community with ranches is more likely to throw out items for children. As a general rule affluent communities have the best trash.

We learned that if we found an incomplete item to pick it up, because another pile may yield the thing needed to make it complete. We brought home an excellent bicycle for our son needing only a new seat. The following day I went out with a wrench and stripped a good seat from a hopelessly rusted bicycle. A Fisher-Price record player without records was matched with records from another source. An old bureau was matched with a can of enamel paint from a separate pile.

We learned that a tremendous amount is discarded because people lack the imagination to envision what something could be—that many items are thrown out for want of a screw.

Our lives would be forever altered by this period of spring cleaning seasons. Since then yard sales and thrift shops pale by comparison. My concept of fun took on a whole new dimension. And a few friends questioned their relationships with us.

We had our yard sale—two actually. Between them we sold a total of $200 worth of things we had picked up on a curb. We also kept a large percentage and are still using them.

If there are no communities in your area that hold this type of event, try to initiate one. Trash picking at the dump is usually outlawed. If you are there and see something of interest, speak with the dump custodian. I know of one individual who actually sneaks into the dump off-hours. He feels a need to respond to a higher moral cause. I have heard a prime trash-picking opportunity occurs in June. The Dumpsters behind the dormitories of affluent colleges hold wonderful finds. Dumpsters behind many businesses and factories offer year-round opportunities.

In many communities trash picking is illegal. If you feel strongly about maintaining your status as a law-abiding citizen, but spot an irresistible treasure in your neighbor's trash, it might be appropriate to knock on their door and ask to take it. You should also do this if you have any question that something was really meant to be thrown away. Children may accidentally leave sleds and bicycles near their families' trash cans.

Another method of trash picking to investigate is the free-for-the-taking pile that some dumps offer.

The most appropriate conclusion for this article is a partial listing of the items we brought home: a bucket of mixed nails, 3 working radio-control cars, 30 partly full quarts of paint, 2 tricycles, 3 floor lamps including 2 of 1920s vintage, 2 director's chairs, books, over 100 canning jars, 3 rolls of Christmas wrap, an an-tique ceramic crock, lumber, an antique bottomless egg box (sold as is for $5), a large rocker, plant stands, an ironing board, a fireplace screen, an antique school desk, an antique iron bed frame, a Rubbermaid trash barrel, a mirror from an old bureau (now providing ambiance in our attic), a doll's wooden high chair, a doll stroller, an applesauce mill, a broken brass bed with pieces missing (sold as is for $20), a wagon, flower pots, kitchen utensils and the complete works of Engelbert Humperdink, which we gave away free with every purchase at the yard sale.

CURBSIDE GLEANING

Dear Amy,

I am forever grateful to you for legitimizing "treasure hunting." I had never done it before. This year we were pressed for time, so I only devoted 6 total hours to the pursuit, all in Bath. We got:

- **A perfectly good barbeque minus the grill**
- **A grill that miraculously fit into the barbecue**
- **A nice bike minus the wheel**
- **A nice wheel minus the bike: the result a nice bike for our son**
- **A push mower that works perfectly, just the thing for our tiny lawn**
- **A sled in perfectly good condition**
- **15 canning jars**
- **A plastic sandbox shaped like a turtle, ugly but sturdy**
- **Men's downhill ski boots, German made, perfect condition**
- **Downhill skis**

A lovely art deco bread box
A terrific sturdy high chair

And we were hardly trying! I would add one piece of advice to your article. Many people treasure hunt primarily by scanning the piles from within their cars. The best way to find the good stuff is to park in the middle of the block, stroll around on foot and dig around in the piles to find what others missed.

By far the most common large item left out during pickup days are old water heaters. Do any readers have ideas about how to use these?

Brad Lemley
Bath, Maine

MAILBOX REVENGE

A small percentage of dim-witted rural teenagers play a sport called "mailbox baseball." The proper rules require a baseball bat, a vehicle, a driver and at least one passenger, a moonless night, and a country road lined with mailboxes.

The object is for the passenger to lean from the moving car and whack the boxes into scrap metal. A similar game involves tossing small explosives known as cherry bombs into the boxes to achieve the same effect.

Mailbox baseball provides considerable entertainment for the teenagers for some curious

reason. And it causes frustration and expense for the persistently harassed mailbox owners. Even the most diligent can't pound the damaged box back into some usable form more than a couple of times.

Corporate America is attempting to cash in by providing mailbox baseball defense systems. A recent ad depicted a bat-proof, bomb-proof mailbox made from space-age plastic that cost over $200.

Word of an ingenious (and less expensive) solution has reached the office of *The Tightwad Gazette.*

Buy a large mailbox and a standard sized mailbox (or reuse your damaged one). Remove the door from the smaller one. Set the large box on end and place the smaller one inside. Fill the cavity between the two boxes with concrete. Once dried, the very heavy mailbox must be bolted to a heavyweight post.

The originator of this solution has reported finding bits of splintered bats in the immediate vicinity of his box.

A large mailbox and a small amount of cement costs under $25, roughly the cost of one Louisville slugger.

No monetary amount can be placed on successful revenge.

A PIRATE BIRTHDAY

The creation of a great but inexpensive birthday party depends on the use of materials and resources readily available. You must be prepared to abandon ideas that do not work or cost too much money. Often the best ideas result from finding yourself backed into a creative corner.

The fall our oldest turned seven we created a party that differed from earlier ones as it relied more heavily on Jim's abilities than mine.

The Theme: Our property, with all its interesting places, provided the perfect setting for a treasure hunt. Months in advance I planted the idea of a pirate party in Alec's head.

The Cake Design: I combined two flat sheet cakes to make one large flat one. I decorated it in off-white and brown frosting to look like a pirate treasure map. (This idea utilized my special ability to bake flat cakes resulting from poor rising.)

The Party Hats: In a precedent-setting move I did not provide some sort of hat or face paint for the guests. I was unable to find large sheets of inexpensive

black paper. The solution to spray paint newspaper hats black fizzled when I discovered all of our cans of black paint were empty. Rather than spending money I abandoned the idea altogether.

The Party Decorations: This is the better idea that came to me after finding myself backed into a creative corner. For earlier parties I had always made some type of paper decorations for the living room. The pirate theme stumped me for weeks. I presented my last-ditch idea to Jim, asking if he could build a pirate ship in the

Sails of old white sheets

Paper pirate flag, actually went up and down

Desk ornament cannon

Alec's telescope

Broken pitchfork with remaining tine stuck in hole of floor

Removable sides of utility trailer lashed together

Masts secured to loft above

Ropes for rigging cleverly used so that none were cut up

Ship's wheel made from wooden barrel top and scrap wood

Barrels and crates for seating, tables and ambiance

Scrounged tug-of-war rope

"No Hunting" signs

large open area of our barn from items we already had.

The morning of the party Jim went to work demonstrating that his wife was not the only parent with a creative knack. (See previous page.) The ship provided entertainment and a place to eat cake and ice cream.

The Activity: The treasure hunt. Jim scrounged a small wooden crate and added rope handles, hinges, a hasp, and a padlock (previously scrounged). I designed the treasure hunt consisting of pictorial clues on small hidden pieces of paper for the children to follow.

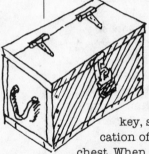

The clues led to a treasure map (drawn on a large sheet of brown wrapping paper), which showed where to find the key, shovel, and the location of the treasure chest. When the children were diverted on the other side of the house Jim threw a cardboard *X* on the site of the buried treasure.

The treasure box with padlock doubled as a birthday present for Alec.

The Take-Home Gift: The treasure box contained 300 chocolate gold coins. The pirate guests split the loot and took home their share in (brand new) Ziploc bags.

The Bottom Line: Alec's party cost under $10. We spent $6 on the coins and the remainder on ice cream, store brand soda, and confectionery sugar. On other occasions I have put together birthdays for under $25, including presents.

PLAY DOUGH

3 cups flour
1½ cups salt
6 tsp cream of tartar
3 cups cool water
3 Tbsp oil
food coloring

Mix dry ingredients together in a big cooking pot. Blend all liquids together in a bowl. Combine with dry ingredients and cook over medium heat, stirring constantly. Remove from heat when dough pulls away from the sides of the pot and can be pinched without sticking (about 5 minutes). Turn onto board or counter and knead until smooth and play dough consistency. Store in airtight container.

Note: The recipe suggests that you do not make double batches. The only reason I can see is that it is very hard to stir near the end of the cooking.

You can add food coloring with the liquid ingredients or carefully add while kneading. Supermarket food coloring works well although it produces uninteresting colors. Professional decorating pastes usually used for cake decorating produce a wider range and more intense color. I usually have an ample supply and have made colors such as hot pinks, deep purples, etc. I also made a camouflage blob as a joke.

Cream of tartar is significantly cheaper when bought in bulk rather than in supermarket-sized containers. Health food stores or food co-ops carry herbs and spices in bulk, such as our local source, Meyers Country Cupboard in Greene, Maine.

This play dough will keep well as long as a year. Occasionally I have made a batch that gets sticky after stored for a while. Maybe I didn't cook it long enough. If a little flour is kneaded in it will return to the original consistency.

If you plan to give these away as a gift (ages 3 to 10) find a nice recycled container and make a custom label with the child's name. If you aren't artistic, mimic a "punk" design.

New converts to tightwaddery write to me asking what they are supposed to do with all this stuff they've just started saving. After all, don't all self-respecting tightwads have an impressive stash of either egg cartons, styrofoam meat trays, toilet paper tubes, or frozen juice lids? My personal impressive stash currently includes 31 egg cartons. (The "Egg Carton Princess Crown" has long since lost its appeal.)

However, it's easy to get the basics of hoarding turned around. We don't save things for the purpose of throwing away less. We save things so that we *buy* less.

Christmas tree ornaments are the most common reuse for the frozen juice lid. Use a hammer and nail to pound a simple design and hang them with a ribbon. This is a better idea than buying more ornaments, but if you already have plenty, why bother?

Some parents like to glue magnets to the lid, put a picture of their child on the front, and put the lid on the front of the refrigerator. I don't like anything stuck to the front of my refrigerator so my inclination would be to throw the thing away before making a magnetized picture frame.

Kindergarten teachers have mastered the art of reuse, creating craft projects out of all sorts of things that are commonly thrown away. It's not that they can't bear to see stuff going to the landfill, but rather by doing so they need to purchase fewer craft materials, thereby stretching a limited budget. (Crafts for kids comprise the bulk of ways to reuse just about anything.)

If you do acquire an impressive stash, develop the habit of looking to it first for a solution. Say you have a table or appliance that is a bit wobbly due to uneven legs. Two or three stacked lids may solve the problem.

People who have limited space have to be selective hoarders, saving only the things they *know* they can reuse, or saving smaller stashes. Ask yourself, "Supposing I were to come up with an extraordinary reuse for the frozen juice lid. How many could I possibly need?" If the answer is 20 juice lids, then only save 20, and throw away the rest with reckless abandon.

THOSE PESKY JUICE LIDS . . .

When I launched a nationwide search for ways to reuse frozen juice lids, ideas poured in from all states of the union (give or take 25). We sorted through the mountain of unparalleled brilliance and have selected the most ingenious ones:

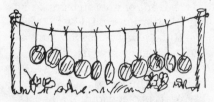

Garden Wind Chimes. Hang lids from a line close enough to clink together . . . to scare away birds. (Linda Sherman, Unadilla, New York)

Reflectors. Use to mark your mailbox or the end of the driveway where there is no streetlight. (Teresa Totaro, Powantan, Virginia)

The Flower Pot Aid. Punch holes and put one in the bottom of a flower pot to keep pebbles in. As it rusts the iron nourishes the plant. (Florence Meitzler, Kresgeville, Pennsylvania)

Coasters. Cover the bottom with felt. Spray paint or decorate if desired. (Judith Kopchak, Murfreesboro, Tennessee)

The Concentration Game. Glue stickers or pictures on lids . . . two of each type. Mix them up and put them on the table facedown. The children take turns finding matches. Mismatched pairs are turned over again and matches are kept until the end of the game. The child with the most matched pairs wins. (Dorothea Howard, Prairie Farm, Wisconsin)

Noisemakers. Nail 2 or 3 lids to a stick of wood, loose enough so that the lids rattle. (Louise Fernandes, Brookline, Massachusetts)

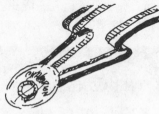

Medals of Achievement. Glue to ribbon to tie around the neck. To make them look more official add gold seal stickers, colored stars, and their name with small letter stickers. (Myra Koch, Merced, California)

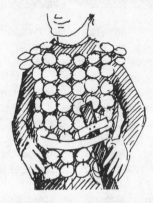

Suits of Armor. Poke holes near the edges and tie together. Start saving now for next Halloween's space warrior costume. (Barbara Winans, Dixon, California)

Toddler Entertainment. Give a stack to a toddler in a highchair. He tosses and giggles. Mom and Dad enjoy relative peace at dinnertime. (Tammy Naquin, Westwego, Louisiana)

When you're done with your lids, take them to the recycling center.

BUDGET WEDDINGS

Undoubtedly the cheapest way to get married is to see a justice of the peace and forgo the stop at Burger King on the way home. By comparison I have attended a wedding rumored to cost about $40,000. This lavish production lasted until 1:00 A.M., about five hours after the guests had suffered beyond their limit.

The vast territory in between would suffice for approximately 99% of the human race.

Weddings are one of the few experiences I feel justify financial investment. The objective is not to spend as little as possible or enough to impress royalty. Rather it is to spend enough to satisfy your reasonable expectations while not going into debt.

The traditional wedding leaves little room for creative budget slashing and fails to reflect changing demographics. Older established singles or couples marrying for the second time comprise a large percentage of today's knot-tiers. Often they pay the bills themselves. Standard wedding gifts of toasters and silver trays do not make sense. These couples already have household items or have formed strong ideas about the things they like.

Therefore my first budget wedding idea is:

The Contribution Wedding Gift: When my uncle married, a friend donated the use of a vintage 1920s Packard for transportation. A relative made a professional cake. I contributed a wedding invitation. Friends played music at the wedding and during the reception.

In other weddings I have attended, linens and silver serving pieces were loaned, centerpieces were made of winter greens, a grandmother's dress was altered.

Establishing this atmosphere of helpfulness depends largely on who will attend your wedding. If people know you plan to pay for this with your own limited funds, they will rise to the occasion.

Along with the contribution wedding gift consider:

The Potluck Reception: Before you gasp at this "tacky" suggestion let me make a case. Budget-catered meals tend to be very poor. Even the better ones offer only two predictable choices and rarely justify the cost. Conversely, wouldn't your guests prefer the opportunity to bring a covered dish that costs a few dollars to prepare rather than a $25 wedding gift?

I have seen four weddings with potluck receptions, including my own. My Yankee/Scotch family took it in stride. I suspect some of Jim's Ukrainian/Polish family politely masked their horror. In each of the four receptions the spread of food was diversified, interesting, and appealing and even superseded the catered meal at the $40,000 wedding.

Potluck, in this case, does not have to mean tuna casserole or

Jell-O in Tupperware. Guests will naturally bring their specialty. Some items may be transferred to more elegant (borrowed) serving dishes for a formal look, if needed.

Organizing who brings what will prove to be the largest obstacle. Solve this by including a note on the RSVP card saying: "We are planning a potluck reception. If you would like to bring a contribution as your wedding gift, please specify." Include a place for them to write in something. Also include a blank next to "I will call for a suggestion." Provide your phone number.

Other Receptions: Summer outdoor receptions, such as at your home or your parents' home, offer a cost-free location. Since they are not as formal, less expensive alternatives, such as paper plates versus rented plates, become acceptable.

Most churches have a hall with adjacent kitchen stocked with dishes and utensils. The women's group might also do the catering, serving, or clean-up for a modest fee. This option generally does not allow for dancing and alcohol.

In some parts of the country wedding receptions take the form of a tea or a hoedown. A sit-down meal is not necessary.

The Attire: Often bridal shops have display or discontinued dresses for as little as $100. This costs less than sewing your own or renting. Check classifieds for

women selling their dresses, which have been worn only one time or not at all. (After the wedding recoup the cost by reselling.) Have your mother's or grandmother's dress altered.

For any member of the bridal party, strongly consider attire that can be worn again. Brides may wear a short white dress or white suit.

When my uncle married, his wife-to-be coordinated outfits with genuine flair. The men wore blue blazers and gray slacks. She reasoned that every man has these already in his closet. Each wore a matching tie and handkerchief. (A tuxedo rental costs about the same as a new jacket.)

For the right couple, yesteryear clothing (items from the '30s and '40s) can be purchased at thrift or vintage clothing shops.

The Rings: Window shop at a jeweler, paying attention to prices. Then go to a pawn shop and look for a bargain. (Only a true tightwad would find a pawn shop romantic.) The rings may not look brand new or come in a fancy box. But shiny new rings gain a used patina quickly.

Consider the heirloom engagement ring. check antique/bric-a-brac shops for estate jewelry. If you don't like diamonds don't buy an engagement ring.

The Invitations: I designed an unconventional invitation for my uncle. Since both are architects they agreed to a blueprint

invitation about 1' × 3' rolled and mailed in a tube. As it unrolled, the invitation read "Plans for a Wedding" with a portrait, then an invitation, directions on how to get to the reception, renderings of their home and church, a map, and a RSVP mailer to cut off. Although the postage cost more, the invitation cost nothing to produce.

A graphic designer might not step forward to offer an inexpensive invitation alternative.

Standard invitations, especially if you select something simple, can be comparatively reasonable. Shop for prices among many printers.

You might also purchase elegant stationery and hand write your invitations. This is suitable for a small group where an RSVP card might not be essential.

Flowers: If you opt for traditional flowers, at least spend the minimum—bouquets for the bride and maid of honor, corsages for the mothers, and a carnation for the men. Obviously some types of flowers cost less than others, especially if you pick flowers in season. Have a precise shopping list and get prices from several florists. Check for wholesale florists in your area.

If possible look to nature for other decorations. My sister in North Carolina planned her wedding when the mountain laurel were in bloom.

Often brides carry a single flower by itself, or in a prayerbook or Bible.

Silk flowers and other reusable accessories rival fresh flowers in price. Custom-made, they serve as permanent mementos or home decorations in the future.

The Cake: A bridal professional suggested having a smaller wedding cake supplemented with your own sheet cake.

Photography: A world of difference separates a professional wedding photographer and your amateur brother-in-law, both in quality and price. A professional photography package can cost about $500. This price makes the work of the amateur more appealing. If you do opt for the amateur have him take several rolls of film so that you have a selection to choose from when assembling your album. Odds are that you know someone with a video camera, too.

Bridal Party Gifts: Let wedding accessories double as the gifts. Bridesmaids and mothers can keep their silk flower corsages. The best man and ushers can keep their matching ties and handkerchiefs.

Negotiating: We are in a recession. Businesses that offer nonessential services hurt first. They may be more flexible to get your business. As one consultant told me, "Ask, ask, ask." If you have a professional service you might be able to barter. If you have a more personal relationship with the business owner you may be able to barter nonprofessional skills such as babysitting or housecleaning.

199

Whenever you barter hold up your end of the deal. If a businessperson has a positive experience he will barter with others in the future.

Or have the vendor do only part of the service. One photographer charges less than half to shoot pictures only. Her clients assume responsibility for developing and album purchasing. To protect yourself you might have the photographer go one step further. Have her develop the film and give you a contact sheet.

One bride, whose financial circumstances diminished prior to the wedding, bought buffet items from a superb caterer and set up a buffet herself, reducing the cost of feeding the 200 invited guests from $8 to $3 each.

Bridal Consultants: If "budget wedding" strikes you as a contradiction in terms and you plan to spend several thousand dollars, professional help can be worth paying for.

One consultant charges a minimum fee of $500 or 15% of the budget, to be included in the total. Because she works regularly with suppliers she can steer you to the best values. You will very likely receive equal services for less than you can find on your own, making her services essentially free. Bridal consultants use vendors regularly, and in return they provide better service. She will help you evenly disperse your budget. As the coordinator of your wedding she'll free your mother or mother-in-law to enjoy the day.

GOOD STUFF THROUGH THE MAIL

Canning Information. If you garden but do not can you might want to rethink before time to order seeds in the spring. I find that people think it is more work than it really is. For a free newsletter called *Pantry* published four times a year send your name and address to Kerr Glass Manufacturing Corp., Attn. Dept. PRA,

THE FIVE-MINUTE COMPOST BIN

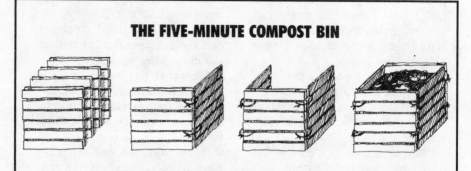

To construct this inexpensive compost bin you will need four wooden pallets and eight hangers. The pallets are usually free or can be purchased for a dollar. Simply wire the four together to form a square. When you wish to remove or stir compost open one side as you would a door.

P.O. Box 76961, Los Angeles, CA 90076. If you send $3.50 they will send you a 112-page paperback guide.

Junk Mail Relief. Send a letter to the Direct Mail & Marketing Association, 6 East 43rd Street, New York, NY 10017 requesting that your name (names) be removed from "all the direct mailing lists they service." This association has several hundred of the largest direct mailing organizations in its program. It will take about three months before you will receive junk mail relief.

A READER QUESTION

Dear Amy,
    How do you reuse/recycle postage stamps?
                    William Cayce
                    Grand Rapids, Michigan

Technically, it's a federal offense to reuse any postage stamp, regardless of whether or not it has ever been through the postal system. Throw away those uncanceled stamps that come through the mail. The price of honesty is very small.

But what if you stamp an envelope, and decide not to use it, and you cannot reuse the envelope? The post office will accept the whole envelope with stamp and exchange it for a new

stamp. They need to see the whole envelope to verify that the stamp has never been through the mail.

We get a large number of SASE's that we cannot use and frequently return them to the post office. I also use post office postcards for much of my correspondence. (I can fit more on them than a scenic or homemade postcard.) I also return any of these that I botch in the writing process.

CUTTING THE COST OF BAKING

As a general rule home-baked foods cost ¼ to ⅓ of the store-bought price. Exceptions include some packaged mixes, as well as some baked goods purchased on sale with double coupons. The cost of home baking can be further minimized using basic strategies.

Flour. For the past two years we have found white flour on sale for $2.88 for 25 lbs during the fall. This equals a 5-lb bag for 57¢, or about half price. (Flour in 25-lb bags generally costs more per pound than 5-lb bags.) Staples rarely go on sale, so when we see these deals we purchase in bulk. Last year we purchased 200 lbs. (Stores reserve the right to limit quantities, but we have never been challenged.)

To keep it from getting "buggy," flour (and other grains for long-term storage) needs to be frozen overnight. Then transfer to an airtight container. We use clean trash barrels or 5-gallon buckets obtained from bulk food stores. This method is common practice in New England. Those in other parts of the country should check with their local Extension Service as I am not certain the method works as well in warmer climates.

Whole Grains. Whole-grain flour, oatmeal, and cornmeal cost more than white flour. But because whole grains combine with other foods to make a protein, they are a good value, so use liberally. Recently we purchased a 50-lb bag of oatmeal at 39¢ a pound compared to 80¢ per pound of Quaker Oats in a small carton. If these quantities are too much for your needs, try to bulk buy with other families.

Add a tablespoon of wheat germ to a cup of white flour as a substitute for wheat flour.

Milk. Use powdered milk in baking. When a recipe calls for cream or condensed milk mix powdered milk with half the water. Buttermilk also comes in powdered form and is almost as cheap as powdered milk. This is handy because it can be stored for a long time. Substitute "sour milk" (a cup of milk to a tablespoon of lemon juice or vinegar) for buttermilk.

One reader sent in the following recipe for sweetened condensed milk:

> 1 cup instant nonfat dry milk
>   solids
> ⅔ cup sugar
> ⅓ cup boiling water
> 3 Tbsp melted margarine

Combine all ingredients in the container of an electric blender (or pour in a bowl and use electric mixer). Process until smooth. Store in refrigerator until ready to use. Yield: about 1¼ cups for 60¢.

The price of powdered milk rises and falls about a year behind the price of whole milk. Here in Maine whole milk prices are low and powdered milk prices are high. Therefore the difference between whole and powdered milk is temporarily only 40¢ per gallon versus the $1.50 per gallon difference of a few years ago.

Eggs and Oil. I group these two together because of the fat content. If you have a cholesterol problem, by all means throw out the yolks. Quadruple bypass operations cost a tad more than a few discarded yolks. The same applies to the use of the more healthy peanut and safflower oils. However, if your doctor looked at your test numbers, eyebrows raised, and said, "Whatever you are doing keep on doing it," then severe limitation of fats is not necessary.

Most egg substitutes are more expensive than throwing away yolks, as are powdered eggs.

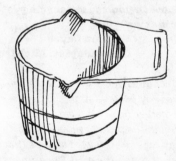

Mary Miller of Lakewood, Colorado, sent in this idea. Substitute one heaping tablespoon of soy flour (or powder) and one tablespoon of water for an egg in baking. She says she has never had a recipe fail. We bought a pound for 99¢ (which yields about 45 heaping tablespoons) and tried it in muffins, pancakes, cornbread, cake, and even meatloaf. We could not detect any difference.

A heaping tablespoon of soy flour costs a tad over 2¢. An egg costs about 10¢ (if you pay $1.20 a dozen). For every egg you eliminate by substituting soy flour you would save a little under 8¢. This means if you substitute soy flour for a dozen eggs, this month you will save $1.

Soy flour is more versatile than eggs, since it does not require refrigeration and takes up less space. Those bakers who like to make up mixes for pancakes and waffles can make mixes with soy flour and powdered milk. They would only need to add water to make a batter. It would be great for camping.

Eggs and oil (or fats) rank among the most expensive and least healthy ingredients in baking. I have discovered, by accidental omission, that you can cut back on eggs and oil (or fat) without significantly changing the final product. Doing this will produce a slightly tougher muffin, for example. Sometimes this can be good for muffins that are too moist and fall apart. Since I always bake double or triple recipes, eliminating one egg is not a problem.

Margarine, shortening, and oil seem to be interchangeable in some types of recipes. On the average the price is comparable unless you buy one on sale and not the other.

Vicki Dely of Allison Park, Pennsylvania, wrote in that you can substitute unsweetened ap-plesauce for oil in some recipes, especially cakes. I have been experimenting with this as well, and in combination with the soy flour.

Substituting applesauce for fat works well when the taste might not compete with other flavors (such as cocoa) or where the fat content might not be critical. Our homemade stuff might be stronger tasting than store-bought applesauce. I liked the applesauce/soy flour combination in cornbread, but it produced a tough oatmeal cookie. I have had more satisfactory results substituting applesauce for half the shortening in cookies.

Depending on prices in your area, or if you make your own applesauce, you can save half or more on the cost of oil in your baking.

Sugars. You can also cut back on the amount of sugar in many recipes. If a recipe calls for brown sugar I may use half brown and half white. You can make brown sugar by mixing 1 tablespoon of molasses to 1 cup of sugar. This is not much cheaper, but works in a pinch. Bulk-purchased molasses is about 50% the cost of small bottles of the name-brand stuff.

Dot Platter of Imperial, Missouri, wrote:

"When shopping for sugar be sure to purchase baking soda. One can save half or more on sugar usage and cost when making pies, cobblers, fruit cakes, and fruit salads by using baking soda to neutralize the acid content in these types of dishes.

"For instance, if one uses ¼ to ½ teaspoon of baking soda in a fruit pie, only about half the usual amount of sugar is needed to get the desired sweetness."

This idea interested me because I frequently make fruit crisps. I put this idea to the "acid test." I made two mixed-fruit crisps of strawberries, apples, rhubarb, and blackberries. I added a teaspoon of baking soda and half the usual sugar to one crisp. The family and a couple of office workers taste-tested both. The crisp with the baking soda and half the sugar was slightly sweeter. Obviously one would have to experiment with different recipes to find the right amount to adjust the sugar and baking soda.

Many use honey because it is not refined. There is a difference of opinion as to whether one form of sugar is healthier than another. Honey can also be dangerous for infants, and any sugar in a sticky form (honey, molasses, raisins) is more likely to cause cavities.

Nuts. I seldom buy these because of the expense; however, they are healthy and therefore a good value. I substitute oatmeal in brownies and raisins or coconut in cookies.

Yeast. Try to find a source of bulk yeast, which costs about 7% of those little packets. If you do not buy yeast in bulk, baking bread may not be cheaper than buying bread at a thrift store.

Herbs and Spices can be remarkably cheap when bought at a natural foods store in bulk. The difference is so great I regard the little jars in grocery stores to be highway robbery. As an alternative look for an inexpensive brand called Spice Time, often found in 5 & 10 stores. In some cases you can save by growing your own herbs or drying orange peel.

Store Brands seem to be of the same quality as any name brand, so buy the cheapest on the shelf. Some stores carry a brand that beats all. Clabber Girl baking powder, which comes in a larger container, costs much less than other well-known brands. Again, you must investigate all the stores in your area.

Baking Powder. Make your own by mixing 1 part baking soda, 2 parts cream of tartar, and 2 parts arrowroot. This eliminates the aluminum found in commercial brands but the cost is roughly 25% more than the best baking powder price that I have, versus making the homemade version with bulk-purchased ingredients.

Convenience Foods. Food manufacturers design recipes that call for their products. The recipes are generally found on the product packaging (such as cold cereal boxes) or in magazine ads. They will drive up your baking costs. Avoid the recipe or try to find a homemade substitute. The same rule applies for recipes that call for a brand-name staple.

Saving on Energy. Baking double batches or baking two items at once can save almost half the energy. You might be able to bake some items as the oven heats up (rather than when already fully heated) and turn the oven off a few minutes early, leaving the items in the oven longer. Do not do this for cakes and other finicky items.

Saving on Time. Establish a "baking center" by grouping baking powder, baking soda, salt, shortening, and other common ingredients in one area. Your baking utensils and measuring equipment should be within reach. I arranged my spices by alphabetical order. A friend has hers grouped together by the type of recipe for which they are used. Either method eliminates the "spice hunt." Preparing double batches saves half the time. Freeze the surplus.

Saving by Choice. Some foods cost more than others while offering little or no nutrition. Therefore, try to choose foods that are cheap *and* healthy. We gave up artificial sweeteners and now simply eat less sugar overall. Sugar is one of our last hold-outs —pumpkin pie just wouldn't taste right without it. But you can choose to make oatmeal raisin cookies instead of gumdrop or chocolate chip. Make carrot cake instead of chocolate. And you can bake fewer desserts altogether in favor of whole-grain breads, rolls, and crackers.

No food that offers little nutritional value is a bargain, even when it is homemade.

Learning to Bake. People have told me that they cannot bake. While mastery of the pie crust may elude some of us, overall baking is simple. It requires experimentation and practice. As a rule I follow recipes precisely the first time, and experiment in subsequent uses. Regard your first frustrating attempts as an investment that will reap future savings.

The Personal Cookbook. Develop your own cookbook to record experiments that work. Also write in recipes used frequently in double or triple batches and alter the amounts accordingly.

BAKING POWDER UPDATE

I gave a recipe on the previous page for a baking powder substitute that costs more than the cheapest commercial baking powder. The advantage was it had no aluminum. Some studies suggest aluminum might be hazardous to your health.

Later we ran out of baking powder, which jogged my brain to test a follow-up tip sent in by a reader: the arrowroot in the homemade version was unnecessary.

I tested this by making two half-batches of muffins—one with commercial baking powder and

one with the homemade, no-arrowroot version—and baked them in the same pan. There was no detectable difference.

Below are prices in my area:

Rumford baking powder (which has no aluminum) costs $1.79 lb.

Clabber Girl baking powder (which has aluminum) costs $1.25 lb.

Home version with 2 parts arrowroot, 2 parts cream of tartar, and 1 part baking soda costs $1.58 lb.

Home version with 2 parts cream of tartar and 1 part baking soda costs $1.34 lb.

The second home version is actually the cheapest of all, because you use less of it. Just ¼ tsp of baking soda and ½ tsp of cream of tarter substitutes for 1 tsp of baking powder. Because you use 25% less, roughly $1 worth equals a pound of the other baking powders. (My calculations are based on store-brand baking soda and cream of tartar at $1.30 lb from a natural foods store.)

My Fannie Farmer cookbook says this version should not be mixed in advance, as it does not keep well. So keep cream of tartar in your "baking center" and add it, and baking soda, individually.

In using this idea I found that on-the-spot computing of odd amounts of baking powder (say 2½ teaspoons) became confusing. So I figured out all the possible baking powder quantities and the equivalent substitutions. I taped this information to the side of my baking powder box, where it would be handy to refer to.

CONTAINER GARDENING

Those of us who live in the country have the advantage of the big garden to help reduce our food bill. However urban or suburban dwellers with little or no space to garden can also supplement their food bills.

Of the many styles of small-scale gardening, container gardening lends itself well to the urban environment.

If you have a rooftop, fire escape, balcony, or patio

that is sheltered and sunny you have a place to garden.

The major advantage to container gardening is that containers can be moved to get maximum sunlight. Most gardens need a minimum of six hours per day. Some gardeners keep their containers on movable carts.

Almost any vegetable can be grown in a container, although you should look for the specific varieties that have been developed for containers.

Containers can include redwood tubs, stone planters, terracotta pots, and half barrels. However, since this is *The Tightwad Gazette* I encourage you to look for less expensive alternatives, such as apple boxes, bushel baskets, or laundry baskets with a trash bag liner. The best inexpensive solution is the 5-gallon bucket. Plastic containers will heat up more and tend to dry out the soil so extra care must be taken.

The 5-gallon bucket can be obtained free from many sources. A health food store or Dunkin' Donuts often has them for the taking.

Container gardens need more drainage than regular gardens. One author suggests drilling holes on the sides near the base, in pairs one above the other every 3 inches. If you have drainage holes in the bottom set your container on blocks off the ground. The bottom of the container should have drainage material, such as peastone gravel, deeper than side drainage holes or at least ½ inch deep for bottom drainage holes.

Soilless mixes, made up of peat moss, vermiculite, and perlite, work well in this application. This mix may become your greatest expense, so you will want to shop for price. The mix can be saved and reused from year to year. If you plan a large-scale operation you may want to learn to mix your own for the sake of economics. Any container must hold a minimum of 6 to 10 inches of soil or mix.

Use a slow-release nutrient to fertilize your garden. Make your own by soaking a handful of dried manure soaked in a jug of water. Not only is this inexpensive but ideal for the novice, as the nutrient is released slowly over a period of time.

To conserve water soak the soil not the foliage. Also water early or late in the day to prevent evaporation. Regular watering is critical. A surplus is better than not enough.

The Portuguese- and Italian-Americans who have settled in our urban areas possess the greatest expertise on urban gardening. Most of you will not be able to snag an expert and should find a book for additional information. A few titles are:

Vegetables by Derek Fell, 1982
Making Vegetables Grow by
    Thalassa Cruso, 1975
Square Foot Gardening by Mel
    Bartholomew, 1981

END SUBSTITUTE ABUSE

For years I have listened in silence to the malicious sneers, the wild and vicious accusations, the snickers, and the low blows. But no more. It is time for someone to take a stand and defend against the onslaught of verbal attacks ... to say with pride, "Dry milk has a place in this world, if nowhere else but in my cupboards!"

Yes, folks, this form of substitute abuse has been allowed to be unchallenged for too long. And I for one am an admitted long-term user of the stuff. Thus I have decided to bring this issue to the forefront of public awareness with this article to examine the attributes of dry milk.

Taste: I would quickly lose credibility if I tried to convince you that the taste of dry milk is indistinguishable from whole milk. I will say that *all* foods are an acquired taste. Chances are that the first time you tasted coffee, tea, diet cola, or wine you did not like them. In all likelihood one of those beverages is a regular part of your diet today.

Dry milk tastes best when chilled overnight and consumed with a meal. Until a few years ago we had been serving our children half dry and half whole. One evening we ran out of whole and served the children straight dry milk. When a child smacked his lips and said "I sure like milk," Jim and I looked at each other in amazed silence, mental gears turning in sync. We have never looked back.

If you wish to switch to dry milk for drinking, mix small amounts of dry to whole and gradually increase the ratio.

Economy: A gallon of whole milk costs $2.19 to $2.59 per gallon. Dry milk, when purchased by the 20-quart store-brand box for $7.00 costs $1.40 per gallon. Even with 100% dry milk use, milk and

juice makes up 30% of our family's expenditure for food. A family that consumes a gallon per day could save $30 per month.

Think of it this way. Every time you finish a box of dry milk you have saved $5.

Health: Dry milk is 100% fat-free. Whole milk has a 4% fat content. By mixing half and half you can make your own 2% milk, which is often more expensive than whole milk.

It was once believed that dry milk was not good for children, who need the fat in their diet. Now you are more likely to pick up a magazine and read about the

growing problem of too much fat in the average child's diet. According to a current government survey it is now known that as many as one in four children is technically obese. The physician I consulted for this article verified that dry milk is absolutely healthy for children over the age of one. (Babies need breast milk or formula.) Children get ample amounts of fat, and often too much, in other parts of their diets.

According to current information children need two cups of

milk per day. Teenagers need three, adults need two, pregnant and lactating women need four. For reasons of health and economy it is not reasonable to allow unrestrained consumption of whole milk. It is easy to do simple math and determine how much milk your family should consume monthly. Including milk used in cooking, our family consumes about 10% over the minimum recommendation. Since we also eat cheese we are well within the guidelines.

Versatility: The attribute I enjoy most about dry milk is its many uses. By mixing with half the water you can make a mock cream that can be substituted for high-fat expensive creams in pies, quiches, and sauces. When a soup recipe calls for cream or milk, mix dry milk in powdered form with saved vegetable broth. If a batter looks too wet, dry milk in powdered form can be added. Vegetarian recipes often include dry milk to boost protein. To make instant hot cocoa mix ⅓ cup of dry milk, 1 teaspoon of sugar, and 1 teaspoon of cocoa to a cup of water. It requires two minutes to heat in the microwave.

Convenience: Think of dry milk as a staple. It does not go bad. We never have to make last-minute trips to the convenience store to buy ridiculously over-priced whole milk because we have run out. In fact we are now able to limit our shopping to one major monthly trip. (Whole milk die-hards can also do this by freezing jugs of milk.)

Rarely will you find absolutes in the pages of *The Tightwad Gazette.* I believe that each individual or family has their own priorities and values. Dry milk use is one exception. It may not be possible or desirable for you to switch your family to 100% dry milk consumption. However, you should at least use it for cooking.

Dry milk is a great bargain. It is not often that you find a food that combines economy, health, versatility, and convenience in such a perfect union. It has a place in every tightwad cupboard.

A RECIPE BREAKDOWN

One of the most frequent reader requests is for inexpensive recipes. Obviously you have to choose recipes that call for inexpensive ingredients. However, you can also learn to interpret an existing recipe to make it less expensive.

On the following page is a recipe for seafood casserole that I use frequently. I have included it in its original form and also shown the changes and choices. It was designed to be a time-saver recipe utilizing expensive ingredients. In the process of altering the recipe I made it less expensive but more time consuming. Counteract this by making double or triple batches and freezing the extra to eat on a busy day. Singles and couples can make single batches in separate smaller casserole dishes and accomplish the same result.

If you were to prepare this recipe with the most expensive ingredient options it would cost about $8.00. The way I prepare it, the casserole costs $1.81. Prepared without white wine would save another 40¢.

Pasta: use any pasta purchased on sale. We get it for 33¢ lb. I increase it by 2 oz. because the recipe makes too much sauce.

Mayonnaise or Salad dressing: Buy store brand for 99¢ per quart. You can make your own mayonnaise but the savings is marginal, and depends on the price of eggs.

Milk or wine: wine is more expensive, but I like the flavor.

Topping: Make your own bread crumbs. Save all your crusts, cereal and cracker crumbs. Store in a bag in the freezer. Process in a blender or food processor.

Seafood: Tuna is the obvious choice. We stock up when it goes on sale for 44¢ per can.

Cheese: use any mild cheese purchased on sale. We always buy it for less than $2 lb. Shredded is usually more expensive, but not always.

Mix-and-Match Seafood Casserole

6 servings

4 to 5 oz pasta
½ cup dry white wine or milk
½ cup mayonnaise or salad dressing
1 cup (4 oz) American cheese, shredded
1 10¾-oz can condensed cream

of celery, shrimp, or mushroom soup
½ tsp dill
6 to 8 oz canned seafood (tuna, salmon, crab, or shrimp), drained
Topping (below)

Preheat the oven to 350°. Prepare the pasta, following the directions on the package; drain and set aside. Mix white wine with mayonnaise. Add the cheese, soup, and dill. Gently combine the noodles and the seafood with the moist ingredients. Pour the mixture into a 1½-quart casserole dish. Cover and bake for 30 minutes. Remove the cover, top with Topping, and bake for an additional 5 minutes. Serve hot.

Topping: Stir 2 Tbsp melted butter into 1 cup of soft bread crumbs. You can also try 1 cup of crushed corn chips, chow mein noodles, or french-fried onions, or ½ cup of sliced almonds.

Condensed Cream Soup: costs 69¢ to $1.11 depending on the type. Instead I make a mock cream of celery soup that costs 15¢. Melt 2 Tbs. of margarine in a sauce pan. Saute 2 Tbs. chopped celery. Blend in 2 Tbs. flour. Add ⅓ cups dry milk powder and ⅔ cups vegetable broth. Add salt and pepper to taste. Cook until smooth.

CANINE CUISINE

After I requested ideas for inexpensive dog food, I received many letters, several of which had conflicting information. This diversity reflects the range of thinking among those who are knowledgeable about dogs.

In light of this I felt that experts needed to be consulted. This article is based on information from Dr. Gail Mason, a doctor of veterinary medicine and Maine's only board-certified veterinary internist. I also received input from two licensed animal health technicians, including Jody L. Burton of Vacaville, California. All of these individuals agreed with periodicals from the library.

Here are some points I learned:

 Major pet food companies have done a great deal of research into animal nutrition. It would be very difficult to make a home petfood that duplicates the combination of protein, fats, and nutrients found in commercial petfoods. While your pet might seem to do well, in the long run it might suffer from a nutrition deficiency, obesity, and/or have a shortened life span. Although I didn't do a cost comparison, I questioned whether some of the home recipes would actually be cheaper because they called for expensive ingredients.

 Dr. Mason says that you don't need to buy a super-premium dog food. Some of the companies that have put a long-term effort into developing good food are Purina, Pedigree Expert, ALPO, and Ken-L Ration. Reader Susan Ballard of Sloatsburg, New York, says she often purchases Purina on sale for $6.99 for 30 lbs. The coupons, often found on previous bags, will lower the price further, as low as $4.99. She also uses rebates.

People I know who breed dogs for show say they wouldn't use Purina. Because their dogs reproduce frequently, and because they want them to be in top condition, these owners opt for a dog food with higher nutrition (and higher price tag) than these ex-

perts felt was necessary for the average dog.

 Stick with name brands. The term "guaranteed analysis" on the packaging is somewhat deceptive. It does guarantee some nutritional standard, but the standard is a loose one. For example, many generics and store brands include hooves and tails as a protein source, which is difficult for dogs to digest. Dr. Mason says some generic brands have been proven to be deficient in some nutrients.

A key way to save money on petfood is to not overfeed your pet. Obesity is one of the most common pet health problems. Begin by following the guidelines on the packaging and adjust as needed. Jody Burton says that you should just be able to feel your pet's ribs, but its backbone should not be too prominent.

A good dry food is generally nutritionally equivalent to a good canned food. Because dry food is cheaper, it is the tightwad choice. Dr. Mason advised against semimoist dog foods, which have dyes and additives to keep them soft. Dry food is better for the dog's teeth, as soft foods tend to stick to teeth.

 A common tightwad practice one might avoid is buying in large quantities and storing for a long period of time. The vitamins tend to degrade during storage. So don't buy more than your pet might eat in a month, and store it in a cool,

dry place such as a garbage can.

 Pets do not need variety in their diet. Switching their foods to keep them from getting bored can actually do harm by upsetting their metabolism. Dr. Mason recommends Purina Puppy Chow for puppies, and then switching to adult food when they are grown.

 Although Dr. Mason advises against homemade dog foods as the main part of the diet, she feels dogs can tolerate an occasional homemade snack.

Attempts to economize by purchasing low-quality food can backfire. Treating a common ailment, like pancreatitis, caused by feeding your dog too many fatty table scraps, can cost at least $150, not to mention the discomfort to your dog.

Our family has a dog and a cat because we feel pets would contribute to the quality of the lives of our children. In bringing the animals into our home we assumed a planned expense necessary to provide a reasonable level of care for them.

THICK TRICK

Don't cook down tomatoes to get thick sauce. Once they are prepared and ready to cook, just put them in the refrigerator overnight. In the morning, use your turkey baster to remove the clear liquid that has floated to the top. Voila!

**Elaine Stalder
Harrisburg, Oregon**

BOOK SMARTS

Before reading this article do the following exercise: count how many books you have in your home that you purchased new. Next count how many of those books you cracked open in the past year ... or five years. My own tally works out to a couple hundred books purchased new that have not been read in over five years.

Jim and I were both readers B.K. (before kids) and brought our own libraries to the marriage. Now my John Updikes gather dust in the attic next to his Robert Ludlums.

Part two of the exercise is to inventory the books you use with regularity. These are the type of books you *need* to own. Based on my results these are the books I recommend for your library:

- A dictionary and thesaurus if you do any amount of writing.
- A general medical volume such as *The A.M.A. Family Medical Guide.* This provides useful information such as how to take a temperature or pinpoint the probability of a strange rash. It also helps judge when a child needs to go to the doctor in the

wee hours of the morning.
- Cookbooks containing basic recipes, like Fannie Farmer or Betty Crocker.
- A basic home maintenance book, especially if you own your own home. If you are remodeling or renovating you should own a book on that subject as well.
- Books covering your special areas of interest, such as the spiritual book of your choice and books relating to your hobby.

Unless you are very lucky, you will not find these books at yard sales. Instead investigate used-book stores. If you are still unable to locate them and your need is pressing, purchase them new. You are likely to save more than the cost of the book.

The following new books I do not recommend:
- Fiction. Last year's best-sellers are soon forgotten and are available at your library.
- Children's books. No parent *wants* to read the same book to their child hundreds of times. If you bring home five library books weekly you will not exhaust your library's shelves before the child goes off to college. These books are also a glut on the yard sale market and can be purchased for a dime.
- Coffee table books. As a graphic designer I am a sucker for these, and the half dozen I have purchased are dusty. They are an attractive and expensive luxury. Stay away from mail-order books, especially the children's books that tend to be poorly crafted. I have responded to the free trial book offers and have found it difficult to cancel my membership. Then I had to pay postage to return books after

I opened the boxes. It was not worth the trouble. Book clubs, which offer free books if you buy two at the regular prices, are still more expensive than if you borrow all these books from the library. And you do not also have the option of browsing through the book before making a purchase.

Jim purchased a brand-new book called *How to Fix Damn Near Anything*. In horror I discovered a $15.95 price tag on the inside of the jacket. Upon interrogation he confessed that he purchased it at the thrift shop for 25¢.

This price difference typifies thrift shops and yard sales. Used-book shops, which have a more reliable selection, charge a little more . . . perhaps $2 for the same book. They will purchase your dusty library in exchange for credit. This allows you to weed out and rebuild a more relevant usable library.

Take advantage of the inter-library loan system. Any library in the United States can borrow a book from any other library. In theory, as long as it is in print, it can be obtained for you in one to three weeks. You only need to provide the title and author. Some libraries offer this as a free service, while others charge a fee to cover postage. If it's free, bear in mind that it isn't free to the library. Especially if your library is small, don't abuse their generosity. If the book you want to read might be of interest to others, you can also ask your librarian if he or she would be interested in purchasing it.

Space, as well as money, is a precious resource. Before pur-chasing any new or used book leaf through the pages to determine the amount of information it contains that is of genuine value to you.

Ironically, the bookstore that raked in my hard-earned cash was located across the street from the Boston Public Library, a place I rarely ventured. Give yourself an inexpensive treat and plan an evening to wander through your own library and marvel at all that is free to borrow.

WHAT TO DO WITH . . .

A Coat Hanger. Make a toilet paper holder. Such a contraption currently graces our yet-to-be-remodeled bathroom. Learn to create solutions to tide you over until you find an inexpensive alternative.

Broccoli Rubber Bands. Save these and cut in half to make two usable rubber bands. (Contributed by Polly Davis, Shirley, Massachusetts)

Butter Wrappers. Save by folding and storing in the butter compartment in your fridge. Then use when buttering cookie sheets, soufflé dishes, etc. before finally throwing away. (Contributed by Leslie Lee, Portland, Oregon)

Frozen Juice Lids. When our daughter was going through her medical phase, Jim pop-riveted a juice lid to a band of elastic to make a doctor's headband.

Watermelon Seeds. Dry and save to mix with bird seed. Musk melon seeds also work. The birds love them. (Contributed by Jim Spaulding, Northfield, Massachusetts)

Bread Bags. Cut in half; use the bottom half as an alternative to expensive sandwich bags. Use the original tab or twist-tie to close.

Old Towels. Fold and use in a clamp handle mop to clean floors. Especially good for corners. (Contributed by Ruth MacPherson, Belfast, Maine)

Potato Peels and Chicken Skins. Mix and fry in the oven (when baking something else). Makes a great treat for dogs, who need extra fat during the winter months. (Contributed by Carolyn Sue Marr, Otisfield, Maine)

An Old Sock. Make a toy for your cat. Sew over any hole and stuff with leftover quilt batting. Sew over the top. (Contributed by Kathy Closson, Wiscassett, Maine)

Old Roll-on Deodorant Bottles. Pry off the cap, rinse, and fill with tempera paint thinned with water. Replace the top. Let children paint with it.

Old Mattress Pads. Cut down to smaller sizes to make changing pads for children. Trim edge with bias tape. Smaller pieces can be used as filler when making potholders. (Contributed by Mrs. Richard Lunden, Haynesville, Maine)

Aquarium Water. Save to water your plants. It is tepid and contains algae and other organic waste, which is nourishing for both house and garden plants.

Cold Cereal Boxes. Make magazine holders for the publications you save. Cut diagonally as shown. (Contributed by Donna McKenna, Casco, Maine) It goes without saying that the cereal was purchased with triple coupons on sale.

Mesh Bags. The type that onions and frozen turkeys come in can be made into scouring pads. Just twist and secure with a rubber band . . . or one of those from broccoli. (This idea was sent in by many readers.)

Summer

THRIFT AND THE ENVIRONMENT

The tightwad bug bit me 10 years ago. A full 6 years would pass before I would fully grasp the profound relationship between thrift and the environment. Despite my ignorance, in the name of penny-pinching, I went about doing most of the right things anyway:

For the first five months after Jim and I married, while we lived near Boston, I rode a bicycle to work. (Pregnancy eventually forced me to abandon this.)

When Alec was born he slept in a crib from the Salvation Army. Within a few weeks we learned he was allergic to disposable diapers, and were forced into cloth diaper use. Despite having to cart soiled diapers to an expensive nearby laundromat they were less work than expected and cost-effective.

When Jim wanted to buy a new vehicle to replace his 12-year-old Chevy Suburban, I successfully argued for the purchase of a small, fuel-efficient car first.

The Navy transferred Jim to Norfolk, Virginia. During these 4 years of suburbia we yard saled with a passion. We came to regret most new purchases of the previous years.

We learned that buying in larger quantities and cooking from scratch would dramatically cut our food bill. We gave up soda and dabbled in vegetarianism.

Jim's parents were generous and brought cases of their home-canned garden produce when they came to visit.

Unlike our neighbors, we did not air-condition our whole house. We resorted to flicking on our small air conditioner to cool our bedroom only on the most sweltering of summer nights.

We hung laundry on a clothesline, took shorter showers, and convinced the landlord to insulate the attic. When I washed dishes I would fill the sink halfway. I baked more than one item at a time and put lids on all pots while cooking.

My passion for pinching extended to the reuse of everything possible. I was aware that many of my efforts would only save a few cents. (How much does a single Baggie cost, anyway?) I rationalized that it was a matter of attitude. If I took care with the small things, I would also pay attention to the larger things.

The military moved us again—this time to Brunswick, Maine. During our 15 months of house hunting, while we lived in a government house, I frequented the public library. It was my practice to scour the how-to shelves for books on a variety of topics that would help us to save more money.

During one of these hunts I found *Reuses* by Carolyn Jabs. The book is subtitled "2,133 Ways to Recycle and Reuse the Things You Ordinarily Throw Away." I checked it out of the library, thinking I would learn new ways to save money.

Instead I was more struck by the brief introduction and conclusion chapters that dealt with the environmental impact of the wasteful habits of our culture.

I was clobbered by facts such as: "Americans represent 5% of the world's population but produce half its waste," and "Each day we generate enough trash to fill the New Orleans Superdome . . . twice." Even more dramatic is the per capita growth of garbage. In 1900 the average person used 58 pounds of paper. In 1973 he used 639 pounds.

I got it. Our efforts to save more on purchases naturally resulted in less consumption of goods. Most of our efforts to cut our food bill, especially eating fewer convenience foods and more home-canned foods, produced less trash —about a third of our neighbors'. The purchasing of used items saved the energy and resources that would have been used to produce new stuff, and also saved space in our overflowing landfills.

The effort to save money on electricity and gasoline resulted in less energy consumption and reduced pollution.

I realized that economy and ecology are like two circles that overlap about 90%. The remaining 10% is the area where doing the right thing for the environment costs more. Buying organically grown food costs more. In most cases solar electricity is not cost-effective.

Sometimes doing the right thing economically is not good for the environment. For example, the use of coupons and rebates can make an overly packaged product less expensive than its equivalent prepared from scratch.

I have become aware of subtle transition in our lives. We've met our house-buying goal, and we have established a prosperous business to support us in Jim's retirement. We do not *have* to be tightwads anymore.

But having successfully blended the areas of economy and ecology in the 90% area, we have found we now have some surplus money, and this surplus gives us economic room to reexamine some of the areas within the 10%.

Not having to work away from home has significantly cut our driving. We can now afford the additional cost of recycled paper for the newsletter. I have even found myself hanging laundry in the attic while employing a room full of people downstairs doing our mail. I am making an environmental choice, and not the economic one.

The understanding of the relationship between thrift and the environment has given me the assurance that efforts to reuse and conserve could not be "too extreme."

People tend to think that environmental damage occurs because of sloppy practices of some factory out there. In fact, we consumers create the demand for what the factories produce.

I have also understood that one family making a supreme effort to live entirely without any harm to the environment makes little impact. But the collective effort of the majority of the population to make smaller, seemingly insignificant changes can make a difference.

The environmentalist enjoys an economic bonus by adopting frugality. We tightwads, whether or not it is a prime motivation, get to wear the cloak of environmentalism, stand tall, and not let anyone tell us we're crazy.

POPSICLE POSSIBILITIES

Summer is Popsicle season. It is the time of year when other neighborhood moms will thwart your attempts to economize. They give your children store bought pops—twin pops, Disney pops, Creamsicles—all of which cost between 10¢ and 22¢ when purchased by the box. Multiply that by the droves that will return to your house for reciprocal offerings and we are talking A LOT of Kool-Aid on a stick. Five per day could add up to $100 during the summer.

Fight back with homemade Popsicles, which are cheap and nutritious. Made from apple juice they cost about 2½¢ each.

OK. This is not exactly startling information and neither is the fact that the droves will not be satiated with such common fare.

So be resourceful. Consider any sweet or wet edible substance for Popsicle possibilities. Raid your cupboards for forgotten ancient commodities and combine them for dangerous new taste sensations. Treat this as another opportunity to use up leftovers. Here are a few ideas:

- homemade plain yogurt (especially what didn't set up well)
- homemade jam (especially what didn't set up well)
- left over Jell-O (especially what didn't set up well)
- juice or syrup left over from canned fruit
- juice left over from a runny berry pie
- fruit or chocolate syrup
- ice tea mix
- sprinkles and jimmies in thicker mixtures
- food coloring
- applesauce
- pudding
- cranberry sauce
- bits of fruit
- coconut

If you can leave the mold open and devise a way to prop the stick, you can make striped Popsicles. (Try aluminum foil for this.) Pour and freeze alternating colors. Tilting the mold will make angled stripes.

Every summer morning take a couple of minutes and create a variety. You will have a cheap and healthful alternative to satiate the thirsty droves.

POPSICLE MOLDS

A friend showed me an ingenious Popsicle mold. She has a surplus of small, neckless prescription bottles. She found that the childproof cap has an inner plastic circle that can be popped out with a knife. The inner plastic circle fits neatly on the top of the prescription bottle. She cuts a slot in the circle to hold a wooden Popsicle stick. These make a Popsicle that is less "klunky" than ones made in a paper cup.

Some might be concerned that the child would associate the prescription bottle with a treat. The labels can be removed or you can just not show the child the bottle when you remove the Popsicle.

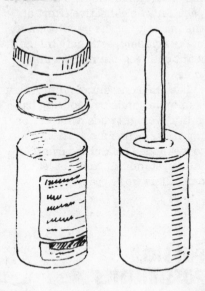

THE FRUGAL ZEALOT GOES TO HOLLYWOOD

It was 9:30 P.M. I was unwinding in a hot tub of water (one of the chinks in my tightwad armor), trying to come down after three consecutive days of interviews with the press (*Boston Globe, Christian Science Monitor,* and a tape interview for PBS radio). During this blissful relaxation I savored the thought that the craziness was at least at a lull. That's when the phone rang.

Jim brought the cordless to me and said, "It's for you. It's *To Tell the Truth.*" I said, "What?"

So there I was, standing on the bath mat, dripping wet, talking to Hollywood as Jim passed towels and a robe.

The woman on the phone told me her name and that she worked for *To Tell the Truth.* I said, "What?" After a few minutes of conversation she asked me if I would like to be on the show. I moved on to a more complex verbal expression. "Ah, come on, is this some kind of joke?"

It wasn't. A week and a half later I boarded a seven-something-seven that would propel me through the friendly skies toward my destination, one of the great capitals of consumer spending on the planet.

I should, at this point, interject that I do not have a high regard for most of television and that I am not sure which I loathe more, game shows or Teenage Mutant Ninja Turtle cartoons. The quality of the newly revived *To Tell the Truth* falls somewhere between *Let's Make a Deal* and *Jeopardy*.

I went knowing that I was selected on the basis of my unusual profession rather than the merits of my message. I accepted the offer because I thought I would regret it if I didn't go. Having done it once I would not feel compelled to do it again.

Did I have fun? It was interesting to see how a show was put together, much as I expected it would be. But of my four days away I spent two very long days traveling and a full day in the studio. My one free day I was somewhat hotel-bound, as it was not within walking distance of anything. And I suffered from jet lag.

I observed several things in Los Angeles. One does not hail a cab as one might in an eastern city. One *calls* a cab (using a telephone). They are extremely expensive. A $20 fare is common. During an attempt to call the Mark Goodson office I bothered some poor woman three times before I finally called the hotel desk to learn I needed to dial a different area code. Los Angeles has three. And the trees are funny there.

I received $80 for food during my stay. I had vowed to try to bring back as much of this as I could. My goal was somewhat undermined as I was limited to the hotel café. I did eat or hoard all that was offered on the plane.

The evening after I arrived I ate with a fellow contestant, a 76-year-old woman from Idaho who counts moose for the forest service. I ordered a $10 turkey club and a glass of water. I learned

how to make a white bread turkey sandwich look more substantial. Cut in quarters, corner to corner, stick in those fancy toothpicks, rearrange so that the four crusts face together to form an inner square and fill the square with potato chips.

From then on the only meal I paid for was breakfast. The café offered a $10 all-you-can-eat breakfast buffet. I ate all I could eat and smuggled muffins out in my pocketbook. This was good for the day.

I hadn't flown in about 10 years. I remember the old days when the movies were free. Now one pays $4.00 for optional headphones. I practiced lip reading. The very same movie was a cable TV option in my hotel room for $6.75.

The hotel included a few freebies. Every morning the daily paper, about the size of the Sunday paper here in Maine, was delivered to every hotel room. This struck me as a waste. They also provided us with trial-size soaps and Vidal Sassoon shampoo and conditioner. I verified my theory

that my bargain brand shampoo makes my hair just as "bouncy and shiny." On my last day I realized that the maid would automatically replace anything that appeared to be used up. Therefore if I had hidden these items on a daily basis I could have brought home three of each.

The trip was my first time away from my children, and I wanted to bring home some West Coast treasures. This was the primary reason I ventured to Universal City (the studio theme park). After a lengthy cost comparison I determined that the airport gift shop, the hotel gift shop, and Universal City gift shop all sold loot for about the same elevated prices. My other shopping option was a $38 tour of the homes of the stars and Rodeo drive. Next time if I decide to buy something I will buy gifts in Maine before I leave.

I noticed another unusual occurrence in Los Angeles—25% to 35% of all people I saw in the airport, hotel, and theme park were Japanese. I was told they now own over half of all the real estate in Los Angeles. In all fairness their prosperity is deserved, as the Japanese people work hard and save a significantly higher percentage of their income than we Americans do. Saving and reinvestment spawn real prosperity. Spending and debt creates a false sense of economic well-being.

On the way over to the studio the day of the taping I shared a limo with Milton Pitts, the barber to President Bush and Ronald Reagan. The following day, when we went our separate ways, Milton Pitts gave me his business card and asked me to send him a newsletter. I mailed six to him, extras for any president or former president who might stop in for a trim.

To Tell the Truth did not let me give an address on the show, although I did squeeze "Leeds, Maine" into one of my answers. I had half a dozen people call for information and received even fewer pieces of mail. I got more mail from a paragraph that appeared in a newspaper in Anchorage, Alaska.

Kitty Carlisle, Orson Bean, and Vicky Lawrence correctly guessed that I was the true tightwad and so I came home with the minimum winning of $334 (plus $40 of my meal allowance).

TIGHTWAD ETHICS OR . . . MUCH ADO ABOUT A MUFFIN

Moments of great horror and pain permanently etch themselves into our memories. When we think back on these events we recall them with amazing clarity.

Such was the case when I read "The Letter" almost a year ago. While waiting in the church parking lot for my daughter to finish her Scout meeting, I browsed through the handful of mail I had just picked up at the post office. A woman wrote criticizing me for an incident of questionable ethics that I had recounted in my then-recent issue. I am sure that I rolled my eyes heavenward and smacked myself in the forehead. She was absolutely correct.

The letter referred to my account of a trip I made to Los Angeles, where I found myself stranded in an expensive hotel and the cheapest breakfast fare was a $10 all-you-can-eat buffet. I had taken one muffin more than I could eat from the buffet. Rather than leaving it behind to be thrown away, in an automatic-doggie-bag-mode I saved it for later consumption. I found it in my purse the following day, dried and crumbled. I never ate it.

Caught up in relating the sport of traveling cheaply, with my trademark humor I embellished my tale to a degree, and my choice of words might have led some to conclude that I had absconded suitcases of muffins. However, in hindsight, I admit that the single muffin was an ethical infraction.

In those awful moments, while reading "The Letter," my entire life passed before my eyes. But rather than the life of crime one might imagine, I saw an ironic contrast—my countless, zealous lectures over the evils of everything from "pilfering paper clips" to the "fudging of insurance claims."

I can offer no explanation for my oversight, except that sometimes, like those plain-as-the-nose-on-your-face typos, things become crystal clear only when someone points them out to you.

It was my hope that the "Smuggled Muffin Affair"—this smudge upon my otherwise spotless tightwad character—would fade into oblivion. However, it reared its ugly head when a journalist included it, against my vehement protest, in a magazine article, and as I predicted, someone wrote a letter to the editor about it.

I must also confess that I internally recall the "Smuggled Muffin Affair" with increasing frequency. Frugality appears to be gaining in acceptance in the '90s. I have found myself an unwitting "expert," and am interviewed on an almost daily basis by journalists and talk-radio hosts. In addition, readers from all over the country send me articles that document this trend.

I should be pleased. But I am also disturbed by what I see as a confusion concerning the ethics of frugality, as recent converts and scoffers alike grapple with this "new concept."

One radio listener called in, not to ask for my "nuggets of frugal wisdom," but to relate how cheap her brother was. It seems that when he invites her for dinner he has her bring the main course. And because his community has a per-bag charge on bags of trash, he drops his off in a community with free pickup service.

An article, which solicited thrifty ideas from area readers, reported such money-saving ideas

as phoning your mother-in-law when you know she's not home, and leaving a message on her answering machine, so that when she calls back, she pays for the long-distance call.

I met a woman who needed a business suit for a single occasion, purchased one, wore it for the day, and then returned it to the store.

Several people have written to me with pride about steaming and reusing uncanceled stamps . . . including one woman who happened to be the wife of a minister.

Because ethics often gets into fuzzy gray areas, no two people would draw the line in the same place. One situation might be clearly wrong, but change a single element of the circumstance and it might be acceptable.

So how do we sort it all out? The relationship between ethics and thrift can be summed up in one sentence. It is wrong to save money at the expense of others. Period.

Small, seemingly insignificant acts such as pilfering, swiping sugar packets, and steaming postage stamps, and fudging income taxes and insurance claims merely pass along your costs to other consumers. It doesn't matter if your boss pays you too little; the restaurant, the post office, or the insurance company charges too much; or if the government doesn't spend funds entirely on programs that you approve of. The collective impact of this raises the cost of living for everyone.

In my dealings with people, both professionally and personally over the past 15 years, I have

been continually astounded at how few purely honest people there are. Nearly everyone, including the spendthrift scoffers who wouldn't stoop to stamp steaming, resort to questionable practices that they feel are justifiable.

People routinely make personal phone calls at work, or use their employer's copy machine for personal business. They "work under the table" to avoid income taxes. Or they accept food stamps and similar programs when they qualify but don't have a genuine need. If they see a clerk is undercharging them, they remain silent.

Beyond practicing sound ethics I see the importance of generosity or consideration for someone else, especially when their income might be less than mine. I believe in tipping when I receive good service. I will almost always dicker at a yard sale. However, I pay the set price if I buy something from a child, or from someone who appears to be raising cash due to lean times. And while I often make a sport out of seeing how well I can do Christmas on a small budget, I have "blown my budget" when a friend or relative was in need.

As individuals, our first economic responsibility is to ourselves and to our families. But meeting this responsibility also serves the larger economic community. We insulate ourselves from the possible financial pitfalls that could cause us to declare bankruptcy or make us dependent on some form of public assistance. Tricky ethical issues come up when we see ourselves as economic islands, separate from the community . . . when we try to save money at the expense of others.

Through my own personal mistake I see another danger. When engaging in such activities we do damage to a worthy cause—one that we hope others will at least accept in us, even if they don't embrace it themselves. As frugality in the '90s takes hold, I anticipate a backlash of doubters who will look to find fault, and take cheap shots. By being consistently honest and generous in our dealings with others we won't give them any ammunition.

I might never have known about the recent letter to the editor, except that it was brought to my attention by a man with whom I have a business relationship. With folded hands and great solemnness he admitted that he agreed with the sentiment of the letter writer . . . as did I. Two days later, I chatted with this same man about my plan to hire a contractor to repair the cracked ceiling in our dining room.

"Hmm . . . ," he said, "is there any way you could write that off as a business expense?"

A FRUGAL MEAL

Beans and rice are a staple of the frugal diet. However, dried beans usually require presoaking and/or lengthy cooking. Many opt for the more expensive canned version to save time. This reader has contributed a 30-minute energy-saving method. We tried it and were pleased to find it works perfectly.

Dear Amy,

In a large pan that fits inside a pressure cooker bring 1 cup beans to a boil, pour off water and add 2 cups fresh water plus 2 Tbsp oil. Place large pan into pressure cooker with 1½ cups water in the bottom of pressure cooker. Place smaller pan down in the bean and water mixture with 1 cup short-grain brown rice and 1½ cups water. Cover both pans with foil. Close pressure cooker and cook 30 minutes after the doodad starts rocking. Then drop pressure under running water and serve.

Flavor the meal however you like. I have enclosed a few suggestions:

Cumin and chili powder with pinto or kidney beans for a Mexican direction.

Curry powder with lentils.

Sage, basil, and bay with split peas or any other bean.

Tomato paste or sauce and Italian herbs with pinto, pink, or kidney beans.

Diane Gilman
Winslow, Washington

(This recipe fed our family of six with leftovers. Singles and couples can freeze the unflavored leftovers in meal-size portions. In subsequent meals try a different variation. FZ)

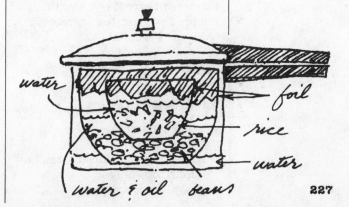

water

foil

rice

water

water & oil   beans

HOMEMADE SALAD DRESSINGS

Toss out those bottled-salad dressing coupons. You can save more by making your own.

The following collection of homemade salad dressing recipes cost 30% to 50% of bottled. For example, 16 oz of bottled name-brand dressing runs between $2.35 and $3.45. These home-made recipes cost between 45¢ (for the Italian) and $1.45 (for the blue cheese) per 16 oz.

Homemade dressings can be prepared in a matter of minutes, providing a healthy savings re-turn for the time spent.

Thousand Island

¾ cup mayonnaise
1 Tbsp sweet pickle relish or finely chopped sweet pickle
2 Tbsp chili sauce or ketchup
2 Tbsp finely chopped green bell pepper
2 Tbsp finely chopped onion
1 Tbsp lemon juice
½ tsp granulated sugar
¼ tsp Worcestershire sauce
1 hard-cooked egg, chopped

Combine all ingredients in a small bowl except egg. Stir in chopped egg last. Refrigerate.
Makes 1⅓ cups.

Ranch Salad Dressing

1 cup mayonnaise
1 cup buttermilk
2 Tbsp finely chopped green on-ions, tops only
¼ tsp onion powder

2 tsp minced parsley
¼ tsp garlic powder or ½ to 1 garlic clove, finely minced
¼ tsp paprika
⅛ tsp cayenne pepper
¼ tsp salt
¼ tsp black pepper

Combine all ingredients in a small bowl. Refrigerate.
Makes 2 cups.

Sweet Tomato-y French

This is for fans of Catalina dressing.

⅔ cup ketchup
½ cup sugar (or to taste)
⅔ cup vegetable oil
½ cup red wine vinegar
salt to taste
1 to 2 cloves garlic (or 1 to 2 tsp)
2 Tbsp finely minced onion

Combine all ingredients in a jar with a tight-fitting lid and shake. This can also be mixed in a blender, although the color be-comes creamier rather than translucent. If preparing in a blender, mix all ingredients ex-cept onion. Stir in finely mixed onion by hand. Refrigerate.
Makes 2 cups.

Cucumber-Buttermilk

1 cup buttermilk
¼ cup grated cucumber
2 Tbsp minced green onions, white and green parts

1 Tbsp Dijon-style mustard
2 tsp minced fresh parsley
2 tsp lemon juice
¼ tsp dried dill
¼ tsp freshly ground black pepper

Combine all ingredients in a small bowl with a tight lid. Stir or shake well. Refrigerate.
Makes 1¼ cups.

Italian Vinaigrette

½ cup red wine vinegar
1½ cups olive oil or vegetable oil or a combination
2 large cloves of garlic, crushed
¾ tsp of salt
¼ to ½ tsp black pepper
1 Tbsp minced parsley
1 tsp dry mustard
½ tsp dried basil or oregano

Combine ingredients in a large jar with a tight-fitting lid. Shake well. The cost comparison is based on vegetable oil.
Makes 1 quart.

Blue Cheese

This recipe makes a large quantity and is very strong. For die-hard blue cheese lovers only.

1 qt (4 cups) mayonnaise
1 cup buttermilk
1 cup small-curd cottage cheese
1 tsp worcestershire sauce
1 tsp garlic salt
1 tsp salt
4 oz. Roquefort or blue cheese, crumbled

Combine all ingredients in a medium bowl except crumbled

DO-IT-YOURSELF CROUTONS & SPROUTS

Croutons

4 slices homemade bread*
2 Tbsp Parmesan cheese
¼ tsp oregano
¼ tsp celery salt
¼ tsp garlic salt
2 Tbsp salad oil

Slice bread into ⅜" cubes and place in a bowl. Add seasonings and oil. Toss well to mix. Place on cookie sheet. Bake at 300° until crisp. Cool. Store in a glass jar. Costs about a third of store bought.

* or French bread from bakery thrift shop
Contributed by Ellen Marston, Brunswick, Maine

Sprouts

Place ¼ cup of mung beans in a quart jar and cover with tepid water. Cover with cheesecloth and tie securely. Soak overnight. Drain water off. Set in a warm dark place. Every day rinse with tepid water and drain. Place in a warm dark place again. Repeat four to five days or until sprouts are as big as you want.

cheese. Mix with electric mixer. Stir in crumbled cheese with a fork. Refrigerate.

Makes 1½ quarts.
—Salad dressing recipes
from The Oregonian

HOW TO AVOID FEELING DEPRIVED

Our brass kerosene lamp gives off a warm glow, enough to provide the additional needed light for our dinner of hot cornmeal biscuits and refrigerator stew made of leftover bean soup and random freezer finds. The children, ruddy from outdoor play, consume without question. Jim's comment that the stew is good bespeaks the chancy nature of leftover cookery. I find myself curbing a smile. I would have the same strange satisfaction had the meal been less successful.

I have the same feeling when I adjust my ancient see-through sock so that the hole doesn't line up with my big toe. When I have time I'll darn it. I can afford new ones, but I have a secret quest to see how long I can make the old ones last.

The feeling occurs again when Jim completes a building project on the table saw that had been intercepted on the way to the dump, overhauled, and mounted on a curb-gleaned frame of a deep-fat fryer.

My attitude has undergone a complete reversal. A decade ago I enjoyed prime rib at the Ritz Carlton and purchased toys for nieces and nephews from F.A.O. Schwartz.

Even today, when excess would not stand between us and our goals, we still enjoy being frugal. In general, we prefer low-cost meals, used acquisitions, and free entertainment.

This attitude reversal lies at the heart of why we have never felt deprived while sustaining our lifestyle for so many years.

The feeling of deprivation will undermine any effort to pursue long-term disciplines.

The dieter will fail as long as he hates low-calorie food. The would-be athlete will fail as long as he hates exertion. The tightwad wannabe will fail as long as he views frugality as a lifestyle he has to endure, or was forced into by circumstance.

To overcome the feeling of deprivation consider the following three points:

First, recognize that you are engaging in the discipline out of choice. You decide to give up something so that you can have something else.

If you think "I eat leftovers because I *have* to," you view yourself as being deprived. Instead think "I eat leftovers because curbing my food bill is something I *can* do to reach my goal."

This attitude adjustment is like the question "Is the glass half empty or half full?" When you recognize that you are making a choice, attitudes change from deprivation to empowerment.

Second, as you cut back, give up expenses in the order of the ones that provide the least value for dollars spent. The order of elimination will differ from tightwad to tightwad.

In the beginning Jim and I ate out more. After a less-than-spectacular meal of stuffed lobster, we agreed to give up restaurant meals altogether. We did not enjoy them enough for the cost. During one of my speaking engagements a woman told me her husband was a chef and loved to eat out. In their case they probably received sufficient value from restaurant meals to continue going out. They needed to find other things to give up first.

View giving up extras as transferring funds from one area of your life to another. I am the first to admit that there is nothing frugal about six kids and a 2,200-square-foot, 100-year-old farmhouse. To afford this we slashed expenses in the areas of food, entertainment, and clothing. Slashing your housing costs to spend more on food, entertainment, and clothing would be equally acceptable as long as you live within your means and are on track in pursuit of your goals.

To assess your values, constantly ask yourself if you received sufficient value for the

Is the glass half empty...

...or half full?

money you spent. It costs $20 to take the kids to a fast-food joint. You could prepare the same meal at home for $2. Is the experience of the fast-food meal 10 times better than the home-cooked meal? Is the convenience worth $18?

People commonly make the mistake of spending money on smaller items that are low on their priority list and, as a result, cannot afford the big things high on their list.

Real deprivation is not being able to afford the things that are high on your priority list. When assessing your values, think back to the concept of transferring funds from one area of your budget to another. Think about the trade-offs and redefine deprivation. Instead of being a matter of eating more leftovers or wearing used clothes, maybe deprivation is having to work a second job you hate, or stress from massive debt or not being able to afford another child.

When you give up the lower priority things first, hopefully your budget will allow you to keep the extras that genuinely give value to your life. However, if you find you still need to cut more, think back to your goal. The chef and his wife had been able to save to buy a home. They needed to measure the value of eating out in relation to the value of home ownership. If they are unwilling to give up the meals out, they need to admit that home ownership must be a lower priority for them.

Third, do not compare your economic situation to those of others. If you are trying to lose weight, it can be frustrating to watch a thin person eat twice as much as you. Having a slow metabolism just means you have to work harder.

If your income is less than someone else's you will have to eliminate more from your priority list to achieve the same goal. Jim and I knew that we had to work harder than our parents and grandparents to afford a similar home. We had nothing to gain by bemoaning today's higher interest rates.

Wringing your hands over economic inequities merely wastes emotional energy that could be better used in a positive way to achieve your goal. Accept the givens in your situation and work with them.

Feeling empowered by recognizing you are choosing to scale down to reach a goal, eliminating expenses in order of least value received, and accepting the givens in your personal economic situation are aspects of "beginner tightwaddery."

Beyond this there is a higher plane of enlightenment . . . "the Zen of Advanced Tightwaddery."

You progress to a state of mind where you develop an aversion to "stupid expenditures," as defined within your personal value system. They become symbols of darkness that have been placed in your path to thwart your efforts . . . hence, my seemingly irrational disdain for Jell-O Pudding Snack Paks.

Likewise, you come to equate aspects of frugality (which our culture regards as deprivation) as symbols for past or future achievements. You know that you have gotten "it" when you discover you prefer refrigerator stew to prime rib, not because it tastes

better, but because more than merely feeding your body it nourishes your soul. You know within yourself that these symbols represent a larger lifestyle that will enable you to acquire (or have enabled you to acquire) the things that are genuinely important to you.

And then when your cousin Wilbur waves a cigar in your face and says, "Eh, lighten up! Would it kill you to take them kids to McDonald's once in a while?" you can curb your smile, wiggle your toe to readjust the sock hole, and silently hold the knowledge that he has yet to reach your plane of higher enlightenment.

HOME HAIRCUTTING FOR BOYS

What I know about cutting hair I have learned from years of watching my own hair being cut. Still, I might never have started cutting my own children's hair if the first had not been born bald on the top with a long scraggly fringe around the edges. I trimmed it and he looked better.

I have learned to cut by trial and error—errors being made before the boys knew any different. I began with a one-length-all-over cut and gradually began to taper for a more traditional look.

Many mothers are closet haircutters with their own method. Mine is the scissors-and-comb technique, which does not require clippers. Before approaching this article I consulted *Scissors and Comb Haircutting* by Bob Ohnstad (You Can Publishing, 1985). The library has other books on home haircutting. These books give a more detailed and intimidating approach. I do it a bit simpler, but the method is the same.

For tools you will need a sharp pair of scissors, a standard (not barber-style) comb, and a towel. I use a pair of barber-style scissors that I have owned forever. I would prefer the shorter-tipped precision scissors that hairstylists use but they cost about $50. A friend and closet haircutter uses Fiskars shears, which come in a variety of sizes at the sewing store. These can be obtained in a set for about $10. The main reason to use haircutting shears is that they are specially designed for that purpose, but other types will work. Traditional barber combs are for clipper cutting. Any regular comb will work with scissors cutting.

The most important rule of this style of haircutting is to cut in the direction of the grain of the hair. In other words, hair grows downward on the back of the head. Cut up and down (holding the scissors vertically), not across. If the hair grows forward on the top don't cut side to side. Cut correctly, the hair will lie like shingles on the side of the house. If you cut cross the grain you will see a horizontal chop line indicating that the layers of hair end in the same place.

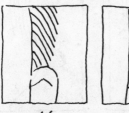

A simple beginner haircut is one with an equal length all over. I find that I can use the comb as a measuring tool. The inch-and-a-half height is about right for a preschooler. The height of the comb and thickness of my index finger is about right for an older child. As long as all the hair is cut to that same measure as pulled away from the scalp you can't go wrong. Continually comb and check for bits of slightly longer hair and trim to the same length.

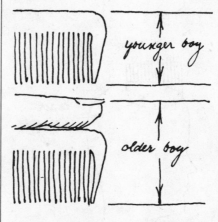

The equal-length-all-over cut tends to look short on the top and long on the sides. I simply vary it by tapering shorter on the sides and longer on the top.

After washing the hair I begin by cutting the crown to the comb

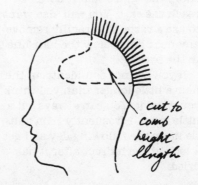

height. Next I taper the sides from comb height to about the thickness of my finger. Finally I taper the top from one comb height to about two comb heights in the front.

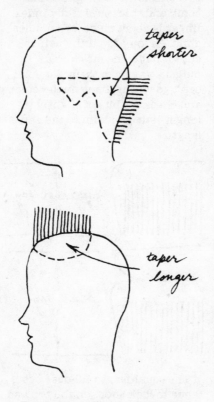

taper shorter

taper longer

The last set is to trim the edges. Comb and cut hair flat against the head. Make sure the sideburns are of equal length. I comb the hair over the ears and trim just short enough so that it doesn't reach the ears. You will also want to use a razor to carefully remove any neck hair below the hair line in the back.

If you are not confident, cut the hair a little longer than you think you want it. You can always cut a little more. I frequently trim a little more the following day as I get a look at the haircut after it has dried.

Very young children won't sit long, and I will cut in stages over few days. With the most impossible toddler I measure out very small sections, holding the measured length between thumb and finger. As hair slacks I can follow his wiggle before snipping. This will not produce as good a cut as when you cut linear sections, but it serves him right.

We estimate that we save about $50 per year for each boy. I find that cutting my children's hair also saves me time. I don't have to chauffeur them to a barber when I can make the time. I can cut while watching TV at my own convenience and as frequently as I want. I can also get a more consistent, predictable look, rather than having a kid go from shaggy to whitewalls in a sitting.

A TRICK FOR CUTTING BANGS

After mastering a boy's haircut, I next attempted my daughter's bangs. Unlike Alec's slightly wavy hair Jamie has very fine straight hair. I found that no matter how careful I was, the blunt cut always seemed to look as though I had done it with pinking shears.

layered

blunt

As I attempted to trim more the bangs got shorter, but not more even.

After several botches I realized why I had this new problem. Boys' bangs are not a true blunt cut—they don't end in the same place, but are layered.

I discovered a trick that works very well. After the blunt cut I separate out vertical sections. I then cut a slight angle as shown. It is important not to cut the bottom of the section as this establishes the hair line. When the hair lies down again it has a softer edge and any original imperfections are no longer visible.

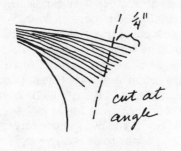

cut at angle

SOCK WISDOM

Dear Amy,

I'm a professional man, and I buy my socks 30 or 40 at a time. Seems like a lot to pay for socks all at once? Maybe so, but I buy them identical—all black poly-cotton. If one wears out beyond

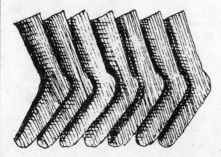

repair, I don't lose a pair . . . just one sock. And I save time (which is money) and bother by not having to match up socks. I just dump all my socks from one washline into one drawer. Any two I pick up will match! Using this method I haven't had to buy new socks since 1980 and expect the present batch to last another five years.

Willard Morris
Lanham-Seabrook, Maryland

PREVENTION

Dear Amy,

In my profession as a cardiac ultrasound technician, I've seen hundreds of people (including hospital employees) killing themselves, and costing them and us big bucks. Preventive medicine is definitely frugal. If everyone stopped smoking, for instance, I'd be out of work.

Diane Shaw
Turner, Maine

SYRUP JUGS

Dear Amy,

I reuse syrup jugs, with the little pop-up lids. My kids use them as canteens, particularly on car trips. Those with handles can be hung from a belt (with a hook) for hiking.

Jamien Morehouse
Rockport, Maine

FRUGAL INHERITANCE

Dear Amy,

Here's my scrapless method of using bath soap bars:

I use the soap until it's about ¼ inch thick or slightly thinner. Next time I take a shower I break out a new bar. I use both bars to lather up, leaving some lather on the bars.

When I'm through showering, I press the small bar on top of the new bar (piggyback), and set them in the soap dish together. The lather dries bonding the two bars together for my next shower.

Each time I take a shower, the bond becomes firmer. When the double bar gets down to ¼ inch thick, I repeat the process with a third bar of soap. And so on, ad infinitum.

Theoretically some of the atoms in this soapy cycle will remain in my bar until my very last shower! When I am gone, my son can continue to use the bar as I have, reflecting that it has traces of the bar I used on the very first Earth Day, when I started recycling soap this way. And thus shall my zealous frugality be passed down from generation to generation as long as my descendents shall lather up.

> Willard Morris
> Lanham-Seabrook, Maryland

HOW TO COMPARE EGG PRICES

Did you ever wonder what size egg is the best value? OK, so I never did either. One reader sent

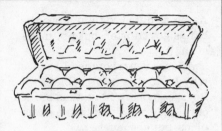

me a packet of material, and this one idea was something I hadn't thought about before.

Eggs are sorted by weight. Jumbo eggs are 30 ounces per dozen, extra large are 27, large are 24, medium are 21, and small are 18 ounces. The weight can exceed these numbers, but not be less. Jumbos can be a great hidden value, since they can be any weight of 30 ounces or over.

One could theorize that there could be some variation in the weight of a dozen eggs within a size group. A dozen large eggs, for example, can be any weight from 24 ounces to just under 27 ounces. If you didn't have anything better to do with your time you could take several boxes and hike the distance from the dairy case to the produce department to weigh them to find the best value.

(You can weigh bags of potatoes, carrots, onions, and heads of lettuce to find any that may be slightly heavier.)

	59¢	69¢	79¢	89¢	99¢	$1.09	$1.19	$1.29	$1.39	$1.49
SMALL	3.3	3.8	4.4	4.9	5.5	6.1	6.6	7.2	7.7	8.3
MEDIUM	2.8	3.3	3.8	4.2	4.7	5.2	5.7	6.1	6.6	7.1
LARGE	2.5	2.9	3.3	3.7	4.1	4.5	5.0	5.4	5.8	6.2
EX-LARGE	2.2	2.6	2.9	3.3	3.7	4.0	4.4	4.8	5.1	5.5
JUMBO	2.0	2.3	2.6	3.0	3.3	3.6	4.0	4.3	4.6	5.0

To determine the best values among different size eggs I have devised the chart on page 236, which shows how many cents per ounce you would pay at the common egg prices.

I have included prices for a dozen eggs from 59¢ to $1.49, but I don't want to perpetuate any myths that food prices are cheaper in Maine. We pay about $1 per dozen for large eggs if we buy from a local farmer.

A photocopy in your billfold might be a handy shopping aid.

A TIGHTWAD PARABLE

The philosopher Diogenes was eating bread and lentils for supper. He was seen by the philosopher Aristippus, who lived comfortably by flattering the king. Said Aristippus, "If you would learn to be subservient to the king you would not have to live on lentils."

Said Diogenes, "Learn to live on lentils and you will not have to be subservient to the king."

The Song of the Bird
by Anthony de Mello

TWO RECIPES FOR KIDS

Homemade Bubble Solution

Many readers sent in a variation of this recipe. Glycerin can be purchased at a drugstore. I recently purchased a 4 oz bottle for $2.25.

Several of the recipes specified Joy dishwashing liquid, perhaps because it is the best for bubbles. The longer you store the bubble solution the better it works. You will want to prepare it weeks (or even months) in advance for a special event.

9 parts water
1 part Joy dishwashing liquid
½ part glycerin

Giant Bubble Maker

Save coffee cans. Cut off tops and bottoms. Hammer the edges smooth. Dip cans in a pan of solution and wave through the air.

Have a contest for the biggest bubble, smallest bubble, and the bubble that floats the highest. (Contributed by Laurie Glendinning, Rohnut Park, California)

Homemade Finger Paints

1 envelope unflavored gelatin
½ cup cornstarch
3 Tbsp sugar
2 cups cold water
food coloring
dishwashing liquid
white shelfpaper

Soak gelatin in ¼ cup warm water and put aside.

In a medium saucepan combine cornstarch and sugar. Gradually add water and cook slowly over low heat, stirring until well blended.

Remove from heat and add softened gelatin. Divide mixture into separate containers for each color.

For each color first add a drop or two of liquid detergent and then add food coloring a drop at a time until you have the shade you want.

Store up to six weeks in the refrigerator.

CHEAP THRILLS

Dear Amy,

Sunday drives through the backwoods of Maine: in the past, when we found a sunny Sunday afternoon, we often drove out to gaze at wished-for farms (with or without attached barns) on back roads to get acquainted with our adopted state. Often we'd stop in antique shops and small restaurants and squander lesser or greater sums (depending on whether these businesses took

Visa). Now when we have a sunny Sunday afternoon, we still go out for a drive, but instead of spending money we try to make some. It's amazing how many beer and soda cans and bottles are strewn along these otherwise beautiful country roads! In less than an hour we have found at least $5 worth, thus more than covering the cost of the gas we use for these trips in our 1984 Escort Pony, and additionally providing us with much self-righteousness in the thought that we're contributing to cleaning up the environment.

Carol M. Petillo
Springvale, Maine

Dear Amy,

Sometimes local high schools have night courses for adults, which meet usually once a week. They are noncredit but you can learn something. I paid $5 registration fee, and though I had to pay $15 for materials for one course, this certainly is inexpensive! One of the courses is introductory welding, which is a very useful skill to be familiar with. I already fixed one tool to make it work better, and plan to make another project.

Dana Morong
Madbury, New Hampshire

Dear Amy,

We live near enough to a college town to be able to enjoy an occasional free concert. Even a recital by music students is a delight. I hear of at least one free event each month.

As has been said before, public libraries are treasure troves of free stuff: information and entertainment. A favorite of mine is books on audio cassette. My husband and I like to listen and visualize Louis L'Amour while cozy in bed.

> Westy Melby
> Boone, Colorado

USED-CAR THEORY

Finding ways to economize on the cost of car ownership is becoming increasingly difficult as the newer cars are often too complex for the average backyard mechanic. Even a proper tune-up requires computerized equipment. As owners of new vehicles we have been hard pressed to come up with ideas other than the obvious, like buying oil on sale or keeping records of mileage and tune-ups.

Two readers, owners of older vehicles, have filled the void with lengthy submissions. I have gleaned the best of their ideas.

Dear Amy,

My philosophy of automobiles is to get a good model and stick with it, learning it, stripping it

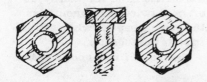

for parts as they rust out, and hauling the rust to a recycling place. Now I subscribe to a newsletter on that car, with useful tips from readers.

Get a good model, get the bottom welded up well, then rebuild the entire brake system (in some cases replace it entirely for safety).

There are four or five curved molded hoses that I got tired of paying crazy prices for (imported). By researching I found alternates (domestic), which are easier to get, less expensive, and work as well.

I spent $4 for a lens, used spare parts, and installed a third brake light in my car to prevent rear-end collisions.

Don't be cheap with engine oil, but replace whenever oil wears out: 5,000 miles for new cars and 3,000 to 4,000 for older cars. I buy several cases of quality oil when on sale (also filters). Those who try to go farther on worn oil only risk wearing the rings (and engine) thus burning more oil, lowering mpg, and polluting the air. Besides, old oil can be saved for recycling.

Every April remove the carpets and air them and the floor for a couple of weeks, to let the floor dry out. Water comes in on the boots in winter, then sets under the carpet and rots the floor in warmer weather. Also hose down the insides of the wheel wells until the water runs clear.

> Dana Morong
> Madbury, New Hampshire

Dear Amy,

The "turnaround" costs connected with replacing a car, including tag transfer, sales tax, expenses of selling, expenses of searching are likely to average more than $200 through the decade. A car that is likely to go to the junkyard within a few months is probably a liability rather than an asset.

Purchasing a car when the appropriate opportunity (a good deal) presents itself is generally wise, even if it means selling a surplus car soon.

If your family owns "n plus one" cars, "n" being the number of drivers, so that there is a spare car, then a reliable mechanic may be willing to repair for less, because a rush is not required.

If there is a teenage driver in the household, the family generally cannot afford to own anything but compact cars too old to justify collision insurance, by reason of the higher premiums for liability insurance for heavier cars. However, if there are no young drivers, the heavy gas guzzler is likely to be the cheapest car for the family driving only a few thousand miles per year.

> John Ewbank
> Southampton, Pennsylvania

NEW-CAR THEORY

There seems to be a discrepancy in car ownership philosophy among the most frugal and expert. A new-car salesman told me never *ever* buy a new car. I have been impressed by letters from people who have never paid more than $500 for a car and have rebuilt engines in their basement. Conventional expert wisdom suggests that the two- or three-year-old car is the best value.

Just when I was feeling like a total clod for our two new pur-chased cars I received a letter from a reader. His theory of new-car ownership exactly reflects my husband's. The letter is very convincing, well written, and long. I have narrowed it down to the major points to save space.

I am convinced that the choice between the new car or old depends on how much you want to spend your winter weekends tinkering on a car in a frigid barn. The single drawback to a two-year-old car is the uncertainty of the care by the previous owner.

Dear Amy,

Two goals of minimizing cost per mile and beating inflation can be achieved by buying a good-quality car new, maintaining it carefully, and driving it for at least 10 years.

Don't wait until your old car dies and you have to rush out in a panic to buy a new one. Take your time and shop around. Get dealers bidding against each other.

When you find a good deal pay cash. Your frugal lifestyle has, of course, allowed you plenty of cash.

Drive your new car straight to an autobody shop for undercoating, or do it yourself with cans of 3M undercoating.

Proceed to the nearest tire dealer and buy a set of top-grade steel-belted radial tires. Now you have nine tires, including the spare. Set up a rotation scheme, rotating properly for even wear. In the year 2000 you'll still be driving on 1991-priced tires.

Most important advice! Change the oil and filter frequently, as often as twice as frequently as the manual says or when the dipstick is unreadable.

Change all fluids once a year.

Ask your service manager of your local dealership about the life expectancy of parts for your model, and replace parts before necessary to save money.

After seven to eight years get it repainted to give you good payback when you sell.

Here is my own experience:

In 1969 I bought a Toyota station wagon for $2,300. Ten years and 170,000 miles later I sold it for $1,000, still running fine and looking very handsome.

In 1979 I bought a new Saab for $8,700. It's going on its 12th year and some 170,000 miles, and I'm still driving it and expect to do so for some time to come.

Ed LaChapelle
Glennallen, Alaska

APPROACHING VEGETARIANISM

If you are like I was only a few years ago, you probably regard vegetarianism as some sort of peculiar diet bordering on a cult. People with that diet, I thought, ate all manner of weird-sounding foods—tofu, alfalfa sprouts, brewer's yeast, soy flour, wheat germ, miso. . . .

What I didn't realize was that I had eaten vegetarian meals nearly every day of my life. Many foods (without strange-sounding names) fall into a category of vegetarianism.

Vegetarianism is simply a diet that relies on the eating of plants as a source of protein. A vegan is someone who eats no protein from an animal source. A lacto-ovo vegetarian gets some of his

protein from eggs and milk products but not from meat.

Meat contains all the amino acids necessary to make a complete protein. The protein that occurs in plant food is not complete in one source. But you can get all the necessary amino acids by combining different foods. It has been generally believed that the right foods must be eaten at the same meal. I have recently read that some nutritionists now believe the combinations do not have to occur within the same meal, just as long as you eat them the same day.

The diagram below shows which foods can be combined to make a complete protein. The solid line indicates combinations that usually combine to make a protein, whereas the broken line indicates combinations that work only some of the time.

Whole grains are grains that have not been processed. White flour and rice have had valuable nutrients removed and will not combine to make a protein. Legumes are any type of dried bean. Seeds include sesame seeds, sunflower seeds, and nuts. Milk products include cheese, yogurt, and ice cream.

Food combining may seem complicated, so remember: it's impor-

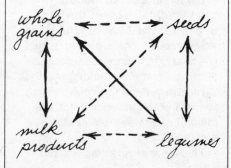

tant not to get too hung up on it. Many Americans were introduced to the idea of vegetarianism by Frances Moore Lappe's *Diet for a Small Planet,* published in 1971. Lappe spends almost the whole book emphasizing the importance of combining foods to create complete proteins. Many readers were left with the impression that vegetarianism was a noble but difficult art.

But in her latest edition, Lappe apologizes for mistakenly giving readers that impression. As she puts it, "If people are getting enough calories, they are virtually certain of getting enough protein." Researchers at institutions from Harvard University to the National Academy of Sciences to the American Dietetic Association now agree: if a variety of healthful foods are eaten, protein is not a problem.

Lack of vitamin B_{12} can be a problem for vegetarians who abstain from eggs and dairy products (vegans), and some nutritionists recommend a B_{12} supplement for them. But vegetarians who do eat eggs and dairy products (lacto-ovo vegetarians) generally get all the vitamins they need from their diet . . . again, if they eat a variety of healthful foods.

If you eat a small amount of meat it will also boost the protein in plant foods. I have found some "vegetarian" cookbooks with recipes that contain small amounts of meat. (Some would dispute that these are vegetarian cookbooks.) Instead of these being meatless meals I call these "less-meat" meals.

There are several vegetarian

meals that are familiar to everyone. For example:

oatmeal and milk
baked beans and brown bread
peanut butter on whole-wheat
   bread
burritos made with refried
   beans (without lard)
corn chowder

So most die-hard meat eaters, without knowing it, have been eating vegetarian meals for years.

Meat is one of the most expensive foods we buy. It is also a food we eat far too much of. Animal fat contributes to high cholesterol and some studies also link it to higher cancer rates. Adults only need a few ounces per day, at most. New nutritional information suggests that we should treat meat more like a side dish rather than the main course. Learning to incorporate more meatless or less-meat meals in our diets makes sense from an economic and health standpoint.

Vegetarianism is also good for the environment for several reasons. Far less water is required to produce protein from plant sources than animal sources. The rainforest is being cut down to make room for grazing land. Meat requires refrigeration.

Eating less meat is another of those triple plays—something you can do that is good for your health, good for the environment, and good for your wallet.

Dried beans are cheaper than the least expensive meats purchased on sale in the family pack. You can even grow your own if you have ample garden space. Without incorporating some legume meals in your diet you will never achieve the rock-bottom food bill.

I am not suggesting that we all make the great leap to a meatless diet, but we can all approach vegetarianism by beginning to include more whole grains, seeds, and dried beans in our diets while reducing the amount of meat we eat.

One reason we eat so much meat is that when we eat the standard meat-and-potatoes meal a five-ounce piece of steak seems the right size. "Disguise" the smaller (more appropriate) meat portions. Look for casseroles that combine small amounts of meat with dried beans, whole grains, seeds, or dairy products. Soups and stir-fry meals accomplish the same objective. You can also serve a small portion of meat along with legumes.

When you reduce meat consumption be sure that you increase the whole grains in your diet. We rarely make pancakes, waffles, muffins, biscuits, or bread without the addition of cornmeal, oatmeal, or whole-wheat flour. You can also add additional dried milk powder to boost protein in baked foods. These additions do increase the cost of your baking, but the decrease in your meat consumption will lower your food bill more. Likewise some meatless recipes call for expensive ingredients, including cheese and other exotic additions. Always do the math to determine if a recipe is truly economical.

When you feed your children breakfasts, they must have adequate protein or they will be lethargic midmorning at school. Breakfasts prepared from white flour without whole grains added (such as waffles or pancakes) will not provide adequate protein. I suggest you give your family milk instead of juice along with a whole-grain meal. Put the juice in their lunch boxes instead—it will keep better than milk.

We dragged our feet a bit in learning to eat more meals with legumes. The beans you buy in a can are not as cheap as the dried type. But the dried type usually requires presoaking and a lengthy cooking time. So our most common legume meal had been bean soup.

Then a reader sent us an energy-saving pressure-cooker method of preparing beans and rice. This can be prepared in about 30 minutes. Now we eat beans and rice when "someone" forgot to thaw meat for our supper. (Since Jim retired, the guilty "someone" is harder to identify.) Beans and rice have become our version of "fast food."

Rather than providing specific recipes I suggest that you get a cookbook from the library. Begin with foods that are familiar to you. In New England baked beans are common. Southerners like pinto beans. Those in the Southwest are familiar with Mexican bean dishes. Our family likes to eat bean soups. There is a 15-bean soup package at the supermarket in the dried bean section that is excellent. Lentil soups are a good place to start because lentils cook up quickly.

Many of the strange-sounding foods no longer sound strange to us. Things like sprouts and wheat germ have found their way into our pantry.

POOCH POTPOURRI

Homemade Dog Biscuits

3½ cups unbleached flour
2 cups whole-wheat flour
1 cup rye flour
2 cups bulgur (cracked wheat)
1 cup cornmeal
½ cup instant nonfat dry milk
4 tsp salt
1 envelope active dry yeast
¼ cup warm water
3 cups chicken broth
1 egg slightly beaten with 1 tsp
   milk

1. Turn oven on to 300°. Mix first seven ingredients with a wooden spoon in a large bowl.

2. Dissolve yeast thoroughly in warm water (110°–115°) in glass measuring cup. Add to dry ingredients.

3. Add chicken broth to flour mixture. Stir until dough forms.

4. Roll out dough until it is ¼″ thick. Cut out bone shapes from dough. Place on greased cookie sheets.

5. Brush dough with egg glaze.

6. Bake bones for 45 minutes. Turn oven off. Biscuits should remain overnight to harden. Makes 30 larger bones at about 40% cheaper than store bought.

The Dog Biscuit Cutter

This recipe originally suggests that you cut bone shapes using a store-bought biscuit as a pattern. However my tuna can cookie cutter idea works for these, too.

You need a can that has a bottom that can be removed with a can opener. After removing both top and bottom shape cutter with two pairs of pliers starting at op-

posite symmetrical points.

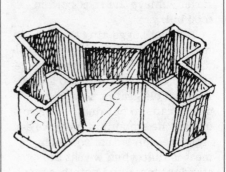

If you do not have a dog consider making these as a gift for someone who does have a dog, especially the hard-to-buy-for elderly person with a precious pooch.

The Pooch Poop Scoop

I developed this out of necessity as the new dog had trouble making the transition to a new home. I used a 20-quart dry milk carton cut diagonally as shown.

This size scoop works well for a shepherd. Use cereal boxes for beagles. Macaroni and cheese boxes for Chihuahuas.

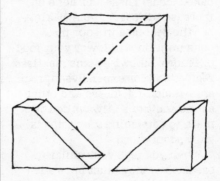

WHEELBARROW METAMORPHOSIS
Or How to Build a Wheelbarrow from Salvaged Materials

Plan 1. When you take your trash to the dump keep your eyes peeled for a discarded wheelbarrow with possibilities. When you spot one ask the dump custodian about it. He will scratch his chin and tell you to take it, as well as another you hadn't noticed. As it happens one will only have a salvageable tub and the other will be good except for a rusted out tub. Bring them both home and let them sit in your barn for several months as you wait for "a good day." This will allow you adequate time to mull your plan to combine the good parts to make one complete wheelbarrow.

Plan 2. By the time the good day arrives you will reject Plan 1. You will decide the wheelbarrow with the "good" tub isn't really very good. Take that wheelbarrow back to the dump. Plan to construct a new tub or body from salvaged lumber. Plan to use all the other parts from the wheelbarrow you kept.

new body

Plan 3. When you disassemble the salvaged wheelbarrow you will notice that the handles are rather flimsy, being made of two pieces of wood held together with a thin metal bracket. You will scratch Plan 2 and make new handles out of salvaged two-by-threes. (This stage requires a little preplanning. First buy a pre-1900 house with attached barn and loads of junk in the attic including old bed springs with hardwood frames. Save the wood and discard the springs.) Shape two-by-threes with a draw-knife to make grips. Construct a new body from salvaged lumber and attach to the handles.

replace handles

Plan 4. After attaching the wheel and axle you will notice that the brackets from the old wheelbarrow will not fit. You will be prepared, having saved brackets for some time from yet another wheelbarrow. When you go to dig those up, an hour-and-a-half's effort yields only one bracket. **Plan 4A.** Make wooden brackets from scraps of two-by-threes.

new brackets

Plan 5. When you try to attach the legs from the salvaged wheelbarrow, they will be a little too long and not wide enough to fit the new plan. About this time your wife, and design consultant, will enter your workshop and second your idea to scrap the old metal legs, on the grounds of a lack of aesthetic appeal. Make new legs out of the remaining two-by-threes. (Note: this design utilizes only the wheel and axle from one of the original two wheelbarrows.) Finally, use your wooden wheelbarrow for a few jobs, and bark your shins several times. **Plan 5A,** move the legs back a few inches and to the outside of the handles.

replace legs

TIGHTWAD PEEVES

An interviewer asked me if there was such a thing as being "too frugal." The answer to that question might be an article in itself, but there are a few common penny-pinching practices that don't wash with me.

The Dilution Solution. Your kid wants yet another glass of juice. You realize that all this juice drinking is driving you to financial ruin, so you decide to fool him. You dilute the juice and he's happy.

Why not do it? Junior should learn that all liquid need not have flavor. This practice will spawn a soda drinker of the future.

Instead tell him he can drink water. Or alternate letting him drink water one time and juice another.

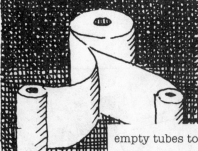

The Paper Split. You've got one roll of two-ply toilet paper and two empty tubes. You separate the two plies and roll them each on the empty tubes to make two rolls of paper.

Why not do it? Because you have better things to do with your life! Besides, what's the first thing you do when you use toilet paper? You fold it, thereby making your one-ply a two-ply again.

Instead educate your family to use fewer two-ply squares.

The Syrup Switch. Your teenager is loyal to Mrs. Butterworth. You know the homemade stuff tastes just as good. For years you've been refilling the same Mrs. Butterworth's bottle. Even though the faded label is a dead giveaway she hasn't noticed yet.

Why not do it? Because you are allowing her to continue believing that brands matter, when in fact, taste preference is acquired.

Tell her to buy her own Mrs. Butterworth's with her babysitting money.

The Packet Swipe. You eat in a restaurant and fill your pockets with extra ketchup and sugar packets.

Why not do it? First, those things were intended for your use in the restaurant, not later at home. Second, what are you doing blowing your money in a restaurant in the first place? A whole cup of sugar costs about 20¢. You just spent about 20 times that amount for lunch.

The Stamp Steam. A letter comes to your home with an uncanceled stamp. You steam it off and reuse it. You figure it's only fair because postal rates just went up.

Why not do it? It happens to be a federal offense. OK, so a fleet of police cars won't converge on your home with sirens, blue lights, and a megaphone. But you're simply passing the cost along to others.

Seems like a better thing to do to aid the postal service in keeping future rates down would be paying for the services that you do use.

The Party Collection. You host as many Tupperware parties as possible to get the free gifts to give away as presents.

Why not do it? The salesperson is trying to make a living. If your friends are tightwads like you, they won't spend. If they're spendthrifts they probably shouldn't spend, but will. (Not to mention that they're throwing away all those Cool Whip containers at home.)

The Card Shark. You send a friend a card, but you sign it in pencil so that they can erase your name and reuse it.

Why not do it? First they can't reuse it anyway because it requires an odd-sized envelope, which they can't replace. Second if you don't think your friend will want to keep the card, why send one at all? Instead send a thoughtful letter . . . using both sides of the paper, naturally.

A SUCCESS STORY

I receive wonderful letters from people. These are enormously important to me since, for the most part, my only connection with readers is through the mail. I wanted to share one particularly good one.

Dear Amy,

Thank you for what you are doing! After receiving my first issue, I promptly sent for all the back issues. When they arrived, I stayed up long past midnight reading every one. It has changed my life!

After receiving the first issue of my subscription, I did a lot of rearranging of my budget and, with some (I thought) severe belt tightening, managed to start saving $200 per month. After my *Gazette* Marathon, I redid my finances, and am now saving $600 per month . . . and my "belt" seems to have gotten lots looser in the process.

It is amazing the difference an attitude change can make in one's life. Before the *Gazette* marathon, I felt poor when I had to "do without" (and rewarded myself for my frugality with expensive clothes, food, and doodads). Now, I feel *smart* for finding fun, creative (and often better) alternatives for little or nothing.

I now shop the garage sales regularly and am finding *great stuff!* My job requires that I dress up every day for work. Recently at a garage sale, I found a beautiful navy wool suit in perfect condition for $5. When I wear it to work, everyone wants to know what special occasion I'm dressing up for. I just give 'em a model's pirouette and a smile.

I started a price book recently and am appalled at how much I've been spending (wasting!) on groceries. I never thought I had time to follow sales. I shopped at stores whose ambiance I liked. I budgeted (and actually spent!) $150 per month on food . . . and I'm a vegetarian! And I live alone! Now, after doing a little research, I discovered it's easier to be frugal. Instead of spending my Saturdays driving to expensive stores in ritzy neighborhoods, I stop by two discount supermarkets that are right on my way home from work, and on my lunch hour I hit the members-only outlet that's near my office. I not only save tons of money but also a whole day as well.

My plans have changed also. I can actually see a time when I'll have my (previously out-of-reach) paid-for little house on five acres in the woods, with a vegetable garden and fruit trees. I have some debts I'm paying off (from my prefrugal days), and when those are gone I'm going to save the money I'm now spending making payments. I will then be saving about half my salary. What this will mean is that for every day I work, I will be paying for one day of financial freedom. This is far more attractive to me than anything I can buy in a store. And the best part is that I can have it all without "sacrificing."

Thank you for giving me control over my life and my future!
(Reader's name withheld by request)

TWO SIDES TO EVERY PAGE

Each month our computer printer spits out great stacks of paper for various reports. Not even four kids, feverishly coloring on one side, can hope to keep up.

The older ones have taken to making "books." Budding authors, you know. They want new paper that is good on both sides, so that their literary works won't be marred with the writings of another.

I've hit upon a simple solution. I fold six papers in half, with printed side on the inside. Then I staple them together on the open edge. Now their books have pages with two clean sides. And because our printer ribbon is so old, the printing on the inside of the pages is faint enough to barely show through.

THE TIGHTWAD CHECKLIST

Several recent magazine articles point to thrift as the new wave of the '90s. As with any trend, there will be those attempting to pass themselves off as genuinely thrifty.

Just how does one distinguish the practitioner of lifelong frugality from those drifting with the current fad? When visiting the homes of individuals in question use this handy checklist to record the telltale signs of a classic tightwad.

❏ A scrubber made from a mesh onion bag.
❏ A squirt bottle of homemade window cleaner.
❏ A new soap bar with a soap sliver adhered. (Any other soap-bit system is acceptable.)
❏ A bundle of old socks in the workshop to be used as grease rags.
❏ A pair of pantyhose minus a bad leg.
❏ A jug of vegetable broth in the refrigerator.
❏ A 20-quart box of powdered milk. (Used only for cooking is acceptable.)
❏ A roll of paper towels cut in half.
❏ Any overturned bottle in the process of draining the last bit out.
❏ A pencil less than three inches long.
❏ A marked-down crushed box of cold cereal.
❏ Any item repaired with a twist-tie, paper clip, or hanger.
❏ A shower curtain repaired with duct tape.
❏ An impressive stash of one of the following items: egg cartons, styrofoam meat trays, toilet paper tubes, or frozen juice lids.
❏ A screwdriver with a tip that has been reground several times.
❏ A started shopping list on the back of a utility bill envelope.

❑ A stockpile of 44¢ per can tuna.

❑ A started container of "refrigerator stew" in the freezer.

❑ An indoor clothesline or a wooden clothes-drying rack.

Any individual scoring 12 or more is likely to be a genuine tightwad, and can be trusted.

WHAT TO DO WITH . . .

Brown Grocery Bags. These are now worth a nickel apiece. Many stores deduct 5¢ from your grocery bill if you bring back and reuse them for your groceries. This makes them too valuable for most any other types of reuse.

Cereal Boxes. Cut out flat sections and punch holes along the edges. Give them to your child along with a shoe lace. They can pretend they are sewing. A very nice set of these might make a gift for a three-year-old. (Contributed by Diane Meyer, St. Louis, Missouri)

Moth-eaten Sweaters. Make mittens from the remaining good sections. Trace a pattern from your hand. Place it on the sweater so that the sweater waist or cuffs become the cuffs of the mitten. Stitch two layers of the sweater on the sewing machine and trim. (Contributed by Eileen Donelan, Enfield, Connecticut)

Old Knee-high Stockings. Cut off the elastic trim neatly. Use for ponytail holders. Murphy's Law dictates that these free ones will not get lost like their 3-for-$1 counterparts. (Contributed by Kristen Mrozinski, Schenectady, New York)

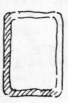

Holey Rubber Gloves. Cut the tips off the fingers to use for picking blackberries or raspberries. The gloves prevent your hands and arms from being scratched, but you can still pick the berries with your fingertips.

Styrofoam Meat Trays. Put them behind wall outlet switch plates for insulation. Trim to fit, and screw tightly for a snug fit.

Coat Hangers. Use to make a hook to hold cookie cutters, canning jar lids, rolls of tape, etc. It can be hooked into an existing peg board. (Contributed by Jamien Morehouse, Camden, Maine)

Old Metal Beds. The head and foot boards can be reused to make great gates, especially around vegetable gardens. (Contributed by Dorothy Lockard, Greenville, Pennsylvania)

ETHICS II:
THE SURVEY

After I ran an article on tightwad ethics, I received a higher-than-normal number of letters from readers pointing to ideas in the newsletter that they thought were unethical.

Clearly, ethics is a tricky area. As I wade through the uncharted waters of tightwaddery, I get letters from vast numbers of people who express opinions on things I have written or published. And frequently the opinions expressed are diametrically opposed.

I felt like I was the only person who was aware of this, so I offered a survey to the readers. My aim was to demonstrate the diversity of what people find ethical.

Because this was the sort of survey that only the most highly ethical person might respond to, and I wanted an accurate sampling, I requested that a few readers with low moral character respond as well.

I got over 1,000 responses. I was particularly interested/amused by those who answered "No to everything," and "Yes to everything." I also chuckled over

the husbands and wives who responded separately with different answers. The possible answers were:

"Yes."

"Yes, but I wouldn't do it."

"No."

"No, but I would do it anyway."

I've also included a typical comment that best expressed the majority viewpoint (I included two comments in number 8 to reflect a fairly evenly split opinion). I have refrained from putting in my own two cents (but, in case you're curious . . . in most cases I agree with the majority view).

Is it ethical to:

1. Secretly switch your spouse's favorite, expensive name brand with store brand to see if they would notice the difference, providing that you eventually let them in on it?

| 76% Yes | 6% Yes, but . . . |
| 14% No | 4% No, but . . . |

"Yes, we both do this all the time."

2. Substitute another receipt to get a rebate if you lost the original receipt? The possible justification here is that you did in fact purchase the product and satisfy

FZ's World

WE LOVED YOUR NEWSLETTER. MY SON LIVES IN THE MIDWEST. AND I WAS TELLING HIM ALL ABOUT IT WHEN I _CALLED_...

HORRORS! DID I REALLY SAY _THAT_ TO THE FRUGAL ZEALOT? SHE'LL THINK I'M A SPENDTHRIFT!

BUT I CALLED HIM WHEN THE RATES WERE CHEAP!

the manufacturer's intention.
70% Yes   5% Yes, but...
19% No   6% No, but...
"Yes, I bought the item."

3. Take all of the unused soap and shampoo from your hotel room?
76% Yes   5% Yes, but...
14% No   5% No, but...
"Yes, but not the light bulbs and rolls of toilet paper."

4. Offer half the asking price and show a wad of cash to encourage the sale when you are making a large purchase from a private individual? This assumes the seller does not appear needy.
72% Yes   12% Yes, but...
15% No   1% No, but...
"Yes, that's just good old Yankee trading."

5. Buy something from a pawn shop, knowing it is likely that someone under economic duress sold the item for a fraction of its real value?
76% Yes   15% Yes, but...
8% No   1% No, but...
"Yes, if the shops did not exist, those in need would have no way to raise quick cash."

6. Return a 10-year-old coat to L. L. Bean, to take advantage of the company's unconditional satisfaction guarantee?
12% Yes   10% Yes, but...
77% No   1% No, but...
"No, this violates the spirit of this guarantee. How can you be dissatisfied after 10 years?"

7. Buy toys for a fraction of their original price from a 10-year-old at a family yard sale?
66% Yes   9% Yes, but...
24% No   1% No, but...

"Yes, assume he prefers the money."

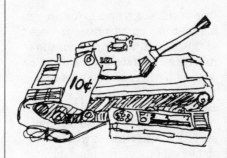

8. Take labels off thrift shop designer clothes and sew them onto new no-name clothes for your kids to wear? This assumes your kids know about it.
35% Yes   17% Yes, but...
45% No   3% No, but...
"Yes, if my kids were under extraordinary pressure from peers, I would see this as beating a stupid system."
"No, You're teaching your children false values."

9. Get Radio Shack's free battery card, and get a once-a-month free battery even though you never plan to buy anything from them?
63% Yes   11% Yes, but...
25% No   1% No, but...
"Yes, they were trying to bait you, and there were no strings."

10. To shop at a thrift shop if you have an average or above-average income? The possible objection is that you would be buying items that poorer people need.
95% Yes   2% Yes, but...
2% No   1% No, but...
"Yes, most thrift shops have too much merchandise. Profits go to a good cause.

SAVING MONEY ON YOUR MORTGAGE

One of the suggestions for an article that has come across my desk is the idea of "buying down the mortgage." I have seen a number of such articles in the past and was reluctant to add my entry. However, the subject recently hit home as we looked into our own situation and what it would take to pay off our mortgage early.

After we had lived in our house for 19 months, we sat down and figured some math. We had been paying $758 per month on a 30-year mortgage (plus taxes and insurance). That worked out to a grand total of $14,402 for the 19 months. Of that amount only $1,804 went toward the principal.

So, we knew this. But in a recent conversation with a friend about to sell her home, I learned that in 12 years she and her husband had paid off only $7,000 of their $39,000 mortgage. I got the feeling that she was completely surprised to find this out.

Most of the mortgages written now are of the 30-year variety. And it makes sense to get one. House buying is tough, and most of us struggle just to buy at all. But you should get one that doesn't penalize you for making extra payments. If your financial circumstances improve, and as inflation reduces the value of the mortgage, you should be able to make extra payments.

One of the common misconceptions about the mortgage is that you shouldn't pay off your mortgage because "you need the tax write-off." However, if you are in the 15% tax bracket you only save about $1.00 on income tax for every $6.66 you lost in interest.

What about investing, instead of using money to pay off a mortgage? In a conversation with an investment counselor, who consistently earned 15% to 20% on his investments, I asked what he thought of the merits of paying off the mortgage early. He told me that the average investor will not earn 9% or 10% on his investment. Therefore, paying off a mortgage early is a great investment strategy.

The exception would be the family with the mortgage at a very low interest rate of 5% or less. They will do better to invest surplus money in any one of a number of safe plans that yields 6% or more.

The chart on page 253 depicts the 30-year mortgage on $75,000 financed at 10%. This illustrates how much goes to pay the interest and principal year by year. Annually the mortgage costs nearly $8,000, but in the first year only $416.95 of the principal is paid off. It isn't until the 24th year that more principal is paid than interest. After 30 years the family will have paid back $236,944.32, and of that $161,944 goes for interest.

Every month the family pays $658.18 for their mortgage. If they were to round the figure up to the nearest hundred, or make payments of $700 per month, they would pay off their mortgage in 22½ years and save $47,944.32 in interest. If this same family set a goal to pay off their mortgage in 15 years they would need to increase their monthly payment by $147.77. By paying off this extra $26,598.60 ($147.77 x 12 months

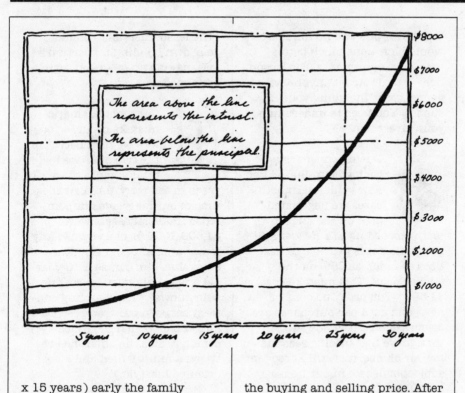

The area above the line represents the interest.

The area below the line represents the principal.

$8000
$7000
$6000
$5000
$4000
$3000
$2000
$1000

5 years   10 years   15 years   20 years   25 years   30 years

x 15 years) early the family would save $91,872.63 in interest.

In other words, after 15 years for every $1.00 paid early (of what the family would have to pay anyway) they would save $3.45. That's a hard investment strategy to beat.

SIX MISTAKES WE MADE

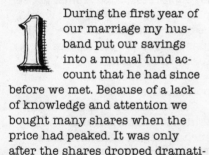

During the first year of our marriage my husband put our savings into a mutual fund account that he had since before we met. Because of a lack of knowledge and attention we bought many shares when the price had peaked. It was only after the shares dropped dramatically that we learned of the gap in the buying and selling price. After nine months of watching we decided to sell out when the shares had partially recovered. (We watched for an additional six months and the price never went higher.) This investment mistake cost us $1,500.

Apparently the pain of our earlier mistake was not severe enough, as we made a similar mistake five years later. This time our sizable nest egg was diversified in long term CDs and half a dozen funds. On the advice of our broker we bought into a fund that was tied to the stock market. Within 60 days the market crashed (Oct. '88). Our fund did not recover before we needed to liquidate. This mistake cost us $800. (At the time we invested, CDs were paying a very high rate. Had we bought all CDs and no funds we would have done much better with our investments. The lesson here is to not trust anyone with your money, including your spouse. You need to understand your investments.)

 During our marriage we have purchased two new vehicles. In both cases we negotiated 20% off the sticker price. According to a *Reader's Digest* article it is possible to negotiate as much as 25% off the sticker price. This mistake cost us $1,500. (The pros and cons of new- and used-car purchases are discussed on pages 239—40. Although we had specific reasons for our choice, it is still a frequent subject of debate in our household.)

 We shopped for a set of secondhand bunkbeds for our children for several months and finally bought a new set that we liked. Within a matter of months they were trashed to the condition of most of the used ones we had seen. This mistake cost us $200. (Children are very hard on furniture, clothing, and toys. We usually try to buy used items, and I have regretted most new purchases.)

 When our offer was accepted on an earlier house we hired a building inspector, who told us what any idiot with a pair of eyes could have seen (had they looked). An entire section of the house had no foundation. This mistake cost us $275.

(The lesson here is to conduct your own building inspection before making an offer and hiring an inspector.)

 Our most dramatic mistake occurred before we met. Between the two of us we had a total of more than 20 years in the work force. At the time of our marriage our combined financial assets were $1,500. Neither of us owned any major appliances or furniture of any value. Jim owned a 10-year-old truck. This mistake cost us ... who knows? (The startling contrast between our track record before and after marriage clearly demonstrates the difference between a fun-oriented and a goal-oriented lifestyle.)

MILK JUG MAGIC

Milk jug plastic is lightweight and can be easily cut, making the jugs highly versatile. Many communities now have recycling programs to accommodate milk jugs. However, the reuse of the jug also benefits the environment because an object fabricated from a jug replaces another object that would be otherwise manufactured. All jugs and plastic scraps can eventually be recycled.

I have included a collection of possibilities.

Cut off the top to make a container to hold children's toys, such as Legos, Matchbox cars, Tinker Toys, etc. The handle makes them easy to carry. The

same idea makes a compost
bucket or a clothespin holder.

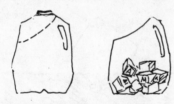

Punch holes in the bottom to
make an irrigation jug. Set into
the ground near plants to be
watered. This allows for slow
watering without evaporation.

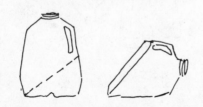

Cut off bottom at an angle to
make a pooper scooper, a bailer,
or a dust pan for the shop.

Cut as shown to make an
Easter basket. Cut the ears out of
extra side panels and staple on.
Mark eyes and nose with a black
marker. Glue on a cotton ball for
a tail.

Cut out a flat panel to make a
pinwheel. Tack to a dowel. Use

markers and glitter to add color.

If you have an X-Acto knife you
can also make simple stencils
from the side panels. Or make
holes with a paper punch to make
sewing cards for children.

Filled with water and dark food
coloring, or painted black, milk
jugs can be stacked to make a
Trombe wall. This functions as an
inexpensive solar collector for a
greenhouse.

Cut the top and handle off to
make a toilet brush holder.

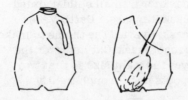

Cut the bottom off to make miniature greenhouses. Remove the
cap during the day. Or use to
cover plants when frost threat-
ens.

Fill with water and put in the toilet tank for a water saver. Or put in the freezer to fill the empty spaces (and improve the energy efficiency).

Fill with sand for weights in the trunk of the car for extra traction during the winter months. Or have a sand jug by the front steps for icy days. Leave cap in place to keep sand dry when not in use.

Cut large holes in the sides to make nonaesthetic but functional bird feeders.

Cut as shown below to make a mask for a small child. Painted black it makes a Darth Vader mask. I varied the theme to make a robot mask. Cut holes for the eyes the right size so that two spouts pop through tightly.

Empty milk jugs with screw caps can be used for buoys.

Cut as shown to make a container for seedlings and a collar to keep cutworms from plants.

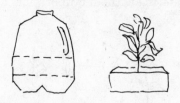

Cut off the bottom to make a megaphone for children.

A COMMENT AND A QUESTION

Linda Van Atta of Scarborough, Maine, submitted this winning idea. She wrote a great comment as well as asked a great question.

THE COMMENT:

"My husband does the mechanical stuff and makes furniture, etc., while my knowledge is in things like growing plants, sewing, creative cooking (the kind you do when it looks like there isn't anything to eat), organization, and cleaning. Sounds sexist, but it really isn't. We do what we do the best and help the other with the rest. And he does a lot of the cooking and some cleaning, too. Teamwork yields some good ideas and saves us money. We can do about anything we need to."

I agree with Linda completely and have always felt that teamwork and compatibility contributed greatly to our ability to save. Couples who often disagree or do not harmonize well expend energy resolving differences. This leaves less energy for working together toward a common goal.

THE QUESTION:

"How do you get your own house cheaply if you are financially responsible, but don't have a big credit history? We've promptly paid thousands in student loans but have been told these don't count. We pay cash, and make our money go much farther than the general public does, but from what we hear banks would rather lend money to people who live beyond their means."

Linda asks two questions. Several methods exist to obtain housing cheaper, such as a state-subsidized loan for low-income families, or buying a two-family house and renting half.

However, the most important aspect of her question concerns establishing credit, without which it is near impossible to get a mortgage, especially in these times of tightening bank regulations.

Establishing credit can be a common tightwad problem, as we like to pay cash for everything to avoid interest charges.

I consulted *Wealth Without Risk* by Charles Givens. He offers three basic strategies for rebuilding credit, which would also work for establishing credit (strategies 57, 58 and 59 in the book).

1. Get a cosigner on a loan to help establish credit. This could either be family or friends. Eventually you will qualify for credit on your own.

2. Get a secured credit card. Secured means that you have a deposit equal to the credit you want. Some banks put this into an interest-earning CD. After you have made payments for six months the deposit will be returned to you. The book offers three sources for secured credit cards.

3. Borrow $1,000 from a bank and put it into a secured savings account in the same bank. Because you cannot withdraw money from the savings account, the bank risks nothing. Pay back the loan with other cash. This costs you interest on the loan, but you earn interest on the savings account. You lose a few percent on your money in exchange for establishing credit.

The last two methods require that you have some savings. They can be attractive to the tightwad who does not want to lose interest money. Other parts of Linda's letter indicated that she and her husband possess remarkable savings ability, putting away a very large percent of a modest income. In our experience we found that large savings accounts impress loan officers. Banks look hard at your ability to save and stay out of debt. Therefore I suggest they couple even a modest credit history with a proven savings track record.

BOOK REVIEW

For all you recently converted tightwads who have succeeded in your newfound restraint, but still feel the itch to part with a few dollars, I have a guilt-free justifiable spend for you.

And for those who have written asking if I would include tightwad recipes, those who are interested in healthful eating, and those for whom the term "sustainable culture" frequently finds its way into your conversation, this is a cookbook for you to add to your shelf.

The *More-with-Less Cookbook* came to my attention some time ago as mentioned in a letter from a reader. But I had not seen a copy until my sister gave it to me for Christmas.

Written by Doris Janzen Longacre, a Mennonite woman who passed away several years ago, the cookbook is in its 38th printing.

She devotes approximately one third of the book to the moral issues surrounding our American dietary habits in relation to the world food crisis, as well as basic nutrition and a general approach to food. Clearly written for the Mennonite people, the first third contains several biblical references. Regardless of your faith you will find the moral issues raised to be absolutely universal.

If this sort of message does not align with your beliefs (or you just want to get to the matter of how to spend less at the grocery store), then move directly to the remaining two thirds of the book. You will find simple and healthful recipes that rely on basic and inexpensive ingredients.

My two most frequent annoyances with many recipes is that they either call for convenience foods or expensive ingredients. As I flip through this cookbook I see many recipes that I can prepare without a shopping trip.

The author includes options to tailor recipes to your own pantry and ways to use up leftovers.

Many recipes contain white sugar, white flour, and red meat. The message is not abstinence but rather a strong suggestion that we attempt to limit these items and substitute more dried beans, whole grains, and fresh or home-preserved fruits and vegetables.

If you are a beginner into the voyage of more healthful eating, you will be quite comfortable with the majority of these recipes, as few call for tofu and sprouts.

You may be able to check out this book at a library. If not, look for it in either a Christian bookstore or a natural-foods store.

SAVING MONEY WHEN YOU HAVE NO TIME

The first year I published *The Tightwad Gazette* overlapped with Jim's last year in the Navy. Our dual careers put added stress on our family. We regarded his retirement date as the light at the end of our tunnel; a beacon signaling a return to more relaxed times.

The Mad Hatter lifestyle gave me a new respect for those who have asked, "But what if you don't have time to do all those thrifty things?"

Yeah, there is no doubt about it. Do-it-yourself furniture reupholstery, rebuilding car engines, rug braiding—many of the best skinflintian practices can be left for those with surplus time. However, investment of significant portions of time is only one of the three basic ways to save money:

1. Be more organized. This will save money as well as time. For example, at certain times of the year different types of merchandise go on sale. Purchasing a marked-down toy in January for a May birthday requires the same amount of time as paying full price at the last minute.

If you plan meals a day in advance you will not have to thaw a frozen piece of meat in the microwave. If you are going to replace your tires in six months, casually watch for a good sale.

Some methods of organization require a relatively small amount of initial investment time, such as setting up a grocery shopping system or organizing a way to pre-buy children's clothing as you run across it at yard sales.

Many forms of record keeping fall into this category, such as keeping a maintenance record for your car.

2. Scale down. Expect to do, have, or spend less. Eliminate the nonessentials. Eat out less. Make something last longer. Buy secondhand instead of new.

I recently bought a "new" handbag at the thrift shop for $1. I expended the same time as if I had bought one at a department store.

One would presume that the loss of surplus time has made our lifestyle more expensive. But we have resisted the temptation to scale up.

Back in my thumb-twiddlin' days I could spend a week preparing a birthday party. This spring we have had parties (if you could call them that) with little more than a cake, a few presents, and a promise for next year.

We've also had to pare down our repertoire of tightwad dinners and eliminate the multistep casseroles in favor of the simpler meals. While the common cuisine would not have excited Julia Child, we did not resort to convenience foods to jazz up meals. As a result our food bill has remained constant.

3. Do those time-consuming thrifty things.

Even those who feel they have little extra time to devote to activities that save money can rethink their use of this strategy.

Focus on using the time you do have on the ways to save that will give you the largest return for time spent. Make it a practice to record the hours spent on an activity and the savings return so that you can best determine the most profitable way for you to spend your time.

When Jim shopped for our Suburban, he contacted 22 car dealerships. Because his approach was organized he only spent an additional nine hours and saved $4,000 off the sticker price. However, he would not stop at 22 department stores to save a few cents on transparent tape.

Sometimes the return in time spent can be weighed by the quality of life achieved. I might spend an hour making a custom birthday card for a friend when I could buy one for $1.25. But a personalized card might have the equivalent impact of an expensive present. Likewise many tightwad strategies are worth doing because they are environmentally sound.

Money-saving activities can conflict with a need to spend quality time with family. Solve this by choosing activities that meet both needs. Our children like to help bake cookies, help plant the garden, or watch their dad build something. In the same way you can choose a personal hobby that will save money (rather than cost money).

Think about the spare minutes as small change that accumulates. Use those moments to accomplish small tasks. A list taped to your refrigerator will help to aid you. Also double up on activities. Have hand sewing to do when watching TV or talking on the phone.

Finally, be certain that you are not working more, to buy more conveniences, because you lack time. In other words don't moonlight to buy TV dinners. Often people fail to calculate how much extra they spend because they work more.

Recently an acquaintance's accountant told her that her part-time $5-per-hour job, when combined with other family income, netted only $2.48 per hour in take-home pay. Had she also factored in gas and commuting time, the figure would be less. Know your real hourly worth and bear that in mind when you think thrifty things aren't worth doing.

Of the three ways to save money, you may be only able to utilize one or two. But being busy does not have to mean spending more.

CHEAP THRILLS

"We worry that you and Jim aren't having enough fun." A relative stunned me with this observation and I replied, "Sure we have fun, like . . . ah . . . ah . . ."

I had to think over the years, way back to our honeymoon, to pinpoint the last shred of traditional expensive fun.

In the year since, I have prepared a better answer. Yes, we do have fun. But it is different from the fun we had when we were single. Somewhere our sense of fun became distorted and it now seems to be centered on conserving funds and working toward goals. Here are a few classic tightwad thrills.

Check out your neighbors' trash after they have cleaned out the garage and left for the evening.

Hold a yard sale. This surpasses the fun of purging by throwing things away.

Beat the supermarket at their own game by challenging yourself to see how much food you can bring home for the fewest dollars. If your sense of fun is greatly distorted, you might enjoy the spectator sport of watching spendthrifts go through the checkout line.

Summers in Maine offer many festivals and free concerts as a way to promote the various towns. They offer such things as bed races and parades. Avoid the temptation of purchasing cans of soda, expensive balloons, and cheap toys.

Gardening. There is something magical about planting seeds, and watching things grow all by themselves. Harvesting is the fun part.

A well-executed child's birthday party—not too much and not too little. The thrill is heightened when you have spent only a few dollars and some kid comes up to you afterwards and says, "This is the best party I ever went to."

Repair, renovation, or refinishing. The more gone the thing is the more fun to bring it back.

When your child catches his first fish, learns to ride his bike without training wheels, or jumps off the bus after his first trauma-free and glorious day of kindergarten and then spends 30 minutes telling you all about it.

CHEAP THRILLS FROM READERS

"I find crossword puzzles and jigsaw puzzles to be some of the cheapest entertainment available. Both provide hours of entertainment and are available for under $5." (Eric May, Racine, Wisconsin)

"The Premiere Dining Club coupon booklet provides two dinners for the price of one with repeat visits allowed. We eat out a fair amount and enjoy the sport of pursuing the greatest quality experience for the least money. We also only drink water in restaurants." (Jon Eberle, Redmond, Washington)

"I have a similar distorted sense of fun. When I get away from the computer or the mail desk I can usually be found fixing electrical appliances, rewebbing lawn chairs we salvaged from the street, or building shelves." (Joe Dominguez, The New Road Map Foundation, Seattle, Washington)

THE TIGHTWAD REFRIGERATOR

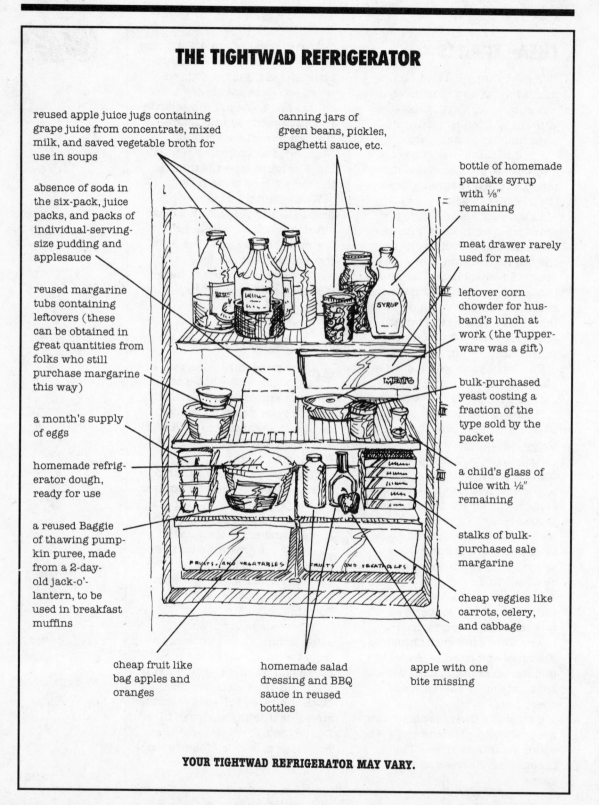

reused apple juice jugs containing grape juice from concentrate, mixed milk, and saved vegetable broth for use in soups

absence of soda in the six-pack, juice packs, and packs of individual-serving-size pudding and applesauce

reused margarine tubs containing leftovers (these can be obtained in great quantities from folks who still purchase margarine this way)

a month's supply of eggs

homemade refrig-erator dough, ready for use

a reused Baggie of thawing pump-kin puree, made from a 2-day-old jack-o'-lantern, to be used in breakfast muffins

canning jars of green beans, pickles, spaghetti sauce, etc.

bottle of homemade pancake syrup with ⅛" remaining

meat drawer rarely used for meat

leftover corn chowder for hus-band's lunch at work (the Tupper-ware was a gift)

bulk-purchased yeast costing a fraction of the type sold by the packet

a child's glass of juice with ½" remaining

stalks of bulk-purchased sale margarine

cheap veggies like carrots, celery, and cabbage

cheap fruit like bag apples and oranges

homemade salad dressing and BBQ sauce in reused bottles

apple with one bite missing

YOUR TIGHTWAD REFRIGERATOR MAY VARY.

HOMEMADE SHAKE & BAKE

Dear Amy,
   This recipe equals 20 store packets at 25% of the price.

   4 cups flour
   4 cups crackermeal (or ground inexpensive crackers)
   4 Tbsp salt
   2 Tbsp sugar
   2 tsp garlic powder
   2 tsp onion powder
   3 Tbsp paprika
   ¼ cup vegetable oil

Mix well and store indefinitely in the refrigerator in a covered container.

                   Ann Davis
                   Andrews, North Carolina

ABOUT SPACE

Dear Amy,
   Do you save almost everything? If so, where do you keep it all? I like to save, but also believe if you haven't worn/used it all year (or five years) get rid of it. I am haunted by stories of people overrun by their own trash. Can you be frugal and neat?

                   Diane Shaw
                   Turner, Maine

Dear Diane,
   Space, like time, energy, and money, is a precious resource. It is hard to be neat when your home is too full of too much. Organization is important to the conserving of time. Time is important to the conserving of money. In other words, the key is to balance all your resources for the maximum quality of life.
   We have a large barn, sheds, and two attics. Space is not a precious resource to us. However, when I do save I make an effort to use those materials first. I design projects around what I have rather than deciding what I want to make and then buying materials. I do not save when I have a surplus or a steady supply of an item. When I purge I try to donate, hold a yard sale, or find someone who wants the items. I feel guilty about what I contribute to the landfill problem. I used to have a similar policy to yours when I was a single apartment dweller. Then I married a packrat. I discovered that saving stuff was more fun than saving space. For the true tightwad few thrills compare with that of making something from salvaged, saved, or leftover materials.

A REMINDER

Dear Amy,
   If one isn't working in a coal mine, why waste water standing in the shower 10 or 15 minutes?
                   Marjorie Lunger
                   Williamsburg, Virginia

(Uh-oh . . . She's on to me. I am very guilty of using the shower as a creative think tank. This has resulted in some very good but expensively obtained ideas for the newsletter. FZ)

THE WHOLE KNEE PATCH

When a child rips the knees in a pair of jeans that otherwise has lots of life, I patch them. I gave up on conventional patches because no sooner had I patched them when the neighboring material would give out.

Now I patch jeans with "the whole knee patch" method.

This is time consuming, and I save the ripping for a time when I am watching TV or visiting with a guest.

Rip out the seam from the bottom to four inches above the tear. Make a new patch from a matching denim scrap that is wider than the pant leg and 5 inches high. Sew the top and bottom edge under ½ inch and then topstitch the patch over the tear. Resew the seams (double seam first from the outside, single seam from the inside).

This patch will outlast the jeans.

Other uses for denim scraps:

- Sew strips to weave a seat for a wooden folding chair.
- Braid a blue jean rug.
- Make a blue jean patchwork quilt for a boy's room.
- Make trendy potholders with gold double topstitched seams
- Make a drawstring sack from a cut-off blue jean leg.

HOLDING A YARD SALE

While running errands on a Saturday afternoon you spot an obscure windblown yard sale sign tacked to a telephone pole on the other side of a busy street. Making great effort to backtrack, you read the sign, deduce the location of the sale, and head off into the unknown. No more signs appear to further guide you, and after 15 minutes of working your way through the suburban maze you luck upon the sale. You think ... There are a few knickknacks on a table and a collection of 1970s vintage adult clothing in a pile next to it. The proprietor, lounging in a lawn chair, kills time, reading behind a newspaper. The newspaper drops down and you find yourself staring into your own face!

Just then you wake up in a cold sweat, your heart racing. It was only a dream—a nightmare of your own yard sale from hell.

How do you avoid sleepless preyard sale nights and the eventual bad yard sale? Think about everything you have disliked about the ones you have attended, and do not repeat the mistakes.

Ideally you want to hold a yard sale in a populated area, and an area where yard sales flourish. Generally an ad will not be essential unless you do not reside on the beaten path. If your location is hopeless, buddy up with a friend in a good location.

Although yard sales go on throughout the summer, the first sunny spring weekend day is your best bet. If you do not place an ad, and if you date your signs at the last minute, you have the option of canceling in poor weather. Do not hold a yard sale on a holiday weekend.

Check to see if your town requires a license. (If you do not get one the Yard Sale Gestapo will not show up. This ordinance is designed to prevent the perpetual yard sale.)

As a graphics person I place a high priority on signs. Good signs have a distinctive quality of their own—something that makes them easy to recognize from the others. Make them all the same. It could be red lettering on cardboard, or tie a balloon to each sign.

The best and fastest method of sign making I have found requires cutting a stencil. Cut out the words YARD SALE in large letters (3″ to 4″) out of lightweight cardboard. Make a second stencil with a large arrow. Use spray paint for a fast job. Put YARD SALE on top and the arrow on the bottom. Use marker to hand write the date and location in the middle. Make half the arrows point one way and half point the other. This way you can place signs from either direction.

Placement of signs is critical. Recall your frustration in trying to follow poorly placed signs.

Place on all the intersections near your home as far as the main road, whatever that is. Put your sign on the side of the road that you want your potential customer to turn.

Begin gathering stuff early. Have a designated yard sale carton and save items in it throughout the year. You won't know if you have enough until you see it all in one place. If your quantity of merchandise seems lean, buddy up with friends. If you learn a neighbor is planning a yard sale, hold yours the same weekend. You will enhance each other's business rather than being in competition.

People will buy nearly anything. During a yard sale my father held, a woman found a rock in our yard and bought it. Anything could be sellable.

In the same way that the retail business uses marketing strategies, so must you. No one likes to see tables of knickknacks and huge piles of clothes. Large items stop cars, so put those things near the road. Hang up as much clothing as possible. Lay out clothing for children according to size so that it is easy to see.

Group similar items together. A box of odd hangers is junk. Simi-

lar hangers neatly bundled becomes good stuff.

When considering pricing, remember that your primary objective is to get rid of stuff, and not to make money. People expect to get a bargain. Generally sell things for between 10% to 50% of a comparable new item. Things that you want to sell the most should be priced lower yet. All items should be clearly priced.

Seasoned yard salers expect to negotiate. Hold firm if you think the item is already cheap enough. Negotiating should be considered at the end of the day rather than at the beginning. Encourage people to return late in the day rather than negotiate early. Do not agree to hold anything for anyone unless they pay first. Even the most sincere-looking person may not return.

After the yard sale put all remaining merchandise back in your yard sale box for next year.

The previous information will help relieve pre-yard sale stress. What of the guilt that leads to post-yard sale nightmares? Take down all of your yard sale signs and sleep comfortably with a clear conscience.

YARD SALE STRATEGY

Dear Amy,
I buy, fix up, and resell yard sale stuff. I just made $40 on two bar stools I got for $20 and sold for $60.

The selling trick is to save store flyers, cut out a picture of the item to be sold, and tape it to the item. Things sell faster when people are reminded of the original selling price.

I find buying things that can be fixed up pays better, as few people want to fix anything themselves. I can buy cheap and with a little paint and ingenuity make them look new.

Dottie Lawrence
Port St. Lucie, Florida

GREAT QUOTES

"You cannot bring about prosperity by discouraging thrift.

You cannot establish sound security on borrowed money.

You cannot keep out of trouble by spending more than you earn."
—Abraham Lincoln

"Junk is the stuff we throw away. Stuff is the junk we save."
—Frank Tyger
The Times, Trenton, New Jersey

WORD PROBLEMS

I have always been a mathematics midget. I am the kind of person who frequently cannot remember that 8 and 5 is . . . uh . . . 13? I married a math whiz. Jim can multiply 27 by 41 in his head and get it right. At least if he's pulling the wool over my eyes I'd never know.

One might think this union of opposites would have caused math atrophy. I have actually improved in recent years, but not because his genius rubbed off. Precision tightwaddery requires continual calculation. Also during my adult years the pocket calculator has become cheap enough to buy with pocket change.

Below are seven real-life word problems. The answers appear on page 268.

1. A heat gun costs about the same as a gallon of paint stripper, or $20. Presuming your electricity costs 9¢ per kilowatt-hour how long could you run a 1,000 kilowatt heat gun before you exceed the cost of the second gallon of paint stripper?

2. The postal service will update your mailing list with nine-digit zip codes for free. This will save .9¢ per piece of bulk mail. However the needed computer program would cost about $325. Presuming a constant monthly mailing of 1,500 how long would it take to recoup the cost of the computer program?

3. A local grocery store runs a special on ground beef: 75% lean costs $1.18 lb, 80% lean costs $1.58 lb, and 85% lean costs $1.88 lb. Presuming you plan to use the beef in such a way as to cook off the extra fat, and in a recipe where the taste difference is not critical, which sale offers the most lean beef per dollar.

4. You buy a battery recharger for $12 and two C rechargeables for $8. You send in for the $2 rebate with a 29¢ stamp. The manufacturer claims that a rechargeable C battery equals 150 disposables (which cost $3 per pair). How much could you save before needing to replace the rechargeables?

5. A 10-oz box of cold cereal costs $1.59. The same brand costs $2.19 for 18 oz. You have a 35¢-off coupon for that brand of cereal and your store offers double coupons. Which size box of cereal is the better value?

6. Generic oatmeal costs 57¢ lb. Assuming that a 1½-oz serving of oatmeal equals a 1½-oz serving of the cold cereal in the previous problem, how much would you save over the course of the year if you fed your family of four oatmeal instead of cold cereal?

7. Blank address labels (1" x 3½") cost $10 per 5,000. Clear tape costs 69¢ for 12½ yards. Business-size envelopes cost 7¢ apiece on sale. The sender of the envelope writes small enough so that the two old addresses can be covered with one label each. You neatly slice the envelope end when opening so that it requires 4" of tape to reclose. Is it cost-effective to reuse business envelopes?

WORD PROBLEM ANSWERS

1. A kilowatt-hour is 1000 watts consumed in one hour. Therefore a 1000 kilowatt appliance uses 9¢ worth of electricity in an hour. You could run a heat gun for 222.22 hours before using up $20 worth of electricity. A heat gun is not the best method of paint removal for every application, but much more economical than chemical stripper.

2. Using the nine-digit zip code would save $13.50 per month and the computer program would be paid for in 24 months. Since we would have to mail in a computer disk monthly it would take 25½ months to recoup the cost.

3. The 75% provides 10 oz of lean for $1. The 80% provides 8 oz for $1, and the 85% provides 7 oz for $1.

4. $431.71

5. The 18-oz box of cereal would cost .083¢ per oz and the 10-oz box would cost .089¢ per oz. That would be 8¢ and 9¢ per oz

respectively if rounded off. Had the prices been closer, the bigger box would still be the better value providing the most cereal at a reduced price.

6. Using the .083¢ figure from the previous problem, the cold cereal would cost about 49.8¢ per day or $181.77 per year. Oatmeal would cost 21¢ a day or $78.01 per year. The oatmeal would save a family of four $103.76 annually.

Although 57¢ lb is a very good price we buy it for 39¢ lb in a 50-lb sack. Our children love oatmeal but will not tolerate it more than four times a week.

7. Labels cost .002¢ each (or .004¢ per envelope) and the tape costs .006¢ per piece of 4" tape. The cost of reusing a business envelope is about a penny, or a savings of 6¢.

(There is no substitution for doing your own homework.)

BULK FRUIT PECTIN

When I mentioned that I learned I could buy bulk pectin to save money on jam making, readers asked me where to get it. Our local health food store buys it from:

Dutch Valley Food Distributors
P.O. Box 465
Meyerstown, PA 17067
(800) 733-4191

BABY-WIPE SOLUTIONS

Many readers have sent me directions on how to make homemade baby wipes using paper towels and a solution of baby oil and baby shampoo. I have always used old washcloths just as previous generations have done before manufacturers invented baby wipes and sold us on this as a "necessity." The cleansing solution may be superior to plain water, but I would prefer not to throw away the paper towels. Here is a letter from a reader that shares my views:

Dear Amy,
   Baby wipes are very expensive. They run $3 to $4 for 80 in our area. These wipes are full of alcohol, fragrances, etc. that are potential irritants to the baby. Instead I "invested" in 12 one-color washcloths in a pack from our local department store ($2.99 for 12). These sit either in the bathroom or at the diaper changing table. I wet one just before the diaper change. Afterward I toss them in the diaper pail to be washed.

**Patricia Hone
Apollo, Pennsylvania**

However, daycare centers require that parents provide disposable baby wipes.

So if you must use them, the homemade version is certainly economical and worthwhile.

This baby wipe recipe was sent by Laurie Kenny of Portland, ME.

   1 roll of Bounty paper towels or
      microwave paper towels
   2¼ cups water
   2 Tbsp baby shampoo or baby
      bath
   1 Tbsp baby oil

Cut the roll of paper towels in half and remove the cardboard center. Mix the water, shampoo or bath, and oil in a plastic container (such as an old baby wipe container). Place half a roll in a container, put the lid on and turn upside down to let the towels thoroughly soak. When ready to use pull the towels from the center of the roll.

OLD THINGS MADE NEW

If you have a good relationship with a body shop you might be able to use it for more than getting a new paint job for your car.

Jim bought a used five-drawer filing cabinet. The paint job was pretty bad and I thought "Ugh, another obviously secondhand piece of office furniture for our already motley-looking office."

He took it to the shop that had just repainted our car. We were able to get the file repainted for $20. It looks brand new. And it certainly looked a long sight better than if we had attempted it with cans of spray paint.

My parents, who live in a different area of the country, had their medicine cabinet sandblasted and repainted by their body shop. I have heard of people getting their refrigerators repainted.

Obviously not all shops will be willing to be bothered or do it for such reasonable prices. I would not approach a chain shop with such a request. This shop accommodated us because we had two cars worked on, and we sent him more business. We were also will-

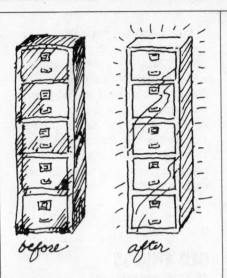

before   *after*

ing to wait until he had a slow time. My father told his shop to paint it when they were going to paint a car the same color as he wanted for the medicine cabinet.

If you need something repainted but do not have an established relationship, you might be able to negotiate in other ways. You might try to barter, for example.

THE USED-CLOTHING FILING SYSTEM

The growth of children occurs subtly enough so that we only notice it when their clothes appear to shrink between wearings. Typically I might begin to dress a two-year-old for church and suddenly all her dresses seem too short. On these occasions we go "shopping in the attic." I am able to locate the proper-sized dress within two minutes.

I developed my used-clothing filing system for kids when I had only two of them. As I collected yard sale finds and as relatives

mailed hand-me-downs, going through the mountain of clothes for the next-sized wardrobe became a tedious task. During this sort, I would invariably discover that I had purchased yard sale clothes when I had sufficient hand-me-downs, or that clothing had become outgrown while in storage. I might also discover that I had failed to purchase enough of something.

Except for sneakers, socks, and some underwear I have never purchased new clothing for any of the children. (OK, once we bought Alec three shirts when he was a toddler.)

Currently my filing system is made up of 30 same-sized boxes. A smaller family could do the same with 4 or fewer boxes per child. The lidded boxes that the newsletters come in from the printer each month are ideal. I have marked each box with the size and sex ... such as 5 YG (i.e., five-year-old girl), or 6 MB. Boys' boxes are on one side of a chimney and girls' on the other. I mark the boxes on the visible facing end with black marker.

I collect clothing years older than my oldest child. Alec is 9 and I have a box for a few teenage freebies that have come my way. However, I *buy* yard sale clothes only a couple years older than the oldest child. I don't buy too far in advance because free hand-me-downs might come along in the meantime. In addition, it can be hard to predict if your child will be a "slim" or a "husky."

At the same time I don't wait to shop for clothes six months in advance because I might not be lucky enough to find everything I need.

I seldom watch for clothes for younger children, as I know that there are ample hand-me-downs from an older sibling, and I am generally given enough things to perk up those tired wardrobes.

By having clothing sorted into same-sized boxes I can quickly gauge if I have too much or not enough clothes for a particular size. I have two full boxes of 3 YR B. Because one box of clothing is sufficient for a young child, I know I can sort the boxes, keeping only the best things. The dregs get donated to a thrift shop. (Some thrift shops sell poor-quality clothing for recycling.)

I graciously accept all clothing that is given to me. I sort later and may only keep a small percentage, depending on the quality of the used items and according to the things I need. I will keep things, even if I don't like the style, or if the item needs repair, when I have a shortage. I don't work on stains or repair clothing until I need to, as it is likely I will find better stuff in time.

I will buy things far in advance if I know they are

hard-to-come-by items such as pants, new shoes that turn up at a yard sale, or coats. I also try to choose items that are likely to be in style in a few years, such as Lee cords and crew-neck sweaters.

I store coats on a rack and shoes in separate boxes.

A used-clothing system such as this saves time, space, and money. I can "file" and retrieve clothes with a minimum of time. I never purchase new clothes or excess used clothes because I know exactly what I have. Because I don't keep more than I need, my system takes up a minimum of space.

THE STAIN RECIPE

This recipe came from an expert, a woman who ran a used-clothing store for children.

Add one cup each of powdered Cascade and Clorox II to five gallons of the hottest water to come out of your faucet. Soak several articles overnight, and launder as usual.

This procedure will remove about 90% of the stains that do not come out with normal laundering. I do not use this recipe for delicate fabrics, or fabrics that are not color-fast. It is particularly good for removing food stains.

ON-THE-JOB SCROUNGE

Dear Amy and Jim,

We always used to get excited and "pat each other on the back" when we found or did something to save a buck. We never had an accurate way to describe it but have now dubbed it the "Tightwad Award."

Just this week my husband brought home a brand-new (in the box) wood folding canvas chair. He works at a lumber company (a great place to find deals) and another company sent it as a promo item. No one ever did anything with it and after asking they gave it to my husband for free.

Earlier this week Michael stopped during the drive home to find a large spool of cord with flagging tape in the middle of the road. Not being one to leave it to rot he brought it home.

To save money my husband has been making a couple of old-fashioned storm windows from cedar wood (scrounged from old pallets and "trash" at work). He happened to stop by to see a friend at work and noticed a couple of large window frames leaning against the Dumpster. He asked and learned they were going to the dump. So he threw them in the back of the truck and home he went. The other glass he needed came from stock windows at work, which had been ordered but not bought. A few weeks before inventory he asked his boss if he could take them off his hands for $2 each (they were worth $50). He needed three windows. When he went to pay he pulled out $5 and fumbled for several minutes looking for another $1 (knowing he had a $20 in his pocket). The boss, being impatient, said, "Oh, just give me the $5."

We have several wood (cedar) Adirondack chairs that Michael has made from free scraps from work. The only expense was the special screws and bolts. We made chairs for my parents at Christmastime. It looked like a gigantic present, but only cost $3 to $4 to make.

We purchased our house 4½ years ago and went through it inside and out restoring it. Because we taught ourselves skills and everything was bartered or bought at a discount we saved a ton.

Amazing what you can do if you have a brain!
Tina Hoag
Alfred, Maine

(Reading this letter one feels as though we are glimpsing the tip of

the iceberg at what this couple has learned to do. They combine a knack for scrounging, knowing how to ask if something is available, and acquired skills to save money. Every place of employment provides unique opportunities to scrounge, although we all wish we had his job. FZ)

WRITE THE MANUFACTURER

Writing a large and distant corporation concerning a product problem is similar to a man standing on the beach of a deserted island. When he throws out the bottle with the message inside he does not really expect a reply. If by chance one does come there is cause for celebration.

The first time I tried this I sent a letter to the manufacturers of the Snickers candy bar with a piece of wood taped to it. I had nearly eaten this. Snickers apologized for the "peanut twig" and sent me coupons for two free bags of candy bars.

My second successful attempt occurred this year. We purchased a "Magidoodle" as a Christmas present for our daughter. Within 10 days of normal use the screen was filled with lines resulting from cracks on the inside. I mailed it back to Ideal with a shameless attempt to extract their sympathy. I truthfully reported it was only one of two new Christmas gifts we had given our four children that year. Ideal promptly called me to ask if I would like a new Magidoodle. I maintained that I wanted my money returned. Although the product was not defective it did not deliver the durability one ought to expect from a $17 present. Ideal responded that it was not their policy to issue refunds, but they did send us a brand-new Magidoodle in the box, which we were able to return to the store without receipt.

Many years ago Jim broke a fishing reel spool. He wrote the manufacturer, Garcia Mitchell, and received no response. Six months later, while his ship was out on a cruise he was upset about a different matter. Making use of this anger he sent the president of Garcia Mitchell a "nasty-gram." He explained that he had already written, received no response, and was going to get rid of all his Garcia Mitchell equipment. A week and a half later he received an entire new reel and a letter of apology.

We are currently using this same strategy to get a response from Sony. We have been unable to get the part to repair our television for 18 months.

To learn who to write to, often you need only to look at the box your defective product came in. If it does not provide the needed information, there are three sources you should consult. I have the 1990 *World Almanac*, which lists names and addresses of corporations, as well as the names of the company presidents. It suggests Standard and Poor's *Register of Corporations, Directors and Executives*. If you don't know the name of the manufacturer consult the *Thomas Register*. Both of these are available in most libraries.

The almanac also suggests a fairly lengthy list of pointers for writing such letters, such as including pertinent information like your name, address, phone number, dates of purchase, copies of paperwork, etc. They suggest that you do not send "nasty-grams." (A lot they know.)

BIRTHDAY SAVINGS

Dear Amy,

* I make sure my charge card doesn't have an annual fee. Why would anyone choose one that does? I charge everything I *have* to buy—birthday presents, clothing, home and garden supplies, etc.—thereby allowing me to earn interest on my money in the bank till the bill comes in.

* There's always extra wallpaper left after finishing a room. I used to save the balance in case I needed to touch up. After many years and many rooms I have *never* needed the paper for this purpose; therefore, I now use the balance for wrapping gifts. I even use the vinyl stuff. This also

makes your gift waterproof during inclement weather.

* Yard sales are the *best* places to get ceramic FTD's decorative florist containers (usually 50¢— someone else has already spent big bucks for this). But, it is almost impossible for you to use these again unless you use a styrofoam florist block and are very good at arranging cut flowers. Take it to a florist and tell them to fill it with $5 worth of flowers and deliver it yourself. You just saved $20.

* I bought a Craftsman ratchet wrench for only 10¢ (it was so rusty it didn't crank). I took it to Sears and got a brand new one in the package ($20 value)! Sears will accept your broken or destroyed Craftsman for a new one.

This birthday my dad's getting a brand new Craftsman ratchet (10¢); of course it's wrapped in only the best vinyl wallpaper (0¢). A floral arrangement for his desk at work ($5) that was of course charged on my Visa (earned 6%). A personalized card that I made on my computer (0¢). A chocolate Pepperidge Farm cake (wouldn't you know I clip coupons); I used a 20¢ manufacturer's coupon at a double coupon market ($1.09 after coupon). It's more expensive to buy a cake and frosting mix and bake it. You can be sure I use my birthday candles at *least* twice.

Cathy Levesque-Gilbert
Woonsocket, Rhode Island

(Cathy touches on two important points about credit cards. I am sure she knows this, and I want to be sure everyone else does. You have to charge at least $50 to recoup the 29¢ it costs to send in the bill. This is an excellent strategy for large purchases or combining many small ones. FZ)

'TIS THE SEASON . . .

. . . to do your Christmas shopping. It is the height of the yard sale season. By shopping now and hoarding in a very disciplined way you can save hundreds of dollars at Christmastime, as well as for birthdays.

Toys can be found in practically brand-new condition. Young entrepreneurs will often sell their wares for pennies, much to the dismay of the parents who bought them.

And don't overlook acceptable used presents for adults, such as collectibles, potential joke presents, or a special old book.

ELECTRICAL TRIVIA

Each month we receive an electric bill that shows the lump sum of our usage. Unlike other bills, like groceries, we do not get a breakdown, which might be of help in showing us where we need to make cutbacks. In short, we feel like we're "in the dark."

As someone who is not knowledgeable about such things, it was helpful for me to receive a free brochure from the electric company, which showed a breakdown of the average costs of using most household appliances. In looking this over I noticed that some of my appliances did not have the same wattage as their example.

However, you can calculate the costs for yourself:

If you use 1,000 watts for 1 hour you've used 1 kilowatt-hour (or KWH). Your utility bill tells how much you pay for a KWH in your area. If you pay 10¢ per KWH hour you can run a 1,000-watt appliance for 60 minutes for 10¢. A 100-watt light bulb costs 1¢ per hour to run. A low-wattage appliance, like a sewing machine, might cost 1/10th of a penny to run per hour.

Appliances have the wattage marked on the bottom. And they don't all have nice easy numbers, so you need the equation:

$$\frac{\text{Watts} \times \text{Hours}}{1,000} = \text{KWH}$$

Example: a 1,400-watt hair dryer used for 2 hours a month:

$$\frac{1,400 \times 2}{1,000} = 2.8 \text{ KWH}$$

If your local KWH rate is 9¢:

$$2.8 \times 9¢ = 25.2¢$$

Appliances that go on and off to maintain a uniform temperature, such as an oven, water heater or freezer are somewhat harder to calculate. This has been something of a frustration for me as I would like to calculate how much energy I am using in baking, for instance . . . or how much it costs to take a shower. The challenge becomes greater with appliances such as ovens, which have several temperatures. In theory, you can calculate it. You would have to peer through your oven window and time how many minutes the oven coils come on during an hour when it's set on 350°, for instance. In these cases I revert back to the brochure and trust their estimates.

If you know how to calculate energy usage you can also roughly figure comparisons between appliances.

If you're boiling water, boil the precise amount you need. If you have a hot-water kettle you can do this by pouring the pre-measured amount in with a funnel.

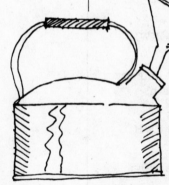

Don't heat water in the microwave. According to our calculations it can require 10% more electricity than boiling water on the stove.

When it comes to cooking solid foods, small appliances are the clear winner. In comparing a couple of recipes (scalloped potatoes and meatloaf) that could be prepared in an oven, a microwave, and a slow cooker, the slow cooker used about one fourth of the energy of the oven, and the microwave used one fifth the energy of the oven. In comparing cooking times of some other foods, the microwave uses less than one tenth of the energy of a conventional oven.

If you're baking something as well as using the range, put your pot

on the surface unit that has the oven vent. The escaping heat will help warm the food. Not all ovens have these types of vents, but if yours does, take advantage of it.

Save electricity by turning the oven off 10 minutes early. Use the same idea for your dryer. Switch it to "air" during the last 15 minutes to take advantage of the hot air built up inside the dryer.

If you have a coffee maker or perker, keep a thermos or insulated carafe nearby. Pour the surplus into it instead of having the coffee maker rewarm the extra. Boil a large pot of water once, and store in the thermos, instead of boiling water several times in a day.

Here are a few more obscure bits of electrical trivia:

Set your water heater to 125°. It needs to be this hot to kill any bacteria in the water tank. Many water heaters are automatically set at 140°. If you don't have a hot water timer on it, do as Karen Godian of Phenix City, Alabama, does—turn the water heater off manually by throwing the switch on your circuit box.

Don't drain the hot water from your tub until it's cold. The heat will warm the bathroom. (Do not leave water in the tub if you have

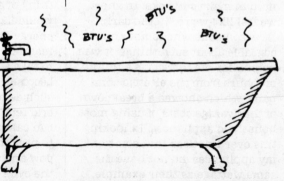

young children.) John Biel of Chesterfield, Ohio, sent me his impressive calculations to show that the equivalent to heat the bathroom with electricity would be worth about 35¢.

One reader wrote of a device called "Extra-Heat" made by De-flecto-o Corp., of Indianapolis, Indiana. It can be purchased for about $6 from a hardware store. It is installed in the dryer duct between the dryer and the outside vent. During cold weather the dryer heat can be diverted indoors. When the dryer is running it produces enough heat to keep a 30′ × 24′ room warm. They've used theirs for nine years, and have been very pleased with it. These devices are generally recommended for electric dryers only.

Low-flow shower heads are great energy savers. Not only do they use less water, but they also have an on/off switch so that you can turn off the water when lathering. Many electric companies offer these free as a part of their energy conservation program.

Use a 3-minute sand timer in your shower. Most people can finish in 6 minutes. Also use the timer to make sure your kids brush their teeth for 3 minutes. You can buy a timer specifically for the shower, with a suction cup, so that it sticks to the shower wall, from Coast Molding Inc., 7965 Dunbrook Road, Suite A, San Diego, CA 92126. Send a $4.95 check or money order. OR just get a regular timer and set it on the shower shelf.

Jim Spaulding of Northfield, Massachusetts, has installed a storage tank in the kitchen near the wood stove, where the tem-perature is often 80 degrees. The water is 40 degrees when it enters the house, and is prewarmed before it goes to the hot water tank.

In some areas of the country the power company offers a Time of Usage plan. The electrical rates are cheaper during off-peak hours. Here in Maine you have to use a very large amount of electricity to get the TOU plan . . . for example if you heat with electricity. I was unable to learn how the plans vary in different parts of the country, but readers have indicated they save as much a 40%.

HOME LITE

Dear Amy,

Today all of the margarine brands have added a reduced-fat product—⅓ less fat or "lite."

Instead I take a pound of regular margarine . . . usually store brand or whatever is on sale. After softening it slightly I gradually add skim milk as I beat it with my electric mixer. Adding the milk slowly, I can add about ⅓ cup of milk to a pound of margarine. The result is a light spreadable product that has increased in quantity by 50%, stays soft in the refrigerator, tastes the same, and has fewer calories.

**Francis Perry
Troy, Maine**

(If you prefer soft margarine, about three minutes of effort can save over $1. FZ)

THE THREE-YEAR SNEAKER PLAN

I own three pair of sneakers— this year's sneakers, last year's sneakers, and the year before's sneakers.

The days that I plan to see anybody at all I wear this year's sneakers, such as when a reporter comes for an interview when I go to the women's quilting meeting at the church, or when I go shopping.

Most days I wear last year's sneakers. The soles have begun to separate from the uppers, and cracks in the suede reveal the colors of the socks I have chosen to wear that day. The purpose of wearing last year's sneakers this year is to keep this year's sneakers looking as good as possible well into next year.

When I garden, mow the lawn, paint the house, or do other very dirty work I wear the year before's sneakers. Not only do these sneakers have the cracks and sole separations but they are marked by paint splatters, grass stains, and garden dirt. The purpose of wearing the year before's sneak-

ers is to keep last year's sneakers looking as good as possible well into next year.

My three-year sneaker plan ensures that I always have presentable footwear. I am able to purchase only one new pair of sneakers per year at a cost of $15 ... $10 if I find a good sale.

When I buy new sneakers they become this year's sneakers, this year's sneakers become last year's sneakers, last year's sneakers become the year before's sneakers, and the year before's sneakers become history.

I have a similar blue jean plan ... this year's blue jeans, last year's blue jeans, and the year before's blue jeans ...

RAZOR EXTENDER

Dear Amy,

 Here's how you can make a double-edge razor blade last longer:

 a. Place the razor blade into a straight-sided drinking glass.

 b. Apply finger pressure in the center of the blade.

 c. With constant pressure move the blade side to side against the glass.

d. Do this ten times, then flip the blade over and do the reverse side.

> Philip L. Masion
> Seattle, Washington

BATTERY IDEAS

Dear Amy,

Many of your readers might not be aware of Radio Shack's generosity. At no charge, Radio Shack will give you a one-year battery card. Each month you can get one free battery. If your spouse gets one you can get 24 free batteries a year.

> Deanna Rhoades
> Auburn, Maine

(This is fine as long as you are aware that they offer this so that you will buy more of their merchandise. Be disciplined and stop only for the battery.

Because of the disposability factor I still prefer rechargeable batteries. FZ)

MARKER PALETTE

Dear Amy,

Take an old block of wood and drill holes in it to permanently secure the caps to children's

Magic Markers . . . transforming the block of wood into an artist's palette of sorts. Your children will not chew on the caps, lose the caps, or forget to put the caps back on. They just pull out the marker when they want to use one, and replace it when through. The markers don't dry out as quickly.

> Suzanne Gage
> Lincoln, Nebraska

REJUVENATING SECONDHAND TOYS

You might be a parent looking to fill in around the edges at Christmas, or a grandparent filling a toy box in anticipation of visiting grandchildren. Get it out of your heads that there is anything wrong with secondhand toys. You'll be way ahead of the game if your children (or grandchildren) become accustomed to them while still young.

Stores charge fantastic prices for a brand-new hunk of plastic. It hurts when that new toy is broken within a week, and you'll breathe a sigh of relief when a toy that was purchased for 25¢ becomes broken.

By the time any kid reaches kindergarten he'll be given 10 times his weight in toys. If the toys are not "reowned" they will take up space at the landfill. Meanwhile toy manufacturers use more resources to make and transport excessively packaged new toys. So if you're really just pinching pennies you can also claim environmental awareness.

If you're a dutiful tightwad you have been picking up "like new" toys. But also develop an eagle eye for toys with rejuvenation possibilities. These items are overlooked by those with a lack of vision and, therefore, are your best buys.

• Fisher-Price toys are remarkably rugged, but they tend to show their wear as the stickers become soiled. These can be completely removed with nail polish remover or rubber cement thinner (always test first). The toys can be left plain or if you are very creative you can make new stickers. Wash toys with warm soapy water and a toothbrush. Scuff marks on plastic can be removed with scouring powder. An emery board or fine sandpaper will remove rough spots. If they are missing parts and the price is very cheap, take a chance. You may turn up what you need at another yard sale. (I got a record player at one and a bag of records at another.) If you do this you may have to hang on to the toy until next year.

• Wooden toys have great repair possibilities. I brought home a doll's high chair that was broken and in pieces. Jim fabricated new pieces out of an old croquet mallet handle with stripes sanded off. He then glued it all back together and refinished it. Shortly thereafter we saw an identical one in a secondhand shop for $18. Mine came from an interesting-looking trash pile.

• Plastic has an interesting property in that it can be screwed to a piece of wood. Therefore, a new wooden piece can be fabricated to replace or reinforce a broken one.

• Often game boxes are beat up even when the contents are new. These can be recovered with paper and rubber cement, or contact paper. I rejuvenated a Spirograph with new pens (on sale) and new paper.

- I generally avoid stuffed animals, because I know of no way to make worn ones look new. If it looks pretty good it can be dressed up with a new ribbon around the neck or other accessories.
- Metal wagons and metal Tonka trucks can be steel wooled and repainted with Rust-Oleum.
- A used bike comes a long way with a new paint job. If you consider doing a bike for a girl be aware that finding pink and lavender spray paints is just about impossible. You can add pinstripes and new accessories. Since this jacks up the price of my bargain I try to make these instead. I have made streamers and baskets. Colored ribbons woven into the spokes gives it a jazzy look.
- A poster with frayed edges can be trimmed with an X-Acto or utility knife. (Use a brand-new blade for best results.) It can also be ironed. (Again, test first.)
- My final suggestion is a long shot. Sometimes two broken toys can be combined to make one good one. I brought home a doll stroller that turned out to be irreparable. Before we threw it out I came across another. Between the two we were able to make a complete stroller.

When you take a chance on a toy in need of rejuvenation you should pay next to nothing for it. You may not be able to salvage your bargain. Try to use materials and paints you already have. If you buy new materials or tools, consider whether you will have other uses for them in the future. If you are a tightwad of extraordinary resourcefulness you will about 99% of the time.

ALTERNATIVE GLIDER

Here's a simple glider you can add to your bag of tightwad tricks to razzle-dazzle your child, niece or nephew, grandchild, or child of a visiting friend.

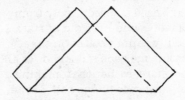

Fold any piece of paper on an angle as shown.

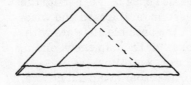

Fold up the folded edge about ½ inch, two times.

Curl the folded edge on the edge of a counter.

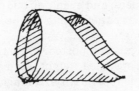

Tuck the ends securely together. Tape is optional.

To fly this glider hold as shown, flip your wrist, and release.

POSTCARD POINTERS

I have learned to always keep a batch of postcards or 19¢ stamps around. Obviously, this saves a dime whenever I have to mail a short message.

If I need a speedy reply from someone who lives out of state, I usually cannot count on them writing me back quickly or at all. Therefore, rather than making a long-distance phone call, I send them a postcard in an envelope. The postcard is stamped and addressed back to me. I write the question on the card and write out the possible answers with boxes for them to check off. Works every time.

One reader (who did not want her name in print) sent me some Christmas postcards she had made from last year's Christmas cards. This saves on the cost of postage as well as Christmas cards. Just cut the "word side" off. Her personalized note was written in red and green marker.

You can make your own postcard out of any stiff card. Tightwads have sent them made out of file folders, and even one out of the front panel from a Grape-Nuts box.

A regulation postcard must meet a specified weight. Find a business reply card in a magazine, feel the thickness, and pick something a little heavier to be sure. It must be no smaller than $3\frac{1}{2}'' \times 5''$ and no larger than $4'' \times 6\frac{1}{4}''$.

A Maine newspaper recently ran a large article about *The Tightwad Gazette*. People interested in a free issue were asked to send a 29¢ stamp. Of the 1,000 or more requests, only two were sent with a postcard. One stamp was hopelessly stuck on, but the other individual, Joyce Leo of Westbrook, Maine, neatly wrapped the stamp in plastic wrap and taped it to the postcard. Bravo!

THE PLASTIC JUG IRRIGATION SYSTEM

For many years we didn't own a lawn sprinkler. Before buying our first home we always rented and were too cheap to pay for the water to keep the landlord's grass green. Had we spotted one at a yard sale we would have bought it, but the purchase eluded us for years.

As a result, on hot days our children had been deprived and their backyard water fun had been limited to the spray of a garden hose dangling over a clothesline.

One summer my desire to remedy this deprivation blended with my mission to recycle plastic jugs. I conceived the plastic jug irrigation system. I had envisioned it as a lying down or prone model but my husband and father-in-law, the pair to whom I had delegated the engineering, got ambitious and constructed this design with a platform.

The first task was to find a jug with a neck size large enough to fit over the threaded end of a garden hose. A well-rinsed gallon bleach jug fit this criterion. A cut piece of old rubber-glove finger slipped over the end of the hose improved the "snugnicity."

Jim drilled a dozen holes in the bottom of the jug with a $\frac{3}{32}''$ drill bit. The platform was constructed of 100% scrap wood. It needed to be 3 inches high so that the hose would have ample bending room.

A simpler version would be a prone jug with holes on the side.

Once it was assembled we ceremoniously turned on the spigot and waited with anticipation as the water level rose to the top and . . . TAH DAH!

Our wonderfully outrageous plastic jug sprinkler shot water jets heavenward

in a seven-foot arched exuberance. (Your arched exuberance may vary depending on your water pressure.)

If this project exceeds your capabilities write to us. We have a few prone models available (rubber glove finger included). Send $19.95, plus $4.00 shipping and handling. Please allow six weeks for delivery. Offer good while supplies last.

A "BY THE GALLON" NONNUTRITIOUS COLD BEVERAGE COMPARISON

These figures are based on average prices of beverage type from a large chain grocery store, movie theater, and fast-food chain in our area. The prices were computed up to what the beverage would cost if purchased in gallon quantities.

Solar iced tea is made by hanging six tea bags in a gallon jug of water. Cover and set in the hot sun until it reaches the desired strength. Sweeten or add lemon to taste.

off the chart with a whopping $14.98 per gallon!

$7.54 — soda purchased at a movie theater minus ice

$7.42 — soda purchased at a fast food chain minus ice

$6.51 — "gourmet" soda in six pack

$6.40 — sparkling water in six pack

$4.99 — soda from a vending machine

$4.51 — "gourmet" soda in 25.4 oz. bottle

$4.28 — sparkling water in liter bottle

$2.63 — soda in six pack

$1.59 — soda in liter bottle

$1.29 — Crystal Light

$1.09 — ice tea mix

60¢ — presweetened koolaid

20¢ — koolaid with your sugar

0¢ — homemade solar iced tea

water

THINK HEAT

In our area heating oil prices drop more than 20¢ off-season. The dealers I spoke to had a difference of opinion as to when prices would hit bottom. It should occur sometime between July and early September. A summer fill-up of a 275-gallon tank can save as much as $55. Plan your cash flow to take advantage of this bargain.

Guessing exactly when to buy can be as tricky as playing the stock market. You will have to monitor prices for many weeks. What you should not do is get your first fill-up in November.

In Maine wood prices seem to be stable year-round, but as in all things, time to shop for the best price can mean savings. If you are able to provide some labor, these prices can be cut in half. This usually means cutting and splitting delivered logs or get-it-yourself cut and split wood.

A LIGHTER NOTE

Q. Why did the tightwad cross the road?

A. To pick up the deposit can on the other side.

THE MEAT TRAY GLIDER

To make this glider you will need two styrofoam meat trays. I used a 14¾" × 8" tray. The tray needs to be of the type that is ¼" thick. You will also need a very sharp utility knife or X-Acto knife. The plans below are drawn to ¼ scale.

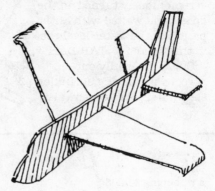

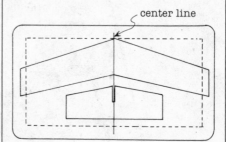

center line

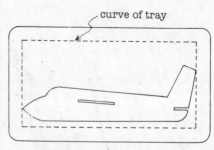

curve of tray

Carefully draw the wings and tail on the bottom of one tray. First find the center line of the tray and measure precisely from there. Include about ½" of the curve of the tray when planning the wings. This curve will give the glider lift. Cut all slots to match the precise thickness of the tray for a snug fit.

Draw and cut the body from the second tray and assemble.

The glider will need paper clips or a small nail in the nose to weigh down the front and help it fly level. If the glider still tends to arch up move the wings back farther.

To decrease the drag and further improve the glider's ability to fly, taper the front and back edges of the wing and tail with a knife or emery board. You can also warm the wing under warm water and bend up slightly on the center line. This will also help it fly straight.

A READER QUESTION

Dear Amy,

Would you please comment on Amway products? We have a friend who is trying to "save us a lot of money" by using the concentrated soaps and other products that he sells. I know there are other companies like Amway with the same claims. Do they really save money or is it a scam?

Nancy Schudalla
Boulder, Colorado

Dear Nancy,

No, it is not a scam, and you may or may not save money.

I have been familiar with Amway for over 20 years. Several friends, family members, and even a man I dated sold it.

One of Amway's good points is that its cleaning products are biodegradable and concentrated . . . two features that make them environmentally friendly. Another feature some people find attractive is that buying from Amway will probably save you time, since the products are delivered directly to you.

Because many of Amway's products are concentrated they are hard to compare in price to more familiar nonconcentrated products. However, about a year ago we did a cost comparison of several cleaning products. We found that the Amway products were generally cheaper than name-brand products, but that Amway could not compete in price with products that are on sale, purchased with a coupon, or that offer rebates.

I am not familiar enough with Amway products to comment on their quality, although my impression is that they tend to be good. I have heard more than one individual complain that they have a skin reaction to the laundry detergent, while the majority of people use it without problem. Also Consumer Reports compared Amway's dishwashing liquid with name brands and found it about twice as expensive to use.

Amway has now branched out into other products, like name-brand clothing, electronic goods, and food. As I cruised through their thick catalog with glossy, color photos, I noted that many of these items are things I would typically try to buy used, or in the case of the convenience foods, I would not buy at all.

In addition to Amway, Shaklee, and similar organizations, a number of buying clubs, like Consumer Buyline, have been making an appearance. Some of these other organizations charge a membership fee. In these cases you have to calculate if your potential savings would justify the fee. Consumer Buyline guarantees to beat supermarket prices on food, with certain limitations. If you buy all your food from one source and don't like to watch prices, it may save money. But these organizations are not a good deal if you compare to buying food at several sources, making one trip to each place per month to pick up bargains.

As a general rule, no one source of goods has the lowest price on everything. You will always save the most money by diversifying. In keeping with this strategy, you'll want to consider Amway a possible source. When you plan a purchase, shop around for the rock-bottom price and then give your Amway distributor a call.

ENERGY SAVER?

Dear Amy,
    I come from a long line of tightwads. My grandmother, an immigrant, took the light bulb out of her fridge because no one could convince her it wasn't on when the fridge door was shut.
        Susan Day
        Gloucester, Massachusetts

WEARERS BEWARE

Dear Amy,
    Someone wrote asking about how to save on contact lens solutions. Contact lenses are not something to be tightwad about. Over the past several years I've treated countless serious eye infections caused by improper contact lens care. I've seen firsthand, people who have suffered permanent vision loss because they took shortcuts for the sake of saving a few dollars. If you want to save money on contact lenses wear glasses instead.
        Toni Powell
        Tacoma, Washington

(This letter went on to discuss contact lens care and potential problems at length. Use brands that your physician recommends, and follow directions precisely. Generics or name brands purchased with a coupon from a discount drugstore will yield the best savings. FZ)

MUSIC REQUEST

Dear Amy,
    When my 16-year-old stepdaughter gave me her birthday list, she had listed more than 20 cassette tapes from her favorite music groups. Instead of buying them, I called a local radio station once or twice a day to request her favorite songs and then taped them. She got all her favorites, and all it cost was a few minutes a day and 50¢ for the tape (I bought top-quality cassette tapes at a clearance sale and paid $1.50 for three).

        Kimberly Hill
        Warren, Michigan

(After printing this idea in the newsletter many readers wrote that they thought the practice was illegal. I spent countless hours researching and consulting with the most expert sources in the country but was unable to come to any conclusion. There is no law that specifically addresses taping from the radio for personal use and it appears to fall under a fuzzy gray area of the copyright law called "fair use." Taping in from the radio for any business purpose is clearly illegal. FZ)

QUICKIE STREAMERS

As happens so often, I did something recently that struck me as normal and boring, and struck others as brilliant. When I made streamers for Jamie's seventh birthday party, I was surprised at how many staffers and mothers of guests had not seen these before.

My homemade streamers are quick to make, and only require 1½ sheets of 8½" × 11" paper to make a streamer that will stretch across a room.

The key to good party decorating is how much you do . . . not how perfectly you do it. Therefore you (or your kids), can work very quickly and use colored scrap paper, such as the notices the school sends home with your kids.

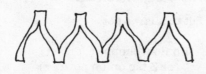

Cut one of the sheets of paper in half the long way. Cut the paper as shown below, leaving ¼" to ½" between cuts. Staple the end of this paper to the next one to make a long streamer.

When you stretch this paper it makes a streamer that looks like this:

If you twist it, it looks like this:

You can make a more dazzling streamer (that uses up more paper) using the same idea, except you fold your half sheet of paper before cutting it:

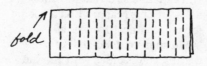

When you stretch it out, the streamer looks like this:

AUGUST BARGAINS

Sylvia Porter's Money Book offers a calendar for bargains. Certain items go on sale during different months of the year.

Good buys for August include: air-conditioners, bathing suits, bedding, camping equipment, new cars, coats, drapes and curtains, fans, furniture, furs, gardening equipment, housewares, lamps, paints, rugs and carpeting, school clothes and supplies, tires, and towels.

Most of these items have other months when they typically go on sale. School supplies go on sale again in October. During one of these months you should buy enough to get you through the school year.

HOMEMADE WORCESTERSHIRE SAUCE

In response to a reader request, I asked if any readers had a recipe for worcestershire sauce.

We spent a good deal of time testing the recipes sent in, and now have several jugs in the refrigerator . . . a 10-year supply for us. Because of the required purchase of things many of us might not normally stock, because of the effort involved, and because most people use it in small quantities the cost savings was not significant. In some cases the homemade version was more expensive than commercial brands.

The best recipe, sent in by Edith Hallet of Brownburg, Indiana, is only slightly cheaper than commercial brands. Using her recipe we substituted ground spices for whole ones, substituted a few ingredients, and came up with an almost-as-good facsimile that costs about 25% of the commercial brands.

Original Worcestershire Sauce

Tie loosely in a cloth:

    1 onion, chopped
    3 Tbsp mustard seed
    ½ tsp red pepper pod
    2 garlic cloves, crushed
    1 tsp peppercorns
    ½ tsp cracked ginger
    1 inch cinnamon bark
    1 tsp whole cloves
    ½ tsp cardamom seeds

Simmer spices in a large, heavy pan with:

    2 cups vinegar
    ½ cup molasses
    ½ cup soy sauce
    ¼ cup tamarind pulp or
    6 Tbsp lemon

Mix in a cup and add:

    3 Tbsp salt
    ½ tsp curry powder
    1 anchovy, mashed
    ½ cup water

While spices are boiling, caramelize ½ cup sugar by putting the sugar in a heavy skillet and stirring over high heat. Move sugar back and forth as it starts to melt and brown. Lower heat. Move sugar continuously and keep chopping at it, breaking the lumps until it is almost black and soupy, not burned.

Take the spice bag from the sauce, squeeze, and carefully pour a little of the boiling liquid into the skillet, stirring briskly until dissolved. Return the liquid sugar to the large pan. Boil briefly. Pour into a bowl, replace the spice bag in the sauce. Place in a covered container in the refrigerator for 2 weeks. Stir from time to time. Strain and bottle. Keep refrigerated or process.

The Cheaper Version

Put in a large pot:

    1 onion, chopped
      (or 3 tsp onion powder)
    3 tsp ground mustard
    ½ tsp red pepper
    2 cloves garlic, crushed
      (or ½ tsp garlic powder)
    ¼ tsp ground cinnamon
    ¼ tsp ground ginger

Add:

2 cups vinegar
½ cup molasses
½ cup soy sauce
6 Tbsp lemon juice

Mix together and add to pot:

3 Tbsp salt
½ tsp curry powder
½ cup water

Bring to boil and simmer ½ hour. While spices are boiling, caramelize ½ cup sugar using procedure given in original recipe. Cook another ½ hour. Store in refrigerator. Flavor will improve with age.

CHECKING UP ON CHECKING FEES

One of the ways that being poor costs money is when you have to pay a service charge on your checking account because you keep your balance below $500.

One of the ways that being stupid costs money is when you have to pay a service charge on your checking account because you keep the balance below $500 . . . and you have money in your savings account.

Banks typically impose service charges on customers who allow their checking accounts to fall below $500. Robin Bullard Carter, a personal money management counselor, says her research indicates that these fees average about $10 per month for maintenance fees and/or per-check fees.

At $10, these fees would add up to $120 per year. So if your average balance is hovering just below $500, you are effectively paying 24% interest . . . even more if your checking account balance tends to be lower.

So if you have money sitting around in a savings account drawing 4% to 5% interest, the smartest thing to do is to move enough of it to your checking account to boost it above your bank's minimum balance.

I would also add that at many credit unions there are no checking fees. Getting into a credit union may be worthwhile to you if you can't keep more than the minimum in a checking account.

(For more information on Carter's counseling services, contact her at Moneysense, 17 Graham Ave., Newbury, MA 01951, [508] 465-3282.)

HOMEMADE CRACKERS

This recipe came from *Yankee* magazine. The crackers taste something like Wheat Thins.

3 cups uncooked oatmeal
2 cups unbleached flour
1 cup wheat germ
3 Tbsp sugar
1 tsp salt
¾ cup oil
1 cup water

Mix ingredients and roll out onto two cookie sheets. (I use a plastic tumbler for this.) Sprinkle with salt, lightly roll again to press salt in. Cut into squares or diamonds. (A pizza cutter works well.) Bake at 350°. After 20 minutes begin checking. The outer ones are usually ready first. Remove crackers as they turn golden brown and hard.

THE CHEAP BIRTHDAY PARTY

Three years ago we celebrated Jim's 40th birthday. For lack of a better theme I designed a Cheap Party. (In this case, the word *cheap* is not to be confused with *thrifty*.)

I used household discards to make decorations and wrap. The same theme used for an office party would take advantage of available office waste, such as used computer paper.

All the presents Jim received cost under $1 and were either joke presents, yard sale finds, or homemade. In one case I finally found the time to make the curtains for his office that he had requested and provided the material for six months earlier. I also made up a standard collection of "Good For" coupons, which were all basically useless and funny.

THE CHEAP BIRTHDAY STREAMER

Paper chain made from sale flyer, newspaper, and brown bag . . . hung haphazardly.

THE CHEAP BIRTHDAY CAKE

Odd or scavenged used candles

Decorated with candies at least 10 years old

THE CHEAP (AND BEAUTY-FUL) BIRTHDAY DECORATION

Multi-reused aluminum-foil

Egg carton section

THE CHEAP PARTY HAT

Toilet paper plastic wrap cut with pinking shears

Brown bag with print side showing

Colored dots cut from junk mail and glued on

Brown bag cut and curled

Sale Flyer

THE CHEAP BIRTHDAY PARTY GAG
The Booby Trap Door

Duct tape

Heavy cord

Plastic bucket filled with wadded trash

Door ajar

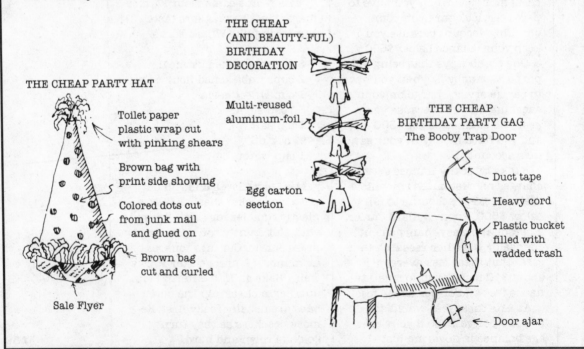

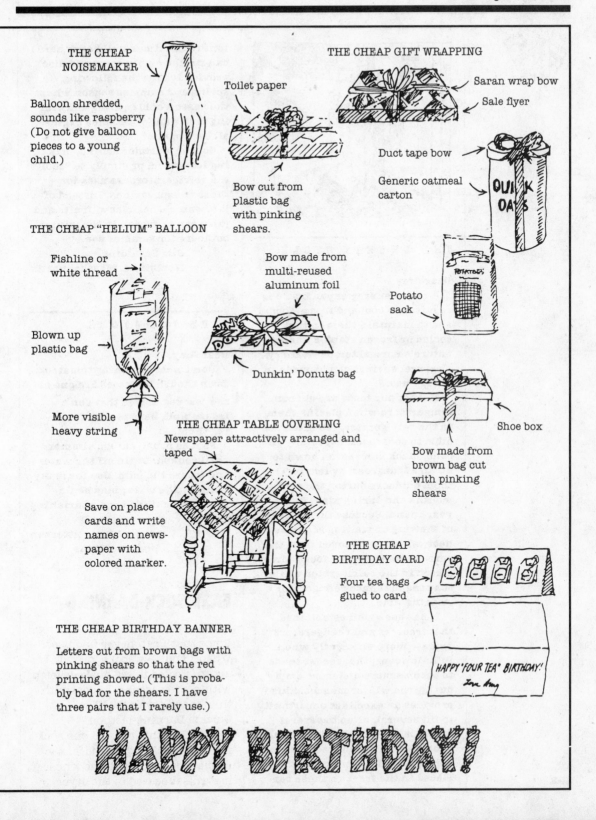

THE CHEAP NOISEMAKER

Balloon shredded, sounds like raspberry (Do not give balloon pieces to a young child.)

Toilet paper

Bow cut from plastic bag with pinking shears.

THE CHEAP GIFT WRAPPING

Saran wrap bow

Sale flyer

Duct tape bow

Generic oatmeal carton

QUICK OATS

THE CHEAP "HELIUM" BALLOON

Fishline or white thread

Blown up plastic bag

More visible heavy string

Bow made from multi-reused aluminum foil

Dunkin' Donuts bag

Potato sack

POTATOES

Shoe box

Bow made from brown bag cut with pinking shears

THE CHEAP TABLE COVERING
Newspaper attractively arranged and taped

Save on place cards and write names on newspaper with colored marker.

THE CHEAP BIRTHDAY CARD

Four tea bags glued to card

HAPPY "FOUR TEA" BIRTHDAY!
Love Amy

THE CHEAP BIRTHDAY BANNER

Letters cut from brown bags with pinking shears so that the red printing showed. (This is probably bad for the shears. I have three pairs that I rarely use.)

HAPPY BIRTHDAY!

THE ENERGY CYCLE

Dear Amy,

A major energy expenditure is required to cool and freeze foods and to maintain them in that cooled or frozen state. By using nature's normal temperature cycles, real savings can be made in energy use.

Most of our foods are at room temperature when placing them in the refrigerator. It's often possible to cool foods, especially in cans, much more, even down to 20° to 25° degrees, by leaving them outdoors during the cold months and during night hours year-round. Because the process of thawing or melting requires heat, which is removed from the surroundings, frozen foods can be placed in the refrigerator while thawing to reduce refrigerator running time.

If has been well established that freezers and refrigerators operate more efficiently when full. However, the freezer tends to become more and more empty during the winter months. This provides an excellent opportunity to fill several, or up to several dozen, milk or fruit juice cartons (not quite full) and freeze them during the cold winter months. Placed in the freezer, these car-tons (sometimes well below zero) can fill the empty spots and also provide ice for the following spring and summer season when the season of blanching and cooling fruits and vegetables begins all over again.

Cooling summer drinks, making ice cream, or simply to "cool" the refrigerator, are uses for these frozen cartons. Instead of just water, Popsicles of fruits and juice can be frozen in the winter outdoors for summer use.

> Jim Spaulding
> Northfield, Massachusetts

RIPE TOMATOES

Dear Amy,

Don't waste ripening tomatoes. Even though tomatoes are one of the few vegetables that don't freeze well, here is a tip for saving them.

Peel as usual, cut up, simmer until cooked. Drain off the water and freeze the pulp. Use for many recipes. The water may be flavored and chilled for a nourishing drink.

> Louise Ware Patterson
> Augusta, Maine

EASY SOCK DARNING

Socks are one of the few clothing items that I can never find used. When I buy new socks for kids I am frustrated to see holes develop within a few weeks. To deal with this I have developed "The Quickie Darning Method."

To utilize this method one sock must be sacrificed. The ideal sacrificial sock would be one whose mate disappeared in the dryer

several years ago. (The Dryer Black Hole functions on the same principle as the Bermuda Triangle.)

Cut a circle from an unworn area of the sacrificial sock. The diameter of the circle should be about ¼" larger than the diameter of the hole to be patched. Use a running stitch to sew the patch in place. Sew around the patch three or four times or until all edges are secure. The process requires only a few minutes.

WHEN YOU DON'T NEED TO BE A TIGHTWAD

It happens. There will probably come a time when you don't need to be a tightwad anymore. The scenario is most frequently played out by a couple who, after decades of pinching pennies, one day finds that the mortgage is paid off, all the kids have completed college, and they've saved a sufficient amount for retirement.

It happens because tightwaddery really does work. But tightwads can be confused as to how to let go of a lifestyle that has brought order and control to their lives and that they have come to enjoy.

The problem is that pressure to spend more increases from all sides. Friends urge you to "lighten up" and buy a sexy car to replace your sensible econobox. Kids' (or grandkids') requests for Sugar Zapper cereal can no longer be squelched with the statement, "We can't afford it." And you start to doubt yourself. You wonder, Does having more money really mean we have to waste it?

The answer is to understand that the tightwad life is not only about spending less . . . it's about spending in a way that reflects your values, and that should not stop if you have a billion dollars. Having more money simply means you can pursue your values in a larger and even more satisfying way.

Note: before abandoning tight-waddery, be sure you have touched all the economic bases. You need sufficient insurance, savings for current emergencies and for all future goals, and no debt whatsoever.

So if you've thought of all that, and still think you don't need to be a tightwad anymore, consider the following: these ideas reflect our values; they may reflect yours, too.

1. Spend in ways that are environmentally sound. Even billionaires need to wash out their Ziploc bags (or at least hire somebody to do it for them). Having surplus income does not grant you the right to be wasteful with the planet's limited resources.

Some environmentally sound

ways to spend money include making long-distance phone calls, hiring a contractor to paint your house, or going out to dinner.

2. If you live in an economically depressed area, buy locally, even if it costs a little more. For example, have a local craftsperson braid a rug for you rather than ordering one from a big mail-order house. This way, you know your money is going where it is needed.

3. Consider charitable giving. Think of it this way: if you're hungry and have a cherry pie, that first slice is very satisfying. The second one tastes good, too. But if you eat the whole pie your enjoyment will diminish with each piece you eat.

Spending all your surplus income on personal gratification can be just as unsatisfying.

I suggest sharing a slice of your pie. You could have a swimming pool put in even though you had previously decided it was a low priority for your family . . . or you could make an anonymous dona-

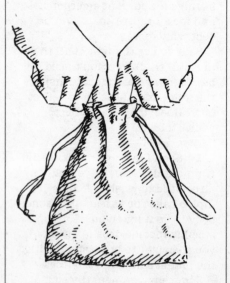

tion to the elderly woman in your community who needs a new water heater.

The recipient, someone who has insufficient funds to satisfy the most basic needs, gets maximum value from your money. You feel good knowing the money was spent well.

4. Even when we can afford to spend more money, we must also consider the legacy we pass on to our children. If we raise them in a lifestyle completely free of want, where everything is brand new, store bought, and expensive, we are raising children who know no economic boundaries.

In all likelihood, children raised in frugality will become young adults who spend as wastefully as children who are raised with excess. It's the nature of that stage of life—they are enjoying their first taste of economic freedom: extra money, no goals.

But children of frugality have an advantage. They grew up watching their parents fixing things, making Halloween costumes, and cooking from scratch. Those images were stored in their "mental banks." If needed, the information is there to retrieve in their adult years.

Because Jim and I were raised by thrifty parents, changing economic gears was a natural process for both of us.

5. Consider retiring early. We're conditioned to think that every breadwinner will work into their sixties. If our work creates extra income we raise our standard of living. However, we can choose to live well beneath our means and invest the surplus. When the interest from the investments equals our cost of living, we reach financial independence.

This strategy is particularly good for singles or childless couples with a large amount of disposable income, and for people who don't like their jobs.

Even if you can't imagine saving up this much, you can increase your degree of financial independence by paying off all your debts and investing in tools, appliances, and other items that will make your life less expensive.

Once freed from having to earn a living, you can devote your time to doing things you find more enriching. You might choose to volunteer or have a low-paying but satisfying career.

The bottom line: spend money in ways that are consistent with your personal values. Don't let others pressure you into spending according to their values.

Think back to your original objective. In our case, we wanted three things—a large family, a large rural home, and time to enjoy our children and home. Our objective was not to amass the largest bank account possible.

I spend extra income in ways that enhance my original objective of achieving a quality family life. In the summer of 1991 we hired a company to put a new roof on our house. It would have been cheaper to do it ourselves, but it also would have taken an entire summer to accomplish given our current time limitations. So, for us, hiring roofers seemed consistent because it enabled us to spend more free time with our children.

Saving money is the means to an end . . . not the end itself.

Index

ABOUT THE AUTHOR

AMY DACYCZYN started a newsletter called "The Tightwad Gazette" in June of 1990, and within two years saw subscriptions climb to over 100,000.

AMY is a graduate of the Vesper George School of Art in Boston. She did free-lance work for many design studios in the Boston area for eight years before her marriage to Jim in 1982. They and their six children live happily and frugally in Leeds, Maine.